ACCADEMIA TOSCANA DI SCIENZE E LETTERE
«LA COLOMBARIA»

«STUDI»
CCXLI

PATRIZIA GRIMALDI PIZZORNO

THE WAYS OF PARADOX FROM LANDO TO DONNE

FIRENZE
LEO S. OLSCHKI EDITORE
MMVII

ISBN 978 88 222 5700 0

To my son Eugenio

PREFACE

The reception of Ortensio Lando's *Paradossi cioè sentenze fuori del co-mun parere* at the Elizabethan Inns of Court is the general subject of this study. *The Defence of Contraries Paradoxes against common opinion*, here reproduced in the appendix, was hastily published in 1593 by Anthony Munday; it contained only 12 paradoxes translated not from the original Italian, but from the French of Charles Estienne who had turned Lando's fideist *Paradossi* into a manual of jocose moot cases for his selected audi-ence, the law apprentices of the Parliament of Paris. Likewise, *The Defence of Contraries*, is addressed to the lawyers and wits at the London Inns of Court, at the time a vital centre of coterie writing, scholarship and patron-age. Paradoxy had always appealed to the legal mind: its cognitive instabil-ity reflected the mishapprension of meaning as well as of people in the legal process; paradoxes used as rhetorical models could stretch both "rational argument" and "commonsense", law's two prerogatives, to the limit of ab-surdity; while arguing *a contrario*, improved forensic dexterity. It was at the Inns of Court that English paradoxy saw both its triumph – in the early 1590s with John Donne's "monarchy of wit" – and its demise in 1618 when in the *Antimasque of Mountebanks*, acted by the students of Gray's Inn to honor Francis Bacon, *Parradox* appeared on stage as the ephemeral Shrovetide monster and the villain "son of a Jesuit father and an Anabap-tist mother."

The late Elizabethan taste for paradox, often described as a "paradox epidemics" was not at all an indistinctive phenomenon: whereas paradox-ical affectation and senseless witticism at the Royal Court was a matter of current fashion, at the Inns of Court sensation in language and ideas was meant to challenge established beliefs. Lawyers were readers and writers of contemporary writing, as well as patrons and benefactors, a fact that lit-erary historians tend to forget. The legal societies, situated as they were outside the city's southwestern walls, alongside the river Thames, were not an insular reality: they were close to the Courts of Law and to the Royal Court and we know that gentlemen students and barristers were actively involved in the rich world of ideas that emanated from both Court and the metropolis. The Inns, addressed by Ben Jonson as "nurseries of humanity," had always represented a distinct cultural sphere with their own specific character; and in an age of intense factionalism they were a haven of religious tolerance and nonconformity where a man was unlikely to be unduly harassed on account of his beliefs. This religious freedom, combined with a humanistic bent and a unique legal training based on the practical application of legal skills did not make lawyers unbelievers. On the contrary, both Catholic and Protestant lawyers shared an Augustinian view of the world and a common piety that stressed the spiritual and inward quality of faith. In their desire to organise the "city of man" in a manner most conducive to salvation they resembled Thomas More, that *jureconsultus perfectus* whose *Utopia* was first translated in Italian by Ortensio Lando.

Lawyers-poets like the young John Donne and his friends lived, like Martial in Domitian's Rome, in a gilded and ferocious age of fear and adulation. From the safehold of the Inns of Court they shot the *pointe assassine* of paradox. Closer in spirit to Lando than to Cicero, their *joco* expressed the pathos of radical change, and the firm belief in the need and possibility of a complete exit from the commonly accepted order of life.

The research and writing process for this study, which may be considered an extended introduction to the *Defence of Contraries*, has stretched over three years, during which time I have acquired many debts. To Quentin Skinner, who first brought to my attention *The Defence of Contraries*, and to Marcello Pagnini who has supported with enthusiasm this project goes my gratitude. I wish to thank John. H. Baker of Cambridge University whose support, advices and comments have been invaluable to wade through the early history of the Inns of Court. Simonetta Adorni-Braccesi, Antonio Corsaro, Silvana Seidel-Menchi who sent me in a neatly packed box all her writings on Lando and the Reformation, deserve special appreciation. My gratitude goes to the colleagues and friends who have helped me in various capacities: J.N. Adams, Warren Boutcher, Antonio Cardini, Ingrid and Sanford Gifford, Susan Halpert, July Holyoke, Coppelia Kahn, Bridget Kendall, Charlie Mayer, Silvana Sciarra, Clare Tame, and my husband Alessandro Pizzorno.

Florence, June, 28 2007

PART ONE

CHAPTER ONE

ORTENSIO LANDO'S *PARADOSSI OF FAITH*

> Et consedimus, ut conloqueremur. Et forte supra
> mensam lusoriam, quae ante nos erat adtendit codi-
> cem: tulit, aperuit, invenit apostolum Paulum, inopi-
> nate sane [...].
>
> AUGUSTINE

> What is convincing though impossible should always
> be preferred to what is possible and unconvincing.
>
> ARISTOTLE

LANDO'S COUNTER-RENAISSANCE

Ortensio Lando (1512-1555 ca.), the author of *Paradossi cioè sentenze fuori del comun parere*, was more than simply a "polygraph" at the service of the 16th-century printing industry. He worked with the vernacular presses in Venice and Lyon as a copyist and editor, and was a freelance author of some success. His output ranges from open denunciations of social injustice and fiercely anti-clerical tracts to lighter pieces written exclusively for profit, and expresses his profound concern with the religious, philosophical, political and social issues of his time. From 1533 until 1553, Lando published 15 original works, mostly anonymously, carried out translations of Erasmus, Luther and More, and produced a respectable number of compilations and editions, so that by 1650 his work had appeared in about 100 editions, including French and English translations.

Together with Anton Francesco Doni and Nicolò Franco, Lando belonged to that mixed group of "young literary adventurers of the pen" who congregated in Venice, attracted by the example of Pietro Aretino and by the relative freedom of the Venetian printing press. This group was known by the pejorative term of *poligrafi*, and long remained outside the literary canon; it is only recently that Reformation historians and literary critics have recognised their importance.[1] It was Lando, more than the others, with his "irregular" writings in Latin and the vernacular, who defied humanist and Renaissance learning and values. He held radical, heterodox views in matters of religion and was associated with the philo-Protestant cause in Italy and above all with the drive for Catholic reform known as Evangelism. This movement, based on the reform of individual Christians, and subsequently of Christian society, through a return to the teachings and spirit of the Gospels and Epistles of St Paul, was at its most animated during his life as a mature writer.[2] The advocates of Evangelism wished to rout out ecclesiastical and political abuses, and to emphasise scripture and the primacy of justification through faith while omitting good works. Here we can discern echoes of the Erasmian ideal Church, conceived of as an invisible congregation of the good. There are also traces of the pre-Lutheran spirituality of the Dutch religious movement *devotio moderna* in Lando's *Paradossi* and *Quattro Libri dei Dubbi* (1552).[3] The ideal of a spiritual community of brothers and sisters united in a life of poverty, good works, education, meditation and personal reading of the Bible was recast in a new language in his last work, *Dialogo della Sacra Scrittura* (1552), inspired by the contemporary Evangelical preachers Bernardino Ochino and Juan de Valdés.[4]

Probably of low birth, Lando joined the Augustinian monastic order in Milan as a young man under the name of Hieremia, a pseudonym that appears in the 1559 *Index of Prohibited Books*.[5] Though there is little docu-

---

[1] For an exhaustive study, see P.F. GRENDEL, *Critics of the Italian World 1530-1560, Anton Francesco Doni, Nicolò Franco e Ortensio Lando*, Madison, University of Wisconsin Press, 1969; A. QUONDAM, *Mercanzia d'Onore, Mercanzia d'Utile, Produzione Libraria e Lavoro Intellettuale a Venezia nel Cinquecento*, in *Libri, editori e pubblico nell'Europa moderna: guida storica e critica*, edited by A. Petrucci, Bari, Laterza, 1977, pp. 53-103. S. Seidel-Menchi has written extensively on Lando in the context of the Reformation, see in particular, *Spiritualismo radicale nelle opere di Ortensio Lando*, «Archiv für Reformationsgeschichte», 65 (1974), pp. 210-277.

[2] That is, until 1542; for the chronology of Evangelism see D. CANTIMORI, *Prospettive di storia ereticale italiana*, Bari, Laterza, 1960, pp. 28-30.

[3] *Quattro libri de dubbi con le solutioni a ciascun dubbio accommodate. La materia del primo è naturale, del secondo è mista (benche per lo piu sia morale) del terzo è amorosa, et del quarto è religiosa*, In Vinegia, appresso Gabriel Giolito de Ferrari, et fratelli, 1552.

[4] The bibliography on Italian evangelism is vast; a classic study is D. CANTIMORI's *Prospettive di storia ereticale italiana del Cinquecento*, Bari, Laterza, 1960, pp. 32-34; E.G. GLEASON, *On the nature of 16th Century Italian Evangelism: scholarship, 1953-1978*, «16th Century Journal», 9, 1978, see in particular, pp. 3-25; On Lando and "spiritualismo filoanabattistico", see SEIDEL – MENCHI, *Spiritualismo radicale*, cit.

[5] Under the name of Hortensius Tranquillus, *alias* Hieremias, *alias* Landus. I thank S. Adorni-Braccesi for allowing me to consult the biography of Lando in manuscript written in collaboration with S. Ragagli and forthcoming in *Enciclopedia Italiana*. For the identification of Lando with a heterodox writer nicknamed "Turchetto", see SEIDEL – MENCHI, *Chi fu Ortensio Lando?*, «Rivista Storica Italiana», v. 106 (1994), pp. 501-564.

mentary evidence on his early years as a monk, we do know that he left the monastery in around 1530 and moved to Bologna to study medicine. He soon found his vocation as a successful freelancer, and by 1541 he was sufficiently distinguished in both Latin and Greek letters for the *Accademia degli Elevati*, in Ferrara, to welcome him with the humanist name of Tranquillus. Characteristically, he thought fit to thank the *Elevati* with a burlesque piece critical of learning, *Dialogo di M. Filalete cittadino di Utopia contra gli huomini letterati* (1541), which was a remake, enriched with autobiographical suggestion, of his *Paradosso* III, "*Meglio è d'esser ignorante che dotto*".[6] But "tranquil" he was most certainly not. In his desire to write free of the suffocating atmosphere of courts and academies, like other penniless *poligrafi* Lando travelled extensively in Italy, Switzerland, France and Germany, occasionally supported by patrons for whom he wrote epistles and other works. His travels brought this enigmatic man, described by the Lyon's printer Sebastianus Gryphius as both inconstant and inconsistent ("vir levissimus" and "vir incostantissimus"), into close contact with European circles of Protestant reformers and Erasmian humanists, with whom he openly shared a disgust for clerical abuses and an intolerance of the pedantry of *Cinquecento* learning.[7]

In 1534, Lando travelled as a fugitive monk to Lyon, where there was no faculty of theology to restrict his freedom. Here he was welcomed by Étienne Dolet and by the city's circle of humanist physicians, such as François Rabelais, which congregated in a veritable enclave of the *Respublica Literaria* at the printing shop of Sebastianus Gryphius. In this half-real, half-ideal society, men who were of different social origins, professions and nationalities, but equals in intelligence, shared common spiritual and intellectual interests ranging from medicine to the Christian Cabala and Hermetism.[8] Dolet was a great admirer of Cicero and involved Lando in the *querelle* of Ciceronian imitation.[9] Lando, whose literary production

---

[6] SEIDEL – MENCHI, *Un Inedito di Ortensio Lando, Il Dialogo contra gli huomini letterati*, «Rivista Storica Svizzera», 27, 1977, pp. 509-527. Cited in GRENDEL's *Critics of the Italian World*, cit., p. 27, n. 25.

[7] SEIDEL – MENCHI, *Chi fu Ortensio Lando?*, cit., p. 516; while in Germany Lando probably translated Luther's *An den christlichen Adel der Deutschen Nation* into Italian.

[8] In 1534 he wrote an introduction for Gryphius to *Cribratio medicamentorum fere omnium* by Symphorien Champier, the doctor and humanist who introduced Ficino's hermetism to France. On the "Republic of Letters" and social circles, see G. SIMMEL, *Gesamtausgabe 11*, «Soziologie», pp. 462-464, Frankfurt am Main, Surkamp, 1992.

[9] Or anti-Ciceronianism, initiated by Erasmus in 1528 with the *Ciceronianus*. The movement spread throughout Europe and only lasted a few decades but in England its echoes still reached Gabriel Harvey, whose *Ciceronianus*, a redefinition of imitation of Cicero, following

is heavily dependent on Erasmus, treated the debate with "studied mockery", and in his *Cicero relegatus, Cicero revocatus*[10] apparently parodies both sides of the question while in fact attempting to reconcile Christ and Tully, Christian knowledge and pagan eloquence. Lando was not a staunch Ciceronian, and – not unlike Erasmus – he always dwelt on the prospect of finding a Christian "middle way" on the question of *imitatio*.[11]

An important event in Lando's life was his meeting with the reform-minded patrician Vincenzo Buonvisi, whose brother Antonio was a banker and patron of letters in London. Through them, Lando became acquainted with the work of their close friend Thomas More. A subsequent period at Buonvisi's villa near Lucca enabled Lando to write at more leisure, and it may have been here that he began his translation of *Utopia*.[12] The paradoxical character of Book II (a "Praise of Nowhere") and More's Augustinian spirituality, with its stress on the inner quality of faith, must have appealed to Lando whose many pseudonyms in the course of his career included those of *Philalethes Polytopiensis civis, Philalestes ex Utopia civis* and *Filalete cittadino d'Utopia*.

Sheer restlessness, or perhaps employment as an informer for the French government, took Lando all over Italy and even beyond the Alps. He parodies contemporary travelogues in his travel diary, *Commentario delle più notabili et mostruose cose d'Italia et altri luoghi, di lingua aramea in italiana tradotto* (Venice 1548), inspired by More's *Utopia*. He is a particularly critical of the Renaissance ideal of *viver civile*. This work, rich in Rabelaisian suggestion, gives an eyewitness account of an Italy that is dynamic but fragmented, disordered and unruly, in sharp contrast with the unrealistic social and linguistic unity the intellectual and aristocratic elites of the time envisaged.

Erasmus and Ramus, was published in 1577. See G. WILLIAMSON, *The Senecan Amble, a Study in Prose from Bacon to Collier*, Chicago, University of Chicago Press, 1951, pp. 1-33.

[10] Its full title is *Cicero relegatus, Cicero revocatus. Dialogi festivissimi* (Lyon, 1534).

[11] See SEIDEL – MENCHI, *Sulla fortuna di Erasmo in Italia: Ortensio Lando e altri eterodossi della prima metà del Cinquecento*, «Rivista Storica Svizzera», 24 (1974), p. 574 ff. GRENDEL, *Critics of the Italian World*, cit., pp. 148-149; E.V. TELLE, *L'Erasmianus Sive Ciceronianus D'Etienne Dolet* (1535), *Introduction-Facsimilé de l'Édition Originale du "De Imitatione Ciceroniana" Commentaires et Appendice*, Geneva, Librairie Droz, 1974.

[12] *Utopia: La repubblica nuovamente ritrovata del governo dell'isola Eutopia [...] Opera di Tommaso Moro cittadino di Londra* (Venice, 1548), was printed anonymously for A. Pincio and edited by his friend Doni. It was the second in a modern vernacular, after the German version. On Lando and Utopia, see SEIDEL – MENCHI, *Ortensio Lando Cittadino di Utopia: un esercizio di lettura*, in *La Fortuna dell'Utopia di Thomas More nel dibattito politico Europeo del '500*, Florence, Olschki, 1996, pp. 95-118.

Lando was at his most prolific during his stay in Venice, between 1548 and 1552. Here he gained access to the lively literary world and printing press of Aretino, which was still unfettered by Roman censorship. He frequently worked with Gabriel Giolito de' Ferrari (d. 1578), a commercially minded entrepreneur who had been swift to adopt typographical innovations. Giolito used his literary judgement to create new clienteles for vernacular literature, specialising in publishing lesser-known contemporary authors. The lively format of these moderately priced dialogues, collections of letters, *novelle*, poetry and satires in the vernacular, along with a selection of modern classics, was very attractive to contemporary readers, and like Lando's books many of these publications ran to subsequent editions. In the urban centres of Europe, print shops such as Giolito's served as miniature "international houses", providing wandering, heterodox scholars with meeting place, sanctuary, cultural centre and literary agency all in one.[13] At the start of their careers, Erasmus, the young canon from Rotterdam, and the young monk and physician Rabelais had found work in print shops, where they made the most of their talents. Similarly, Lando was able to emerge from monastic obscurity and win patrons and public recognition, first through Gryphius, the printer of medical literature for whom Rabelais had also worked as an editor, and later through Giolito. In May 1554, the *Index* banned the books of *Hortensius Tranquillus* and *Philatetis civis Utopiensis*, alongside those of Erasmus and Rabelais.

The way in which Lando moved within the spheres of the "Counter-Renaissance"[14] is quite extraordinary. From his early association with the Erasmian/Augustinian monastic community in Milan onward, Lando's works reveal his lifelong involvement in the anti-intellectual, anti-moralistic movement of the 16th-century. Whether in science or religion, in ethics or aesthetics, he shared the epistemological scepticism of Agrippa von Nettesheim's (1486-1535) *De incertitudine et vanitate scientiarum declamatio invectiva* (1539), and of Erasmus's *Encomium Moriae* (1508). Lando believed the sole key to knowledge (and thus salvation) was the word of God. His model was Socrates, who like the prophets of Israel prepares for the advent of the Gospel. Like Socrates, he favoured the representation of deformity and grotesqueness, and using Alcibiade's comparison of Socrates to an ugly Silenus in the *Symposium* presented himself as being

---

[13] E.L. EISENSTEIN, *The Printing Revolution in Early Modern Europe*, Vol. I, Cambridge, Cambridge University Press, 1983, p. 140.

[14] The term "Counter-Renaissance" was coined by H. HAYDN, in *The Counter-Renaissance*, New York, Harcourt, Brace & World, 1950, Chap. I.

ugly and of a sickly disposition,[15] comparing himself and his works to the grotesque *silènes* (the apothecaries' trick boxes containing precious medicines), as Rabelais had done in the Prologue of *Gargantua*.[16]

His scant biography leaves much of his life shrouded in mystery. However, after leaving the order of Saint Augustine in Milan, he may have continued his own spiritual apostolate, casting his vocation in the Augustinian model of the Christian orator who interprets his calling as an apostolic expression of the Word. In an age of intense religious turmoil, he became involved in promoting the causes of the Reformation and Evangelism, albeit always concealing his identity, either with anonymity or by writing under a series of Latinate pen names.[17]

Lando's writings seem to reveal that his religious and political beliefs were distinctly more radical than those held by moderate *spirituali* such as Cardinal Reginald Pole and Margherite de Navarre. This group practiced a form of Nicodemism based more on circumstances than on any coherent theory of dissimulation;[18] they emphasised the inner quality of religious experience and privately disociated themselves from traditional doctrine and sacramental theology; they treated Catholic practices as *adiaphorus* (morally indifferent for salvation, neither good nor bad), and took the anonymous Calvinist tract *Il Beneficio di Cristo* (1543) as their confessional manifesto and devotional and meditational text.

THE MANY CONTEXTS OF *PARADOSSI*

Lando's first work in vernacular, *Paradossi cioè sentenze fuori del comun parere*,[19] was published in Lyon during his second stay in the city

---

[15] See *Paradosso* II, A. CORSARO, *Paradossi cioè sentenze fuori del comun parere*, Rome, Edizioni di Storia e Letteratura, 2000, pp. 96-100.

[16] A reference to Erasmus's adage on *Sileni Alcibiadis* III, iii, I, and F. RABELAIS, *Gargantua*, Geneva, Librarie Droz, 1970, pp. 8-18.

[17] Landi Hortensius dictus Tranquillus, alias Landus, Hortensius, alias Hortensius Mediolanensis alias Lando, Geremia (Hieremias) alias Hortensius Tranquillus (Mediolanensis) alias Ortensio (Hortensio) detto il Tranquillo (Lando, Milanese) alias Hortensius Appianus, alias Andronico Collodio alias Philalethes Polytopiensis civis, Philalestes ex Utopia civis, Filalete cittadino d'Utopia. See SEIDEL – MENCHI, *Chi fu Ortensio Lando?*, cit., p. 516.

[18] On the "Nicodemite" position in matters of religious persuasion, Cantimori's research has been carried on by his former student C. GINSBURG, in *Nicodemismo: Simulazione e dissimulazione religiosa nell'Europa del '500*, Turin, Einaudi, 1970. For a list of Lando's allusions to men and women of high rank involved in the Italian Evangelical movement see, A. CORSARO, *Paradossi*, cit., p. 19.

[19] *Che Miglior sia la povertà che la ricchezza; Che meglio sia l'essere brutto che bello; Meglio è*

in 1543. The following year it was printed in Venice by B. Bindoni,[20] and dedicated to the "Erasmian" Cardinals Cristoforo Madruzzo and Nicola Maria Caracciolo. Lando, who signed this work as *Ludebat Hortensius*, written backwards, concealed his moral, religious and political creed under the cloak of his sour wit (*acri ingegno*), and promoted, as has been convincingly argued, the heterodox beliefs of "spiritualismo filoanabattistico".[21] Such beliefs were opposed by both the Reformed and Roman Church, and came under fierce attack from Calvin in 1544 in his *Brière Instruction pour armer tous bons fideles contre les erreurs de la secte commune de Anabaptiste*, and again in 1545 in *Contre la secte phantastique et furieuse des Libertins, qui se nomment spirituelz*. In both pamphlets, the Geneva reformer condemned the "secte de Libertins", or "spiritual Libertines", as "forcenez et hors de sens", "phantastique" and "furieuse". The apparent contradiction in the expression "spiritual Libertins" reveals that at the core of Calvin's attack lies the fear of religious and moral topsy-turviness in which "such furious people come then to turn upside down all order and all distinctions". The great names of his times, Agrippa von Nettesheim, Simon de Villeneuve, Étienne Dolet, Rabelais, the "morosophs" and followers of Lucian, were all denounced as metaphysical and moral libertines. They are described as heretics who share a pragmatic and reductive view of religion and as egalitarians who believe in a revolutionary and metaphysical conception of freedom that is against all forms of social hierarchy.

Lando's *Paradossi* would have also appeared to Calvin as the ravings of a dangerous and extravagant fool, promoting monstrous opinions. For

---

d'esser ignorante che dotto; Meglio è d'esser ceco che illuminato; Meglio è d'esser pazzo che savio; Che mala cosa non sia se un principe perda il stato; Esser miglior l'imbriachezza che la sobrietà; Meglio è d'aver la moglie sterile che feconda; Meglio è vivere mandato in esiglio che nella patria longamente dimorare; Meglio è l'esser debole e mal sano che robusto e gagliardo; Non esser cosa detestabile né odiosa la moglie disonesta; Meglio è di piangere che ridere; Esser miglior la carestia che l'abbondanza; Meglio è morire che lungamente campare; Che meglio sia nascere ne' luoghi piccioli che nelle populose città; Che meglio sia abitare nell'umil case che ne' gran palagi; Che mala cosa non sia l'esser ferito e battuto; Non è cosa biasimevole né odiosa l'esser bastardo; Meglio è d'essere in prigione che in libertà; Esser miglior la guerra che la pace; Non esser da dolersi se la moglie si muoia e troppo stoltamente far chiunque la piagne; Meglio è non aver servidori che averne; Che meglio sia nascere di gente umile che di chiara e illustre; Esser miglior la vita parca della splendida e sontuosa; Che la donna è di maggior eccellenza che l'uomo; Che meglio sia d'esser timido che animoso e ardito; Che l'opere del Bocaccio non sieno degne d'esser lette, ispezialmente le dieci giornate; Che l'opere quali al presente abbiamo sotto nome di Aristotele non sieno di Aristotele; Che Aristotele fusse non solo un ignorante ma anche lo più malvagio uomo di quella età; Che M. Tullio sia non sol ignorante de filosofia, ma di retorica, di cosmografia e dell'istoria.

[20] The same publisher of *Il Beneficio di Cristo* (1543).

[21] That is, a mixture of Anabaptism, Nicodemism and Spiritualism. See SEIDEL – MENCHI, *Spiritualismo radicale*, cit., pp. 210-277.

2

Paradossi advocates precisely the very *liberté* Calvin execrated. Lando's Menippean spirit, the humanitarian and even egalitarian tone of his social criticism, the disputational and rationalistic bent of his writings and his humanistic and scientific training all constituted "scandals", which Calvin forcefully denounced in the *Traité des scandales* (1550).[22] *Paradossi* was published at the very onset of Calvin's attacks on libertinism, but it is hard to judge whether or not the work contains covert allusions to these attacks. *Paradosso* XIX, "*Meglio è d'essere in prigione che in libertà*", may also refer to the question of "spiritual Libertinism".[23] Like Queen Margherite, who was notorious for her moral and intellectual "nonchalance", Lando defends true "spiritual" liberty and offers a "consolation" to those imprisoned for their "liberated" and reformed faith.[24]

Paradossi is related to the classical genre of the Stoic paradoxical declamations, encomiums and satirical eulogies, which was revived by Erasmus in his *Moriæ encomium* (1511).[25] As the full title obliquely indicates, *Paradossi* is written in the tradition of Cicero's *Paradoxa Stoicorum*, which consists of literary paradoxes argued against received opinion. In *Paradoxa*, Cicero restates the ethical doctrines of the Stoics, which in his hypocritical society had become *contra opinionem omnium*, and thus paradoxical: virtue as the sole good and unique requisite for happiness; that all good deeds are equally meritorious and all bad deeds equally heinous; that folly is insanity and slavery; and that wisdom is the only freedom and the only form of riches. Writing a few years after the publication of *Cicero relegatus Cicero revocatus*, Lando's dependence on the great Latin *auctor* is, however, apparent only in the last paradox, where Cicero is discredited as "ignorant of philosophy, rhetoric, cosmography and history".

Lando's signature, *Ludebat Hortensius* – written backwards at the end of the book – may allude to that other Hortensius, Cicero's great rival at

---

[22] On Calvin and Libertinism, see J.C. MARGOLIN, *Réflexions sur l'emploi du terme libertin au XVI siècle*, in *Aspects du Libertinisme au XVIe siècle*, Paris, Vrin, 1974, pp. 1-33. On the history of libertinism see R. PINTARD, *Le Libertinage érudit dans la première moitié du XVIIe siècle*, 2nd edn., Geneva and Paris, Slatkine, 1983, pp. XIII--XLIII.

[23] Much like a passage of *Thèatre profane*, by Margherite de Navarre, which may be interpreted as a response to Calvin.

[24] The quality of "freedom" in this paradox echoes T. MORE's *Dialogue of Comfort*, written in the Tower in 1534. Lando may have known this work through More's friends, Vincent and Antonio Buonvisi, whose names are given respectively to the two characters in the dialogue, the old man in prison and his young cousin.

[25] For a complete historical review of paradox in literature and philosophy, see the classic study by R. COLIE, *Paradoxia Epidemica: The Renaissance Tradition of Paradox*, Princeton, N.J., Princeton University Press, 1966.

the bar and champion of the optimates, and may imply that, like an original version of Quintus Hortensius, he has "outdone" Cicero in the art of paradox.[26] Lando questions the very principle of intellectual authority in *Paradosso XXVIII*, "*Che L'opere quali al presente abbiamo sotto nome di Aristotele non sieno di Aristotele*", when he takes up Peter Ramus's thesis that "*quaecumque ab Aristotele dicta essent, commentitia esse*", and subjects the supreme Greek *auctor* to bitter criticism declaring in the XXIX, "*Che Aristotele fusse non solo un ignorante ma anche lo più malvagio uomo di quelle età*".[27] Neither is his *damnatio Aristotelis* limited to academic scientific questions or to logic, as in Ramus's confutations, *Aristotelicae animadversiones*, published in Paris the same year as *Paradossi:* Lando's perspective appears to be primarily ethical and religious, and is conducted from the standpoint of Christian truth. In the last three *Paradossi*, the comic element is suddenly abandoned; the language becomes strong and at times bitter, the tone admonitory. The author, who is now playing his cards face up and revealing his ideological perspectives, seems to urge the reader to return to the beginning and search for the truth behind the laughter.

Lando favoured forms of stylistic inversion, and linguistic and rhetorical estrangement, and concealed his moral and didactic intentions beneath a lively mixture, and inversion, of dialogical forms and discursive genres. *Paradossi*, written in Lombard Italian, was quite at odds with the Tuscan norm; and the stylistic shifts from the *acutum dicendi genus*, with its tropes, paradoxes, irony, hyperbole, emphasis and oxymorons, to the *humile* and *admirabile*, produce a comic effect.[28] Each paradox constitutes a thought-provoking riddle that prompts the reader to bridge the gap between text and its apparent meaning. *Paradossi* and his "lighter" pieces, such as the grotesque sermons on the death of animals, in mock oratorical style, the *Commentario* and *Quattro libri de' Dubbi*, are complex texts that resonate with older literary traditions and are dialogically oriented toward a number of verbal and ideological horizons. Lando's parodic stylisation of various levels and genres of literary language is, as in Rabelais, not an abstract sys-

---

[26] On "outdoing" and the *auctores*, see E.R. CURTIUS, *European Literature and the Latin Middle Ages*, translated by W.R. Trask, Princeton, N.J., Bollingen Series, 1973, pp. 160-162; *Hortensius* is also the title of Cicero's treatise on the praise of philosophy with which Augustine began his process of conversion.

[27] *That the works attributed to Aristotele are not his; That Aristotle was not just ignorant but also the most evil man of his times.*

[28] See *Paradosso XXVII*; on Lando's rejection of Boccaccio, see CORSARO, *Paradossi*, cit., p. 240 ff.

tem of normative forms but a concrete, heterological opinion of the world where, in the words of Bakhtin:

> Every word gives off the scent of a profession, a genre, a current, a party, a particular work, a particular man, a generation, an era [...]. Every word smells of the *context* and *contexts* in which it has lived its intense social life; all words and all forms are inhabited by intentions.[29]

The most immediate context of *Paradossi* is the Stoic discussion on virtue as the supreme good, originating in Aristotle's *Nicomachean Ethics*, a key text for Lando.[30] For both Aristotle and the Stoics, happiness was an activity of the soul in accordance with perfect virtue. Aristotle accepted different senses of the word "good", and believed that "external goods" such as "noble birth, numerous friends, good friends, good children, numerous children, a good old age; further, bodily excellences, such as health, beauty, strength, stature, fitness for athletic contests, a good reputation, honour, good luck [and] virtue"[31] were required for a happy life. By contrast, Stoics such as Zeno and Chrysippus deemed virtue to be the sole and supreme good. They held that external goods could not affect virtue, and that consequently these were not morally relevant and should be treated as morally indifferent (*adiaphora*).

However, the Stoics deem some of the *adiaphora* "preferables", insofar as they accord with nature, while others are "rejected" as contrary to nature. The former include such attributes as life, fame, health and beauty; the latter include their opposites: death, ignominy, sickness and ugliness. Although the "preferables" are morally neutral, the wise man will make use of them if they are available, since they are the material upon which virtuous action is based. In the last instance, however, they are not indispensable for the wise man, whose virtue remains intact even if he enjoys none of these advantages. Opponents of early Stoic ethical theory argued

---

[29] In M. BAKHTIN's *Discourse in the Novel*, in *The Dialogical Imagination, Four Essays by M. Bakhtin*, edited by M. Holquist, Austin, University of Texas Press, 1981, pp. 259-422. This author's italics. For the complexity and range of Lando's intertexts, allusions and references, see Corsaro's exhaustive commentary.

[30] Lando's inspiration is wholly classical and rhetorical; his paradoxes are not in the tradition of the medieval commentaries on *insolubilia* developed from Aristotle's mention of the liar paradox in *De Sophisticis Elenchis* 180*b*. For a useful historical review of the logical paradox see E.J. ASHWORTH, *The Treatment of Semantic Paradoxes from 1400 to 1700*, «Notre Dame Journal of Formal Logic», Vol. XIII, Number 1 (January 1972), pp. 34-52.

[31] *"Art" of Rhetoric* (1360*b* 3-4), Cambridge, Mass., Harvard University Press, Loeb Edition, 1982, p. 49.

that the problem with the Stoic notion of the relation of preferred things to the supreme good is that either the "preferables" should be considered goods, and therefore accorded some moral status, as in Aristotle, or a more radical approach to the supreme good needs to be taken in order to avoid contradiction.

In his *Paradossi* Lando treats the matter with irony, taking a radical and unprecedented approach by employing the typically Stoic mode of reasoning while turning Aristotle's external goods upside down so that the qualities of life, wealth, fame, health and beauty are rejected in favour of death, poverty, ignominy, sickness and ugliness. He pushes the doctrine of *adiaphora* to its extreme, neutralising and ridiculing it by giving moral value to what should be rejected and rejecting what should be preferred.[32] He contends that it is better to be poor than rich, ugly than beautiful, ignorant than wise, drunk than sober; that is preferable to have a dishonest or barren wife; that is better to die than to live a long life, and to live in a humble house than in a mansion; that it is not discreditable to be a bastard; that is better to be at war than at peace, to be exiled than to live in one's own country; and that is better to cry than to laugh.

Like the great "morosophs", Lando exalted ignorance, humbleness and folly, expressing a reformed Christian vocation guided by a belief in man's utter helplessness rather than by intellectual agnosticism. At a time of intense academic debate on the state of the Italian language, Lando's appeal to *sola fide* found linguistic expression in Saint Augustine's anti-rhetoric of the *sermo humilis*, or simple language. In the context of the paradox of the Incarnation, lowly, everyday questions lose their humbleness and are treated in the high style; conversely, the most exalted mysteries of faith may be expressed in simple words that all can understand.[33] Unlike Erasmus, who viewed the *studia humanitatis* as a means to achieve "true nobility" and even social preferment, Lando did not believe in a pragmatic use of intellectual and scientific knowledge. Thus, despite his vast knowledge and appreciation of Greek and Latin culture, in his *Enchiridion*, or manual for Christians, Augustine, openly advises against intellectual pursuit and scientific investigation as ways of fashioning one's identity. In *Paradosso*

---

[32] On *adiaphora* and the rhetoric of prudence in Machiavelli and Reginald Pole, see V. KAHN, *Revising the History of Machiavellism: English Machiavellism and the Doctrine of Things Indifferent*, «Renaissance Quarterly», Vol. 46 (1993), pp. 526-561.

[33] E. AUERBACH, *Literary Language and its Public in Late Latin Antiquity and in the Middle Ages*, translated by R. Manheim, Princeton, N.J., Princeton University Press, 1993, Chap. I; *Paradosso* III, V, in CORSARO, *Paradossi*, cit., pp. 101-114; 122-130.

III, *"Meglio è d'esser ignorante che dotto"*, in praise of ignorance, Lando quotes from St Augustine's *Confessions*, to remind the reader that:

> [...] uneducated people are rising up and capturing heaven, and we with our high culture without any heart – see where we roll in the mud of flesh and blood.[34]

Augustine's quest for the *beata quippe vita est gaudium in veritate* ("the happy life that is joy based on truth"),[35] inspires Lando's *lusus* or "play", and his use of paradox as the cognitive instrument of reformed Christian language. This defrocked Augustinian monk, who had adhered to scripture throughout his religious and literary life, now found himself, in middle age, shipwrecked on the shores of "new doctrine". Together with the two most outstanding converts to Christianity, Paul and Augustine, Lando believed in the inseperableness of epistemology and linguistic theory, and that Christian revelation, the true subject of the Christian orator, cannot be subjected to the pagan divisions of *genera elocutionis*. Paul, the soldier turned apostle, and Augustine, the *Poenus orator* turned Christian pastor and theologian, were his models; and the followers of a more radical form of Evangelism, which stressed Bible-reading and the Pauline Epistles, were his audience.

Throughout *Paradossi*, the inspired tone beneath the laughter suggests a mock-homiletic dimension to the text. In this respect, the sustained parody of *adiaphora* is resonant of the continuing controversy generated by Melancthon's theological system of *adiaphora*, whereby men of good sense can agree that Catholic practices, as "things indifferent", are not doctrinally necessary and may therefore be changed from one place and time to another without endangering the unity of Christendom.[36] *Paradosso* XXIX, against Aristotele, contains an explicit criticism of preaching as "indifferent", and consequently of unreformed Roman Catholic homiletics. In a personal reminiscence, Lando relates how in Padua, Pietro Bembo told him that he had no wish to listen to preachers who had reduced the Gospel to mere scholastic disquisitions. Christian humanism is then reviled for its dependence on Aristotle in the interpretation of Scripture, while Luther is explicitly praised because:

---

[34] AUGUSTINE, *Confessions*, translated by H. Chadwick, Oxford, Oxford University Press, 1991, VIII, viii, p. 146.

[35] AUGUSTINE, *Confessions*, cit., X, xxiiii, p. 199.

[36] On *adiaphora* and Anglican "via media", see V. KAHN, *Revising the History of Machiavellism*, cit., pp. 526-561.

[...] without Aristotle, in his own way and without Scotus' formalities, equipped only with holy Scripture, Luther disbanded all the eminent theologians [...] and proved them how wrong it was to take the chaff for the wheat.[37]

Between 1530 and 1542, reform-minded bishops instructed preachers to abandon the divine rhetoric of the medieval *artes praedicandi* and to emphasise the discussion and commentary on the gospel (*explanatio Evangeli*) in their sermons, a devotional practice that evoked the "exercise of piety" of Thomas a Kempis and the mystical anti-intellectualism of *De Imitatione Christi* (1450 ca.). When the first Italian translation of the New Testament was published in Venice in 1530, Lando may well have been part of the study circles of Pauline Epistles held there and in other Italian cities by the so-called Erasmian cardinals, influential members of the nobility, professionals and merchants.[38] The mock-homiletic quality of *Paradossi* is reminiscent of the *sermons joyeux*, or parodic sermons of late medieval drama, where comedy arises from the incongruity of using the structure of *ars sermocinandi* as a container for absurd or lewd *thema* and *exempla*.[39] A paradoxical *thema* is developed using the *exempla* and the method of probatory division and amplification of divine rhetoric. As "witty preaching", *Paradossi* to some extent anticipates the *gusto espagnol* of the Counter-Reformation: that is, the revival in preaching of the "mannerism" of the patristic tradition.[40]

Lando's extreme rhetorical practice, clearly anti-courtly, stands against the ideological context of Renaissance *civility* and of *sprezzatura* (nonchalance). The rhetorical paradox in vernacular literature was a sophisticated form addressed to a learned coterie and appreciated by a select group of men and women practising the art of *civil conversazione*. In Castiglione's *Cortegiano*[41] paradoxical wit is described as a necessary complement of *sprezzatura*, and as Lady Emilia suggests, paradox is a *giuoco* devoid of

---

[37] *Paradossi*, p. 259, this author's translation.

[38] See R. CESSI, *Paolinismo preluterano*, «Rendiconti dell'Accademia dei Lincei, classe di scienze morali, storiche e filologiche», 12 (1957), pp. 3-30.

[39] On mock sermons, see J.-C. AUBAILLY, *Le monologue le dialogue et la sottie essais sur quelques genres dramatiques de la fin du moyen âge et du début du XVIe siécle*, Paris, Librairie Honouré Champion, 1984.

[40] On the mannerism of late Roman antiquity in Saint Augustine, see E.R. CURTIUS, *European Literature and the Latin Middle Ages*, cit., pp. 279-301.

[41] B. CASTIGLIONE, *Il Libro del Cortegiano*, Napoli-Milano, Riccardo Ricciardi Editore, 1960.

any psychological or ideological commitment to a presumed "truth", an apparently effortless form of verbal acrobatics.

Owing to the "adiaphorous" quality of the detachment it imposes on courtly behaviour, *sprezzatura* is a mode of "presentation of the self" particularly alien to Lando, who throughout his work was passionate in his criticism of princes and courts. Lando's *Paradossi* and his keen rhetoric of estrangement is the opposite of Castiglione's controlled manipulation of the rules of language and conduct in society.[42] At a time when humanists were raising the "threshold of embarassment and shame", and when manners, together with models of speech, were being codified and controlled, Lando's *evangelical* paradoxes turn the essence of courtesy and civility (*civiltà, civilité*) upside down and challenge the very "observation of difference".[43] Lando's unwillingness to identify with any of the social groups of his world and his refusal to speak *comme il faut* to a courtly élite are a consequence of his radical religious creed: he speaks to those who wished to be saved. Indeed, it was Paul who said:

For after that in the wisdom of God the world by wisdom knew not God, it pleased God by the foolishness of preaching to save them that believe.[44]

METAPHOR, PARADOX AND CONVERSION

Lando had absorbed Augustine's verbal theory of the knowledge of God, and eccentrically adapted the questions of cognition through speech and the expression of the Word in the light of contemporary issues. In the context of Augustinian verbal theory, the *Paradossi* are metaphorical and function like *aenigma*, a figure of speech that became extremely influential in Augustine's theory of signification. In the "redeemed rhetoric outcome of a revealed wisdom", *aenigma* was to the converted Augustine both the linguistic means of transformation and the moral impediment to direct vision, as in Paul's "*videmus nunc per speculum in aenigmatae, tunc autem*

---

[42] And also, for that matter, of Erasmus's pretense of detachment, *qua* humanist, from all social groups.

[43] N. ELIAS, *The Civilizing Process*, translated by Edmund Jephcott, New York, Urizen Books, 1978, pp. 70-84; 109-113.

[44] *I Corinthians*, 1, 21; also quoted by Erasmus in in *The Praise of Folly*, translated from the Latin, with an Essay & Commentary, by H.H. Hudson, Princeton, N.J., Princeton University Press, 1941, pp. 89-93.

facie ad faciem".[45] In the medieval theory of verbal signs, where human speech is recast as a Pauline mirror, *aenigma* worked as a *signum translatum*,[46] a "thing which causes us to think of something beyond the impression that the thing in itself makes upon the senses".[47] It worked, therefore, as a *translatio*, or metaphor, as the Latin rhetoricians called it.

Aristotle had been the first to describe metaphor as an *aenigma* and to discuss its capacity "to name the unnamed". Metaphors are therefore creative and help our understanding insofar as they fill what linguists call "lexical gaps".[48] Their function is to instruct by combining elements that have not previously been put together; and their power, Aristotle says, is inseparable from paradox:

> And *clever riddles* are agreeable for the same reason; for some thing is learnt, and the expression is also metaphorical [...] novel expressions arise when what follows is *paradoxical*, and not in accordance with our previous expectations.[49]

Metaphor's *dramatic* power to make things *visible*, *alive* and *actual* is, as Aristotle says, inseparable from either a *logical relation* of *proportion* (A : B = C : D) or a *comparison*. Metaphor is therefore "proportional" and consists of a "transference" of sense. Lando's metaphorical use of paradox may be described in terms of Aristotle's description of the functioning of metaphor, in which a contrary strategy of discourse applies. One can say that the dramatic power of his metaphorical *Paradossi* is inseparable from an *illogical relation* of *disproportion* and *dissimilarity*. The proportional transference of sense is in fact not in a relationship of similarity (*simile*), as is the case with metaphor, but of dissimilarity (*contrarium*). *Paradossi*, do indeed signify reality, but present us not with "likeness", as in metaphor, but with dissimilarity; that is, the horizon of Augustine's *regio dissimilitudinis*, or region of unlikeness: a world out of joint.[50]

---

[45] "For now we see through a glass darkly; but then face to face". On the theory of language in Saint Augustine, see M.L. COLISH, *The Mirror of Language, A Study in the Medieval Theory of Knowledge*, Chap. 1, New Haven, Yale University Press, 1968. The term *aenigma* returns in Cicero who discusses it in *De Oratore* among the standard list of metaphors and rhetorical tropes and defines it as a "species of metaphor".

[46] *De Doctrina Cristiana* II, I 1 CC, 32, 32.

[47] COLISH, *op. cit.*, p. 74.

[48] "*Art*" *of Rhetoric*, III, ii, 12-13, Cambridge, Mass., Harvard University Press, Loeb Edition, 1982. On this and the subject of religion see J.M. SOSKICE, *Metaphor and Religious Language*, Oxford, Clarendon Press, 1985.

[49] "*Art*" *of Rhetoric*, cit., III, xi, 6.

[50] "And I found myself far from you in the region of dissimilarity [...]", *Confessions* VII, 10,16.

The view that knowledge by faith alone was firm and certain, albeit partial, and the belief that cognition should be mediated through signs, is the basis of the medieval fascination with figurative speech and symbolism. Symbolism expressed a need to organise language and the world in terms of *proportion*. In the Middle Ages symbolism was a form of "realism" and its highest form in the root-metaphor of the world was the *Book*.[51] The Book of God's Word, the Bible, was a mirror (*speculum*) of the *Book* of his work, Nature. The *artes liberales*, in the *trivium* (grammar, dialectics and rhetoric), and the *quadrivium* (music, arithmetic, geometry and astronomy) are developments of the Book metaphor that had provided a structure for the universe and the basis of the medieval educational system. In deriding Scholasticism and the Renaissance Christian-humanistic preoccupation with universal proportion, design, purpose and degree, Lando's poetics of disproportion goes well beyond that "*defective* translation into images of secret connections dimly felt"[52] of the waning of the Middle Ages. He challenges the dominant paradigm of the universe as an immense "chain of being" arranged in hierarchical order from the lowliest to the highest kind of creature, which spans Plotinus and Leibnitz.[53]

The *Paradossi* was written in the years immediately following the sack of Rome, and published the same year as Copernicus's *De Revolutionibus Orbium Caelestium* and three years after the institution of the Inquisition and the *Index*. It expresses that "essential tension" felt by artists and creative scientists alike, who like Lando "must be able to live in a state of crisis and in a world out of joint".[54] Kuhn's concept of "essential tension" as a response to crisis linguistically recalls the working of tensive/generative metaphor and of all figures of thought, or tropes, in which the duality of reference, the transference or *carrying-over* of a term from one *realm* into another, from one *system* into another, always involves *tension*.[55] Insofar as the subject of metaphor is a system rather than a word or sentence, "ten-

---

[51] J.M. GELLRICH, *The Idea of the Book in the Middle Ages*, Ithaca, Cornell University Press, 1985.

[52] J. HUIZINGA, *The Waning of the Middle Ages*, New York, Doubleday Anchor Books, 1954, Chap. XV. This author's italics.

[53] A.O. LOVEJOY, *The Great Chain of Being*, Cambridge, Mass., Harvard University Press, 1936, pp. 58-59.

[54] On paradigm-rejection and transition, see T.S. KUHN, *The Structure of Scientific Revolutions*, Chicago, University of Chicago Press, 1970, pp. 77-91; *The essential tension*, Chicago University of Chicago Press, 1977, pp. 225-239.

[55] For the tensive view of metaphor see I.A. RICHARDS, *The Philosophy of Rhetoric*, New York, Oxford University Press, 1936, p. 93.

sion" or "interaction" may be said to construct meaning and generate new knowledge.[56]

For Kenneth Burke, the social function of the *tensive* and generative process of tropes, defined as a "metaphorical extension of perspective by incongruity", consists of the resolution of conflict, in ecological balance. Metaphor, says Burke,[57] may *resolve* ethical ambiguity or confusion by indicating a "moral" by means of semantic incongruities. As the expression of an "essential tension" and as a response to crisis, Lando's metaphorical paradoxes can be said to work as a strategy for handling existential moments, and to reveal a *via negativa* for the discovery and description of truth. This was the route later followed by Montaigne, who gave a powerful demonstration of the impotence of human reason in his *Apologie de Raymond Sebond* (1575).[58]

---

[56] M. BLACK, *More about Metaphors*, in *Metaphor and Thought*, edited by A. Ortonty, 2nd edn. Cambridge and New York, Cambridge University Press, 1993, p. 28.

[57] K. BURKE, *On Symbol and Society*, edited and with an introduction by J.R. Gusfield, Chicago, University of Chicago Press, 1989, p. 6. On metaphor and resolution of conflict, see also, P. RICŒUR, *The Rule of Metaphor: The Creation of Meaning in Language*, translated by R. Czerny with K. McLaughlin and J. Costello (London and New York, Routledge, 2003), 2nd edn.

[58] MONTAIGNE, *Essays*, Paris, Librairie Garnier Fréres, 1943, vol. II, p. 115.

CHAPTER TWO

THE FRENCH *PARADOXES*

> Ce temps n'est propre à nous amender qu'à recu-
> lons, par disconvenance plus que par accord, par dif-
> férence que par similitude...
>
> MONTAIGNE

CHARLES ESTIENNE'S PARADOXES

Lando's *Paradossi* were an immediate and international success. In 1543, some of them were circulated in pirated manuscript in the French translations of Maurice Scève.[1] In the years between the Lyon edition of *Paradossi* and Charles Estienne's *Paradoxes* in 1553,[2] the literary genre of the paradox had become distinctly popular in France. The "age of bluff" was in full swing, and the *blazons de la goutte, d'Honneur et de la Quarte* testify to the flowering of this genre.[3] Similarly, the contemporary French debate on the status and character of women, or the *querelle des femmes*, quite possibly initiated by Jean de Meung, had developed more into an intellectual controversy on lady friends, or a *querelle des amyes*, conducted in a satirical and paradoxical tone. It was a serio-comic exam-ination of the behaviour of the courtly lady and an expression of the anti-*Courtier* trend. Lando's friend the humanist printer Étienne Dolet, who had revised a translation of the *Courtier*, published two books in

---

[1] He had urged Lando to publish them anonymously in Lyon with the Italian printer Gio-vanni Pullone, see CORSARO, *op. cit.*, p. 7.

[2] Its full title is *Paradoxes, ce sont propos contre la commune opinion: debatus, en forme de Declamations forenses: pour exerciter les jeunes advocats, en causes difficiles.*

[3] B.C. BOWEN, *The Age of Bluff: Paradox and Ambiguity in Rabelais and Montaigne*, Urba-na, University of Illinois Press, 1972; A.M. TOMARKEN, *The Smile of Truth. The French Satirical Eulogy and its Antecedents*, Princeton, N.J., Princeton University Press, 1990; H.K. MILLER, *The Paradoxical Encomium with Special Reference to Its Vogue in England, 1600-1800*, «Modern Phi-lology», 53. 3, Feb., 1956, pp. 145-178.

the *querelle* genre: Bertrand de la Borderie's, *Amye de court* (1541), and Antoine Héroet's *Parfaite amie* (1542). Philibert de Vienne's *Philosophe de Court* (1547) was yet another paradoxical eulogy of courtliness as a definition of virtue. Many of the works classified as part of the *querelle des femmes* argument were not in fact serious polemics but exercises in paradox. In 1599, when the *querelle* was far from settled, Alexandre de Pontaymeri adapted Agrippa's *De Nobilitate* and published in Paris his *Paradoxe apologétique, où il est fidellement démonstré que la femme est beaucoup plus parfaicte que l'homme en toute action de vertu*.[4] The fashion for paradox affected du Bellay, who in 1556 wrote his *Hymne de la Surdité*; and in 1577 the lawyer Jean Bodin produced a seminal essay that contributed to the *querelle* on price inflation initiated by the Seigneur de Malestroict, with the first paradox in economics.[5] In 1582, Agrippa's invective *De Incertitudine*, known in intellectual circles as a sceptical and fideistic text and quoted on several occasions by Montaigne in his *Apologie de Raymond Sebond*,[6] acquired paradoxical overtones in its first French translation.

Charles Estienne (1504-1564), son of the royal printer and scholar Henri *le grand* (d. 1520) and the founder of three generations of great humanist printers, was the French translator of *Paradossi*.[7] He transformed Lando's complex and heterodox paradoxes into a collection of intellectual curiosities and ludic rhetorical devices for an accomplished professional clientele. In an unadorned yet polished French, *Paradoxes* was intended as a serious, albeit light, rhetorical tool for law students who wished to learn how to plead extremely difficult cases *a contrario* before the courts.

---

[4] According to R. Colie (*Paradoxia Epidemica*, cit., p. 103), all humanist defences of women including those by Agrippa, Erasmus, Vivés, and Pontaymeri, are paradoxical. From the "Encomie du corbeau" to that of "La Grenouille" examples of the paradoxical encomium in Renaissance France can be found in the works of both the Marotic poets and those of the Pléiade. Rabelais, was a master of the genre, with Panurge's praise of debts and debtors, and a panegiric of the codpiece.

[5] J. BODIN, *Response to the Paradoxes of Malestroit*, translated and edited by H. Tudor and R.W. Dyson, Bristol, Thoemmes Press, 1997. On MALESTROICT, see *Jehan Cherruyt, seigneur de Malestroict, Paradoxes inédits du seigneur de Malestroit touchant les monnoyes: avec la Response du president de La Tourette*, edited by L. Einaudi, Turin, Einaudi, 1937.

[6] It was presented as "[...] *A Work Which Can Be Profitable and Which Will Bring satisfaction to Those Who Frequent the Courts of the Nobility, and Who Wish to Learn to reason on an Infinity of Topics against Commonly Held Opinion*". See M. VAN DE POEL, *The French translation of Agrippa von Nettesheim's Declamatio de incertitudine et vanitate scientiarum et artium: Declamatio as Paradox*, in *Translation and the Trasmission of culture Between 1300 and 1600*, edited by J. Beer and K. Llyod-Jones, Michigan, Medieval Institute Publications, 1995, pp. 305-329.

[7] [CHARLES ESTIENNE], *Paradoxes*, edited by T. Peach, Geneva, Droz, 1998.

Such a pedagogic intention is declared in the title of the first edition, *"pour exerciter les jeunes advocats, en causes difficiles"*.[8]

By erasing Lando's linguistic, ideological and religious meanings and placing emphasis on the importance of sound reasoning, Estienne brought the rhetorical paradox back to its original, sophistic usage and the legal milieu of the courtroom. *Paradoxes* is therefore presented as a manual of jocose moot cases for young lawyers. Estienne amplifies the epideictic character of Lando's satirical eulogies and stresses the judicial tone to the point where his paradoxes resemble a lawyer's harangue. While preserving the original dialogical and indeed comic element, the French humanist encourages an *esprit de corps*, punctuating the work with addresses to both court and auditors (*messieurs*), and with legal jargon. He gives the *exempla* the topicality and piquancy of a *cause grasse*, which greatly appealed to the law apprentices of the parliament of Paris who congregated in the *sociétés joyeuses* of the *Basoche*.[9]

Estienne neutralised the two potentially subversive Erasmian principles that constitute the original framework of *Paradossi*, giving the text a didactic structure and a practical function. The first principle, of the poverty of Christ, which is amplified in *Paradosso* I (*"Che miglior sia la Povertà che la Ricchezza"*), receives a rather cool treatment from Estienne, who breaks up Lando's emotional declamation into a series of arguable units. In general, the homiletic elements, such as Latin sentences from the Gospels and Lando's appeals to Christ, are not translated. The second Erasmian principle, that of the divorce between wisdom and eloquence that permeates the *Paradossi*, becomes "technically" irrelevant. Moreover, Estienne, who like his father and his brother Robert made an important contribution to the transmission of classical learning, was unaffected by the crisis of exemplarity and authority that characterises Lando's works. For instance, he does not translate the paradoxes against Boccaccio, Aristotle and Cicero or *Paradosso* XI (*"Non esser detestabile né odiosa la moglie dishonesta"*), which is considered too improper to be included in his collection. *Paradoxes* ends instead with a new paradox, penned by Estienne himself and based on the tradition of satirical invectives against lawyers, *"Que le plaider est chose tresutile et necessaire à la vie des hommes"*.

---

[8] For a complete list of the French editions, see PEACH, *op. cit.*, pp. 37-43; later editions enlarge the audience to address the *jeunes esprit* and *toutes gens*.

[9] Estienne carefully avoids lewd allusions; see for instance how the example of a "giovanetto toscano", in *Paradosso* II – an indirect reference to Florentine homosexuality – becomes "jeune fille de Perigod" (p. 81). On other aspects of Estienne's translation, see L. ZILLI, *I Paradossi di Ortensio Lando rivisitati da Charles Estienne*, in *Parcours et Rencontres Mélanges de langue, d'histoire et de littérature françaises offert à Enea Balmas*, Paris, 1993, pp. 665-674.

Linguistically, Estienne's aim is to "domesticate" Lando's unruly text. The careful avoidance of Italianisms indicates that his efforts are geared to exalt the superiority of the French language over competing vernaculars while concealing its foreign original.[10] Charles Estienne never forgets his selected audience of lawyers; he alters Italian names and incidents to French examples and is very careful in fashioning his translation down to the last detail. In *Declamation V*, for instance, Lando's *nobilissimi ingegni* -- the authorities for his own praise of folly – is translated as *"deus excellens advocates"*. Where Estienne's translation is characterised by a professional concern, Lando's *Paradossi*, with its bold rejection of the ideals of Renaissance humanism, expresses a marked anti-professional and anti-vocational stance. From the little we know of his monastic experience, medical studies and academic affiliations, it appears that Lando shunned lasting professional commitments. His sharp critique of courtly life and his refusal to be on the payroll of a prince not only indicate his "political" beliefs but may also be seen as a refusal to identify with any "professional status" and a rejection of Castiglione's ideal of courtiership as a secular, "modern" profession.[11]

By contrast, Estienne, himself a printer and physician and thus both humanist and professional, was particularly responsive to the intellectual needs of the emerging professions. Besides *Paradoxes*, which was addressed to the *gens de justice*, he composed a number of how-to books, among them a road guide for French merchants, a handbook for landed proprietors and Galen's *Anatomical Procedures*.[12] One key aspect of Estienne's involvement in professional literature is the question of the adaptation of *studia humanitatis* outside the classroom to the practical needs of the real world. Writing as a professional, for professionals, Estienne attempted to shape the abstract ideals of humanist *paideia* for personal

---

[10] His nephew, Henry Estienne (1531-1598) was the most distinguished Hellenist of his generation, a theoretician and practitioner of the humanist translation and author of *Deux dialogues du nouveau langage françois: italianizé et autrement desguizé, principalement entre les courtisans de ce temps: de plusieurs nouveautez qui ont accompagné ceste nouveauté de langage: de quelques courtisanismes modernes, et de quelques singularitez courtisanesques*, edited by P.-M. Smith, Geneva, Slatkine, 1980.

[11] *Paradossi* deserves more attention as a parody of the rhetoric of civil *conversazione*. On the courtier and professions and related bibliography, see D. BIOW, *Doctors, Ambassadors, Secretaries: humanism and professions in Renaissance Italy*, Chicago, University of Chicago Press, 2002, pp. 10-12. During his stay in Lyon, Lando was in close contact with Estienne Dolet and the circle of intellectuals who were involved in the translation of *Il Cortegiano*, but were also critical of Castiglione's courtly values.

[12] See J.C. MARGOLIN, *Science, humanisme et société, le cas de Charles Estienne*, in *Parcours et rencontres*, cit., pp. 423-441.

growth into a pedagogical programme to meet the actual needs of those practising professions in 16th-century Europe. This practical and professional linking up of humanist learning helped shape the nature of Renaissance humanism in Europe and was the major binding force of that international *Respublica Literaria* or "Republic of Letters"[13] that embraced a linguistically and religiously heterogeneous community.

In the context of the early modern printing industry, Estienne's "professional" publications are an example of the sort of publishing strategy whereby the press created new cultural networks by creating new clienteles. By the middle of the 16th-century, printers in France were starting to gauge the special needs of their reading public rather than to extend that public *per se*. Chartier argues that such systems "categorised the products of the printing trade in cultural terms, thus fragmenting the market into clienteles presumed to be discrete and establishing new cultural frontiers".[14]

PARADOXES JOYEUSES

As a book for both oratorical practice and amusement, *Paradoxes* was addressed to the *jeunes avocats*, the young barristers and law apprentices of Paris, the so-called clerks to the *procureur* (much the same as a modern English solicitor). After studying three years for a licence in the Faculty of Law, during their subsequent training (*stage*) they joined the *sociétés joyeuses* of the "Kingdom of the *Basoche*".[15] This was indeed the most famous confraternity on account of its pre-eminence in the variegated universe of late medieval youth organisations, and for the impulse it lent to French co-

---

[13] On the history and contexts of the "Republic of Letters", see H. BOTS – F. WAQUET, *La République des Lettres*, Paris, Belin-De Boek, 1997.

[14] R. CHARTIER, *The Cultural Uses of Print in Early Modern France*, Princeton, N.J., Princeton University Press, 1987, p. 182.

[15] I believe that the etymology of the term *Basoche*, of unknown origin, is from *bas* (low) and *soçon, soichon*, n.m. *compagnon, associé* (fellow) with wordplay on *cochon* (young pig). *Bas* may refer to their place in the legal profession, as well as to the actual lower level of the *Palais de Justice*, near the famous kitchens, where students used to meet. For the history of the *Basoche* and their dramatic production, see H.G. HARVEY, *The Theatre of the Basoche*, Parts I-III, Cambridge, Mass., Harvard University Press, 1941; J.-C. AUBAILLY, *Le théâtre médiéval, profane et comique*, Paris, Larousse Université, 1975, Vol. II, Chapters I, II, V, 1984. On youth groups like the *Basoche*, the use of imaginary kingdoms and the anthropological *rites de passage*, see N. ZEMON DAVIS, *Society and Culture in Early Modern France*, Stanford, Ca., Stanford University Press, 1975; D.A. BELL, *Lawyers and Citizens, The Making of a Political Elite in Old Regime France*, Oxford, Oxford University Press, 1994; P. GRIMALDI PIZZORNO, *Justice at Play or the Play of Justice*, «Ludica», 8, 2002, pp. 115-127.

3

medy in general. Well before the birth of any cohesive corporate body of barristers (ca. 1660), the *Basoche* was first organised by the royal magistrates into a formal and permanent society with the objective of imposing a professional discipline on these young, unmarried men and regulating the conditions of their apprenticeship. It took the form of a miniature kingdom, with all the administrative and judicial machinery that a kingdom required; it had a king, and even an independent system of coinage. The jurisdiction of the Court of the *Basoche* was real, albeit limited, and its reality lent a seriousness to the petty proceedings that afforded excellent practice for the apprentices of law.

With the youth organisation of the *Basoche*, education and the nature of legal practice played their part in bonding a socially diverse group of young men that by the mid-14th-century had begun to challenge ecclesiastical jurisdiction. By the end of the 15th-century, professional, bourgeois jurists had replaced the untrained nobles and clergymen of the judicial branches of Philip the Fair's Council. A newly organised intellectual class had succeeded in the competition with the clerical jurists and could challenge the University of Bologna in the game of jurisprudence and legal erudition. There were about 10,000 *Basochiens* in Paris, and each High Court had its own separate division. It was here, within the culturally sophisticated circles of the new *noblesse de robe* in France, that professional comic drama originated.

Petty lawsuits gave the *Basochiens* excellent opportunities to practice writing and to play farce. Soon they began to prepare burlesque lawsuits, called *causes grasses* because they were performed at Carnival time. On the day appointed for the *cause grasse* (sometimes mockingly referred to as a *cause solennelle*), the High Court appeared in full splendour to try the most scandalous or ridiculous case the clerks of law could find to bring before it. The especially privileged and privately performed *causes grasses* of the *Basoche* of Paris were already famous in the 15th-century, and their fame was still considerable two centuries later. Local, real-life scandals were sometime chosen for the mock trial, as was the case for the *cause grasse* presented to the court on Fat Tuesday in Grenoble in the year 1605. The humour in the mock trials arose from the incongruity between the elaborate processes of justice and the learning of judges and advocates, and the trivial, paradoxical case. The technical language of the law was mixed with other languages and syntaxes to concoct a sort of *fricassée de mots*. The best example is the scene of the *grand delirium* in the legal farce *Mâtre Pathelin*. This monologue is written in a mishmash of Flemish and Anglo-German that is unintelligible to the modern reader, and the early medieval nonsense tradition of the *fatrasies* and *resveries* is pushed to its limits. The mock court scene in the second part of the farce, where the travelling judge, together with Agnelet (the culprit), the draper, the plaintiff and the lawyer, are all assembled on the stage, represents a legalistic carnival in which *drapperie* and *bergerie* are constantly confused in a whirlwind of legal and linguistic nonsense and *tromperie*. The administration of justice, however, was not satirised; in mixing "high" and "low" culture, the *causes grasses* primarily expressed a taste for judicial and epideictic paradox whose origin was not entirely "popular".

The *Basoche* met once a year at Carnival time to perform plays in private, but as early as 1424 they began to perform in public on other festive occasions and to include comic plays in their performances. In 1442 the *Confrères de la Passion* invited the law students to assist them with comic interludes to be presented between the *journées* of their mystery plays, and from that moment on the *Basochiens* and the *Confrères* had the almost exclusive privilege of producing and staging comic plays in Paris. In conjunction with the performance of religious plays, the *Confrères*, *Basochiens* and *Enfants-sans-souci* played moralities, farces, and *sotties* to the general public in Paris at the *Hôtel de la Trinité* and later at the *Hôtel de Bourgogne* until the end of the 16th-century. Of all the authors of the *Basoche*, Guillaume Coquillart (d. 1510 ca.) enjoyed a considerable and enduring success. He took a baccalaureate in Canon Law, became an *avocat* at the Châtelet de Paris and later moved to Rheims, where he pursued a brilliant legal career, becoming a judge in the ecclesiastical courts and an important figure in civil life. Today Coquillart's lampooning of his profession is almost forgotten, but in 1548 his books were bought by men of law, and in the preface to *La comédie du sacrifice or Les Abusez*[16] Estienne still classed him, *avecq' son plaidoye*, and the author of *Mâtre Pathelin* among the best poets of France.[17]

---

[16] *La Comédie à l'époque d'Henri II et de Charles IX* (*Théâtre français de la Renaissance, Première Série*, 6 1541-1554), edited by L. Zilli et al., Florence, Leo S. Olschki, and Paris, PUF, 1994, p. 95.

[17] B.C. BOWEN, *Les characteristiques essentielles de la farce française*, Urbana, University of Illinois Press, 1964. In Coquillart's poetry the lawyer is represented as "Regnaud Prens-tout" or "Reginald grab-all" and "Oudard de la main garnie" or "Edward of the well-oiled palm" see J.V. ALTER, *Les origines de la satire anti-bourgeoise en France*, Geneva, Droz, 1966, pp. 166 ff.

CHAPTER THREE

TRANSLATION AND THE BUSINESS OF LETTERS

> even the best translation, is, for mere necessitie, but
> an evill imped wing to flie withall, or a hevie stompe
> leg of wood to go withal
>
> ROGER ASCHAM

TUDOR TRANSLATION AND GRUB STREET

At the close of the 15th-century, English played no part whatsoever in the curricula of the universities; there was no composition in English and only a few progressive grammar schools had started to use books with English words, phrases, and sentences to be translated into Latin. At around this time, Robert Whittington, teacher and author of a renowned Latin grammar, and the translator of Cicero's *Paradoxes*, claimed that:

> [...] many yonge persones very studyous of knowledge of thynges, and be vehemently bente to rede newe workes, and in especyall [those] that be translated into the vulgare tonge.[1]

The intensive study and painstaking practice of a genuine Latinity, which eschews the "barbarous" Latin of the later Middle Ages and conforms more or less to the diction and style of the "best" authors of classical and early Christian literature, almost inevitably demanded the use of the vernacular for translation. Apprenticeship in the art of vernacular translation was based on the twofold process of translating first from the Latin into English and then from the English into Latin. This method, advocated by Roger Ascham in his *Schoolmaster*,[2] which only a small minority fa-

---

[1] Here and *passim*, see H.S. BENNETT's two classical studies, *English Books and Readers 1475 to 1557*, Cambridge, Cambridge University Press, 1952, and *English Books and Readers 1558 to 1603*, Cambridge, Cambridge University Press, 1965.

[2] *The scholemaster or plaine and perfite way of teachyng children, to vnderstand, write, and*

voured by birth, wealth or talent could practise, did however guarantee the attainment of proficiency in sound Latin composition, and indirectly improved written English. Somewhat paradoxically, the insistence on the attainment of proficiency in sound Latin composition by humanists such as John Colet, Sir Thomas More, Thomas Lupset and Sir Thomas Elyot was what gave composition in English a firm, albeit secondary, place in the early Tudor emphasis on education, thus contributing to the development of an original English expository prose.

The years from the introduction of printing to the advent of the New Learning, 1477-1517, is the essentially medieval period, when Boethius, "Cato", and "Aesop" were translated, and Ovid and Virgil appeared in summaries and *rifacimenti*. The following 40 years, until 1557, are marked by the many translations from the Greek moralists, especially Lucian and Plutarch, under the influence of Erasmus and his group, and by a number of translations of historians. Under Henry VIII, translations of classical works reflected the religious designs and utilitarian aims of the king and his councillors. Works dealing with philosophy, science, political strategy and military science, and tracts on moral and civic virtues intended to improve the body politic, greatly outnumbered those lacking any clear moral or didactic purpose. Since the publication of the *Miscellany*, a collection of early Tudor court poetry, by Tottel,[3] who was responsible for the publication of nearly all the existing verse translations with the exception of Virgil, the demand for translations in prose and verse, from ancient and modern authors, continued to grow. Under Elizabeth I, translations made up a significant part of the output of the book trade, running to over 1,000 works. During the latter part of the Tudor age, the intense and varied nature of the translating business is proof of the wider uses of writing and printing, and of a changing and growing readership.

One significant aim of Henry VIII's politico-cultural programme was to popularise the royal supremacy and discredit papal authority and practice in England. This was achieved by means of a court-centred system of patronage and the press. Since the creation of the Office of the King's Printer,[4]

---

speake, the Latin tong but specially purposed for the priuate bryngyng vp of youth in ientlemen and noble mens houses, and commodious also for all such, as haue forgot the Latin tonge..., 1570 STC (2nd ed.) /832.

   [3] Richard Tottel (1528-1593) was both printer and bookseller of common-law books.

   [4] For a synthesis of the question and the establishment of the Office of the King's Printer,

instituted by Henry VII, the press could be used as a mechanism of government control. Henry began to develop it in the 1530s, in collaboration with his Secretary of State and subsequently Lord Privy Seal Thomas Cromwell.[5] Government action was systematic and planned, and the propaganda campaign was conducted in several stages and with a range of printed propaganda. The Office of the King's Printer was used "intensively, carefully and purposefully, to back up political action".[6]

The pulpit occupied a key place in the government's press campaign, via the King's Printer, and Thomas Wolsey incorporated its management into the general system for supervising the work of the clergy, whose propagandistic activities became indispensable for the enforcement of the new order. Cromwell, inspired probably by Richard Morison, his secretary and a leading pamphleteer, also used the stage for propaganda purposes and organised and financed travelling acting companies that performed plays written by the new Protestant authors. With community drama and other traditional ceremonies and practices, "intellectual" work in general was appropriated to encourage adherence to the royal cause, as new forms of group identity began to compete with the old order.[7] In 1562, John Foxe, the author of *The Book of Martyrs*, wrote:

> [...] players, printers and preachers be set up of God as a triple bulwark against the triple crown of the Pope, to bring him down.[8]

During the early Tudor period "humanistic translation" was generally confined to the circles and servants of Privy Councillors, courtiers, members of the Inns, and prominent political figures in the establishment and local government and university scholars. Aware of the enormous power wielded by translation in the construction of national identity, they imposed constraints on it that extended from method and the choice of source material to the "utility" of the book for the classroom, the pulpit

---

see P. Neville-Sington, *Press, Politics and Religion*, in *The Cambridge History of the Book in Britain*, edited by L. Hellinga and J.B. Trapp, Vol. III, Cambridge, Cambridge University Press, 1999, pp. 576-577.

[5] G.R. Elton, *Policy and Police: The Enforcement of the Reformation in the Age of Thomas Cromwell*, Cambridge, Cambridge University Press, 1972, Chap. 4.

[6] Id., *Policy and Police*, cit., p. 206.

[7] *Ivi*, pp. 171-216; E.L. Eisenstein, *The Printing Revolution in Early Modern Europe*, Cambridge, Cambridge University Press, 1983, p. 96.

[8] E. Duffy, *The Stripping of the Altars traditional religion in England*, c. 1400-c. 1580, New Haven, Yale University Press, 2005, p. 23.

or government. By 1531 the common lawyer Thomas Cromwell, under the patronage of Thomas Wolsey and in collaboration with the "King's Printer", Thomas Berthelet, was emerging as a "semi-official" sponsor of translations of Erasmus. Alongside the most prolific populariser of Erasmus, Richard Taverner, Cromwell's leading pamphleteers, Richard Morison and Thomas Starkey, were university men trained in Padua and connected to the Inns of, Court who worked following the official line. Among Cromwell's last and most distinguished recruits for his translating circle were Thomas More's brother-in-law, the author, printer and barrister of the Middle Temple John Rastell (d. 1536), and his son William (d. 1565), a student of Lincoln's Inn and later a judge. With their output of printed translations of common law books,[9] these two made an impressive contribution.

The lawyers' humanist activity served the Protestant cause for religious, political and educational purposes, and translations of classical texts of practical utility for the "Commonweale" were much the easiest – and safest – means of courting royal favour.[10] Cromwell also backed the publication in translation of two key anti-papal tracts, Lorenzo Valla's *Donation of Constantine* (1534) and the first printed edition of Marsiglio of Padua's *Defensor pacis* (1535). Translating these works into English gave the campaign a respectable and scholarly European backing.[11] It was within the closed circles of influential and royal patronage that humanism and Erasmianism made their way. By the time the royal divorce went through, government policy had succeeded in bringing Erasmus before the general public, and his translations could be purchased on English bookstalls.[12] Belief in evangelical humanism as the expression of a "middle way", the encouragement of educational reform, the advocacy of utilitarian writings, and the control

---

[9] On learning and lawyers in early Tudor England, see E.W. Ives, *The Common Lawyers*, in *Profession, Vocation and Culture in Late Medieval England*, edited by C.H. Clough, Liverpool, Liverpool University Press, pp. 181-217. J.H. Baker, *The Books of the Common Law*, in *The Cambridge History of the Book in Britain*, edited by L. Hellinga and J.B. Trapp, Vol. III, Cambridge, Cambridge University Press, 1999, pp. 411-432.

[10] G.R. Elton, *Policy and Police*, cit., p. 186 and J.K. McConica, *English Humanists and Reformation Politics under Henry VIII and Edward VI*, Oxford, Clarendon Press, 1965, p. 119. On English law students in Italy, see J. Woolfson, *Padua and the Tudors*, Cambridge, J. Clarke & Co., 1998, Chap. 2; C.H. Conley, *The First English Translators of the Classics*, New Haven, Yale University Press, 1927, Chap III; H. Burrowes Lathrop, *Translations from the Classics into English from Caxton to Chapman 1477-1620*, Madison, University of Wisconsin, 1933, p. 35.

[11] Elton, *Policy and Police*, cit., p. 186.

[12] J.K. McConica, *English Humanists and Reformation Politics*, cit., Chap. 3.

of the printing presses remained Elizabeth's chief instruments in training a new generation of civil servants, while unifying public opinion and maintaining public support. According to her tutor, Roger Ascham, Elizabeth had "perfect readiness" in Italian, French and Spanish. Herself an accomplished translator, she wished to bring a halt to the decline in formal learning brought about by the Dissolution under Henry VIII and Edward VI, and by the Marian persecutions. The improvement of the quality of a more organic English language that could express an independent national ethos was essential for the Queen's project of forming a new generation of educated men able to produce books and take up positions in government.

In keeping with the cultural programme of the early Tudor period, the new Elizabethan aristocracy actively cooperated in rebuilding the religious and national identity of England, and in fostering patriotic and Protestant values by supporting learning. Translators, even those with only a basic knowledge of modern languages, enthusiastically participated in this programme, and were supported and directed more by a system of aristocratic patronage than directly by the court. Discriminating patrons such as William Cecil, Lord Burghley and Robert Dudley, Earl of Leicester, although rivals, operated an almost indistinguishable cultural policy across a broad front in the interests of scholarship and reform. They sponsored translations of Calvin and supported the publication of books on policy, civil courtesy and history ancient and modern, as well as translations of classical texts and works on medicine, astronomy, mathematics and chronology. The authors, who were often rewarded with courtly or academic preferment, in turn dedicated their books to these patrons.[13]

By the end of the 16th-century, with the emergence of a public literary sphere, books of all kinds helped reshape the outlook and manners of the English élite. With the spread of literacy and the expansion of the public stage, in the 1570s the number of translations produced for non-élite readers increased rapidly. Translators and the new "professional" authors did not attempt to demonstrate their ability as linguists and scholars but to give evidence of their zeal to serve their masters. One of them was Anthony Munday (bap. 1560, d. 1633), the translator, from the French of Estienne, of Lando's *Paradossi*, of which 12 were collected under the title *The Defence of Contraries*.[14] Munday courted all manner of readers and, always

---

[13] On patronage and humanism in Elizabethan England, see E. ROSENBERG, *Leicester, Patron of Letters*, New York, Columbia University Press, 1955, and *Patronage in the Renaissance*, edited by G. Lytle and S. Orgel, Princeton, N.J., Princeton University Press, 1981.

[14] *The Defence of Contraries Paradoxes against common opinion, debated in forme of decla-*

obsequious before powerful patrons, constantly advertised his work in pursuit of his twin goals, money and preferment. He worked for profit-seeking printers such as John Allde and John Charlewood, Giordano Bruno's printer, and for the arch-pirate of the Elizabethan printing press, John Wolfe. His writing, which often plumbed the literary depths, was not altogether cut off from higher seats of power and learning, and belonged to the interconnected network of practices that defined early-modern print culture.[15]

When examining the work of translation in early modern England, and the occupational groups involved in it, one should consider that the term "print culture" – understood as the revolution in communications that influenced almost all aspects of life since the development of movable type in the 15th-century – should not be used in its global sense. On the contrary, particular local cases, with interconnected networks of specific communities of readers, patrons, writers and book producers, should be taken into account.[16] The work of translators and the diffusion of translated works in the Elizabethan period were in fact carried out by men recruited from throughout the ranks of society, with little in common. They ranged from obscure and often invisible "professional" translators with a very approximate knowledge of modern languages, who toiled for booksellers, to continental French and Italian émigrés, exiles or refugees, to collegiate amateurs, aristocrats, gentlemen lawyers and learned women.[17]

---

mations in place of publike censure: only to exercise yong wittes in difficult matters. Wherein is no offence to Gods honour, the estate of princes, or priuate mens honest actions: but pleasant recreation to beguile the iniquity of time. Translated out of French by A.M. one of the messengers of her Maiesties Chamber. London, John Windet for Simon Waterson, 1593. It was republished in 1602 as Paradoxes against common opinion: debated in form of Declamations in place of Publique censure, with a new title page. The only, defective, known copy is in the Bodleian Library (formerly STC 16661). The Defence of Contraries contains only twelve paradoxes: For Povertie, For the Hard-favoured face or fowle Complexion, For the ignorant. For Blindneße, For the Foole, For him that hath lost his worldlie goods, honours and Preferments, For Drinkers, For Sterillitie, For the Exiled, For infirmitie of the body, For Teares, For Dearth. At the end of the volume Munday promises a second part – no longer extant, if ever produced – that includes Estienne's own paradox "That a Lawyer is a most profitable member in a Commonweale".

[15] R. DARNTON, The Literary Underground of the Old Regime, Cambridge, Mass., Harvard University Press, 1982. See also, Society and Culture in Early Modern France, edited by N. Zemon Davis, Stanford, Ca., Stanford University Press, 1975, pp. 97-123.

[16] R. CHARTIER, The Cultural Uses of Print in Early Modern France, cit., Chap. V. For a lively description of the interplay of actors in the work of translation, see T. NASHE's address To The Gentlemen Students of Both Universities, edited by R.B. McKerrow, Vol. III, Oxford, Blackwell, 1966, pp. 311-325.

[17] London print shops perpetuated the continental practice of giving sanctuary to destitute scholars who offered their editorial services, alongside the locally hired professionals, in exchange for board and lodging. In London Giordano Bruno and Lodovico Castelveltro had both had experiences similar to those of Ortensio Lando who was offered work and hospitality by Giolito

In post-Tridentine Europe, imperial, national and papal authorities viewed translation with suspicion, and edicts issued by these authorities effectively prevented the printing of Bibles in the vernacular. By contrast, in Reformed England, translation flourished and was deemed consistent with the evangelical belief that the "Gospel truth" should not be withheld from ordinary men. Indeed, the lay evangelism of the Protestants coincided with the patriotic and democratic interests of versatile occupational groups engaged in the production and distribution of printed material for a lay readership. These groups challenged academic monopolies and professional élites bent on preventing the diffusion of esoteric knowledge in Greek, Latin and law-French to a wider, non-aristocratic public. With the stamp of government approval, both education and religion were cast in the same uniform and colloquial mould, with the vernacular Bible and the *Book of Common Prayer*, grammars, primers, legal and scientific texts being churned out by printers for the lay reader.[18]

With the incorporation of the London Stationers in around the year 1577, the book trade was suddenly faced with a larger and more eager reading public that demanded not only works of philosophy, religious devotion and moral education, but also literary fiction, entertainment and news. For example, the volume of "literature" published for the Elizabethan middle class was three times that for the period 1475-1558.[19] Not only had the demand increased, but it had become more selective. Chaucer and the medieval authors and genres once in favour were now less fashionable, and new trends in poetry or prose appealed to the bourgeois reader intent on his or her own social betterment. With the growing availability of low-cost books, the strategies adopted by individual printers were increasingly governed – book censorship permitting – by the criterion of profit, so that printers paid greater attention to the demand for translation from classical and modern languages into modern English. The bookstalls of Paris and Rome, and

---

and Griphius in Venice and Lyon. On similar arrangements practiced by John Wolfe, see S. MASSAI, *John Wolfe and the Impact of Exemplary Go-between on Early Modern Print Culture*, in *Renaissance Go-Betweens Cultural Exchange in Early Modern Europe*, edited by A. Höfele and W. von Koppenfels, Berlin, de Gruyter, 2005, pp. 104-118.

[18] E.L. EISENSTEIN, *The Printing Press as an Agent of Change Communications and Cultural Transformations in Early Modern Europe*, Vol. II, New York, Cambridge University Press, 1979, Chap. 4; H.S. BENNETT, *English Books and Readers 1475 to 1557*, cit., 1952, pp. 16-17. See also, W. BOUTCHER, *The Oxford Guide to Literature in English Translation*, edited by P. France, Oxford, Oxford University Press, 2000, pp. 45-55.

[19] In the sense of "light literature" *OED*, LIGHT 19. said of dramatic works, music, etc., requiring little mental work, amusing and entertaining. On the changing meaning of "literature" see *OED* LITERATURE.

the Frankfurt spring book fair, were literally ransacked by printers, booksellers and translators searching for suitable material for an English reading public among the works of French, Spanish, Portuguese and Italian authors. On the bookstalls of Saint Paul's churchyard in London one could purchase translations of the books on the Catholic Church's list of prohibited works, the *Index Librorum Prohibitorum*. It was precisely this sort of text that was sought after by profit-seeking printers such as John Wolfe and John Charlewood, who exploited the foreign trade in forbidden books to break into a business previously monopolised by a few privileged firms.

Translations of works of history, philosophy, poetry and romance became thus more numerous, but at the end of the 16th-century the majority of outstanding classical works were not yet available in English. For example, the three great writers of Greek tragedy remained unpublished. It was only from 1592 onwards that large projects were courageously undertaken, and although the period includes Chapman's seminal translation of Homer, most of the important translations consisted of serious historical and ethical prose. To the 16th-century reader, the great classical past was the imperial age, in which the order of human life had been best understood and organised by the intelligence of man. It gave a fixed norm. By contrast, in France, works of classical philosophy, history, poetry and drama had been made available to a wider public through lexicographical and encyclopedic developments in which the dynasty of the Paris master-printer Henri Estienne (Henri *le grand*, 1470-1520), supported by the king, played a prominent role. Whatever the language of a text, French mediated the European literary tradition for the English to the extent that in 1598 the Italophile Sir Robert Dallington (1561-1638) censured the current tendency to be satisfied with French versions of any foreign text.[20]

ANTHONY MUNDAY, A COMMON MAN OF LETTERS

The "Englishing" of law and letters was then the result of the complex interplay of diverse actors and elements, with a range of different producers and consumers. From the great merchant-publishers to the disreputable printer-bookseller, from government control to aristocratic patronage and Puritan pressure groups, from the translators and readers at the Inns of Court, and university scholars, to the "hired pens" of the Elizabethan

---

[20] R. DALLINGTON, *The View of France*, reprint London, Oxford University Press, 1936.

"Grub Street" and the London theatres, the scenario of the book trade was indeed a complex one.[21] Late Elizabethan translations addressed a range of readerships, from the aristocratic and bourgeois elites to a broader and more heterogeneous mass audience that cut across divisions and political factions. The English reception of the continental genre of paradox, and the life and work of Anthony Munday, are indicative of this complexity.

In around 1531, during the early age of print culture, the term "intelligence" was, in the words of Thomas Elyot (1490-1546?), "communication" and "interchange of knowledge or mutual conveyance of information".[22] "Intelligence," he claimed, was "now used for an elegant worde, where there is mutual treaties or appoyntementes, either by letter or message".[23] By 1587, however, the term "intelligence" had come to mean the accumulation of secrets by political, commercial and cultural dealings with foreign cultures old and new. At around the same time it also began to mean "espionage" as the communication of secret or private agents; hence "intelligencer" *qua* spy, or at best, newsmonger. By the end of the century John Florio, in his introduction to his translation of Montaigne's *Essays*, uses the word to denote the special knowledge acquired through translation in the sense of the "discovery and use of ancient wisdom".[24] Anthony Munday was involved in both "communication" and "intelligence" in more than one sense. He was a translator of popular continental romances and essays, a secret agent abroad, a balladeer, a news reporter in the Protestant cause, a chronicler, an actor, a playwright and, later in life, a deviser of pageants for the City of London, so that in the words of Ben Jonson, "a worser cannot be had".[25] Munday belonged to the Grub Street of Elizabethan England and was the quintessential *traduttore-traditore*. Unknown

---

[21] On Grub Street and the literary profession of Elizabethan times, see E.H. MILLER, *The Professional Writer in Elizabethan England: A Study of Non-Dramatic Literature*, Cambridge, Mass., Harvard University Press, 1959, pp. 203-241. P. SHEAVYN, *The Literary Profession in Elizabethan England*, 2nd edn., revised by J.W. Saunders, Manchester, Manchester University Press, 1967, Chap. III; J.W. SAUNDERS, *The Profession of English Letters*, London, Routledge & Kegan Paul, 1964.

[22] See Elyot cited in the *Oxford English Dictionary*, «Intelligence», 5.

[23] *A critical edition of Sir Thomas Elyot's The Boke named the Governour*, edited by D.W. Rude, New York, Garland Pub., 1992.

[24] On Florio, see W. BOUTCHER, *Vernacular Humanism in the 16th Century*, in *The Cambridge Companion to Renaissance Humanism*, edited by J. Kraye, Cambridge, Cambridge University Press, 2003, pp. 189-202. *Essays*, translated by John Florio, London, J.M. Dent, 1942.

[25] Munday is presented as pitifully disqualified for the profession of dramatist – as Antonio Balladino, "pageant-poet to the city of Milan" – in BEN JONSON's *Case Is Altered*, I, i, edited by C.H. Herford and P.E. Simpson (1925-1952), Chicago, Hollister Brothers, 1902.

in earlier days, when "literature" was a private, aristocratic diversion and the circulation of manuscript books was limited to restricted circles, Grub Street, was the by-product of the growing printing industry. Profit-seeking printers and expanding literacy created new opportunities for the middle-class young men seeking fame and fortune in London. They were often "foreigners", that is to say, men who like their betters Shakespeare or Marlowe had come to the metropolis from the provinces in search of fame and fortune. Some of them, such as Robert Greene, Gabriel Harvey, Thomas Nashe and Thomas Lodge, were well educated or had attended the grammar schools; some, such as Munday, were Londoners and free members of livery companies. All were engaged, often anonymously or under pseudonyms, in a range of literary lines, and their biographies illustrate how these enterprising, unscrupulous but not particularly talented young men managed to make a living in the tough world of the Elizabethan literary profession.[26]

Anthony Munday, the son of Christopher Munday, a freeman of the Drapers' Company, was orphaned at the age of 16 and articled himself to the stationer-printer John Allde, with whom he remained until he applied to cancel his indenture in order to travel abroad in 1578.[27] During his first continental journey he kept a diary, *The English Roman Life* (1582), often cited as his single best work, in which he motivates this decision with a "desire to see strange countries, as also affection to learn the languages".[28] The truth of the matter is that he was on a secret mission as an informer for the Elizabethan secret service, headed by Sir Francis Walsingham. In 1573, a year after the St Bartholomew's Eve massacre of French Protestants by the followers of the Duke of Guise, Elizabeth recalled Walsingham from his post as English ambassador in Paris and made him Secretary of State, a key position that this adept of Machiavellian political cunning was to hold for more than 16 years until his death, in 1590. In 1580, Walsingham created his own secret service dedicated to the penetration and exposure of Catholic groups at home and abroad. Below the

---

[26] On the Elizabethan "Grub Street" see, E.H. MILLER, *op. cit.*

[27] D.M. BERGERON, *Munday, Anthony (bap. 1560, d. 1633)*, «Oxford Dictionary of National Biography», Oxford University Press, 2004; C.J. TURNER, *Anthony Mundy, an Elizabethan Man of Letters*, Berkeley, Ca., University of California Publications in English, II, 1928.

[28] *The English Roman Life*, edited by P.J. Ayers, Oxford, Clarendon Press, 1980; M. ORD, *Representing Rome and the Self in Anthony Munday's 'The English Roman Life'*, in *Travels and Translations in the 16th Century*, edited by M. Pincombe, Burlington, Ashgate, 2004, pp. 45-61.

rank of Walsingham and his close aides, we find the shifting legion of free-lancers who provided the raw material of anti-Catholic "intelligence" or espionage. Among them, literary globetrotters such as Munday[29] or the wild, *déracinés*, penniless "university wits" such as Christopher Marlowe, viewed government employment as a way of supporting their literary am-bitions while satisfying a desire to travel abroad.

The English Roman Life is rich in conspiratorial elements, and the nar-rator, like an agent provocateur or "projector", observes, reports and even provokes the Catholics in the newly established English (Jesuit) College in Rome, where he was a guest and student for three months in 1579 under the Latinised pseudonym of Antonius Auleus. On his return to London, in 1580, Munday continued his anti-Catholic activity under the protection of Robert Dudley, Earl of Leicester. At a time of particularly intense anti-Catholic feeling, after the arrival of the Jesuit mission, he wrote an eyewit-ness account of the capture of Edmund Campion. His anti-Jesuit pamphlets, *A View of Soundry Examples* (1580), a chap-book of sensational news, and *Brief Discourse of the taking of Edmund Champion and divers other pa-pists in Barkeshire* (1581), together with his response to two publications that attacked the validity of his evidence and discredited him as a news-monger, were stimulated more by the desire to obtain government ap-proval than by the need to exploit a profitable literary market. He contin-ued his government activity until at least 1612. At last, in his much sought-after official role of "Servant to the Queenes most excellent Maiestie" and "Messenger of her Maiesties Chamber", he hunted [Catholic] recusants, under Richard Topcliffe, and Martinists during the Matrepelate contro-versy. However, despite his anti-Catholic writings and his foray into the field of Calvinist publications, his later publishing ventures include several genres that earned him the public disapproval of the Puritans, and which reveal him as an opportunist and canny businessman of letters rather than a disinterested advocate of religious principles.

His reputation for deceit also won him enemies. Nashe detested himm, Ben Jonson worked with him on pageants and poked fun at him, referring to him on one occasion as "our best plotter".[30] In his unabashed disloyalty, Munday, who had been also an actor, joined in the chorus of Puritan at-

---

[29] In around the year 1585, Munday began to enter the outer fringes of this environment, and Thomas Walsingham, second cousin of Francis Walsingham, was Marlowe's patron and an important link in the chain of espionage from France.

[30] C.J. TURNER, *Anthony Mundy*, cit., p. 23.

tacks on the popular stage, only to return to it a few years later, in the words of a leading enemy of the stage, Stephen Gosson, "like a dog to his own vomit".[31] In the early 1580s, when control of the stage by local authorities was rapidly increasing, Munday, under the pseudonym of "Anglophile Eutheo", published *A Second and Third Blast of Retrait from Plaies and Theatres* (1580?). This was a petty and venomous compilation of excerpts from anti-theatrical tracts, one of which was from the well-known *School of Abuse* (1579) by his critic Gosson. Notwithstanding this publication, in around the year 1593, he collaborated in the six-hands play *The Booke of Sir Thomas Moore*.[32] In 1598, Munday was named in a list of distinguished playwrights of comedy (including Shakespeare), and from Philip Henslowe's famous diary we know that throughout the 1590s he was one of those writing for performances at the Rose theatre.

Munday's translating activity was neither extemporaneous nor dictated solely by the marketing strategies of his printers, but was part of the Tudor cultural intent to harness the popular press and scholarship to policy by the means of a controlled system of literary patronage. Hired translators who, like Munday, Edward Aggas and Anthony Chute, had acquired their linguistic abilities "on the job", were much in demand. John Wolfe alone must have provided a good deal of such employment, for he entered no fewer than 77 translations in the Stationer's Register. Standards were not particularly high, and little more than a lively version of the original in a plain conversational style was required. What mattered for noble patrons, printers and booksellers alike was not the quality of the translation but its supposed utility for the Commonwealth. Munday, like his fellow translators – those "shifting companions that runne through every Art and thrive by none [...] that could scarcely Latinise their neck verse..."[33] – was mainly concerned with the exciting nature of the narrative and the novelty of what was offered to the readers.

His choices frequently combined all these requirements.[34] In his first translation, *Galien of France* (1578), "badly Englished" from the French, Munday deliberately exploited the commercially successful market of belles-lettres, such as foreign romantic tales. For over two decades he en-

---

31 E.K. CHAMBERS, *The Elizabethan Stage*, Vol. I, Oxford, Clarendon Press, 1923.

32 *The Book of Sir Thomas More*, edited by V. Gabrieli and G. Melchiori, Bari, Adriatica, 1981. The alleged "Hand D" in the manuscript has been identified as that of Shakespeare.

33 T. NASHE, *To the Gentlemen Students of Both Universities*, cit., p. 315.

34 E.L. EISENSTEIN, *The Printing Press*, cit., Vol. I, pp. 136-159, 413 ff.

tertained readers who considered themselves too genteel for old-fashioned English romance with his translation of Claude Colet's story *Palmerin d'Oliva* (1581-1597) and the remarkable adventures of the protagonist's offspring. Like other translators who used their work for personal advancement, he was constantly at pains to emphasise the practical, didactic and moral value of his writings. In *The Famous, pleasant, and variable Histoire of Palladine of England* (1588), Munday was careful to preface his work with a declaration that it did not contain any encouragement "to the loose by lascivious matter". Puritans considered all *ephemera* – cheap medieval fiction, ballads and poems – in the same way as they did all things medieval connected to the Catholic past: that is, as enfeebling to the intellect and pernicious to sound morals. Once more, it is Thomas Nashe who gives us an idea of how writers such as Munday were reputed obscurantists who:

voide of all knowledge, endevour continually to publish their follie [...such] Idlebies should betake to a new trade [...] the Presse should be farre better employed [...][35]

Munday's production was made of "idle bookes and riffe raffe", that is to say, belles-lettres and *ephemera*. He was certainly not alone in writing romances, plays and ballads, in prose or verse, that were at the time considered unworthy of a gentleman's library. Belles-lettres, which took in virtually all of English poetry and drama, with a few exceptions such as Chaucer, Sidney and Spenser, were meant for exclusively private diversion. The audience for belles-lettres was the rising professional classes and educated women, who were beginning to purchase these works by the late 16th-century.[36] Such daring, collegiate ladies attracted the attention of Ben Jonson, who in his *Epicœne or the silent woman* (1609) represented them as monsters of fashion and superficial learning, voicing the common male opinion that women's literacy constituted a potential moral danger to society.[37]

---

[35] T. NASHE, *The Anatomie of Absurditie*, edited by R.B. McKerrow, Vol. I, 10, Oxford, Blackwell, 1966.

[36] *The Palace of Pleasure* was published again in 1640 with a new introduction "for the profit and delight of the ingenious English of both sexes". On the question of the survival of this type of texts and the higher class prejudices, see P. SHEAVYN, *The Literary Profession in Elizabethan England*, cit., pp. 147-208. On the *belles-lettres* aspect of Elizabethan humanism, see M. PINCOMBE's *Introduction*, in *Elizabethan Humanism: Literature and Learning in the Later 16th Century*, New York and London, Longman, 2001.

[37] On reading-only literacy for women, see H. BRAYMAN HACKEL, *'Boasting of silence': women readers in a patriarchal state*, in *Reading, Society and Politics in Early Modern England*, edited

Anthony Munday's publishing strategies are best exemplified by the way in which he traded on what was then considered a British "classic", the *Mirrour for Magistrates* (1559-1561), written by William Baldwin and other prominent lawyers at the Inns of Court.[38] This was a product of "high" culture originating from Lydgate's *Fall of Princes*. Munday's *Mirrour of Mutabilitie*, printed by his former master, John Allde, was an imitation not at all suitable for attachment to the original version of the 1559 *Mirrour*. The fact that Munday was an obsequious timeserver adds to the significance of his *Mirrour*, both as an indication of contemporary tastes and of the way in which the popular press appropriated "high" culture. Munday structures his *Mirrour* according to the seven deadly sins and prefaces each tale with an adornment of admonitory verses whose initial letters spell the sins that then lead to tragedy. The result is a mixture of injunctions not to sin and injunctions to be cautious; the author's declared goal is to entertain his reader with "excellent Historyes, both pleasant and profitable". In 1580, Anthony Munday again capitalised on the idea of worldly punishment for sin, and published a hasty compilation, this time not of tragic stories of outstanding figures from the past, but contemporary stories of news about ordinary human beings and of marvellous, but contemporary, happenings. His *A view of sundry Examples. Reporting many strange murthers* is a perfect example of exploitation of the popular taste for tragic justice and, despite the moral tone, of the way "history" could be transformed into popular and readable pleasantries.

Hack writers often published their "idle books" anonymously or under a pseudonym. Moreover, they frequently tailored the subject matter to the appetites of their alleged patrons in order to win approval and support even to the extent of disguising the book's true contents. In both *The Defence of Contraries*, and his second and longer "oratorical" translation, *The*

---

by K. Sharpe and S.N. Zwicker, Cambridge, Cambridge University Press, 2003, pp. 101-121; on Shakespeare's representations of women readers and sexual transgression, see L. JARDINE, *Reading Shakespeare Historically*, London and New York, Routledge, 1996, pp. 48-63; *Lando's Quattro Libri de Dubbi*, translated by W. Painter (1540?-1594) as *Delectable demaundes, and pleasaunt questions, with their seuerall aunswers, in matters of loue, naturall causes, with morall and politique deuises. Newely translated out of Frenche into Englishe, this present yere of our Lorde God. 1566; STC (2ⁿᵈ edn.)/ 5060/* was meant to appeal to women readers; a second edition was published, significantly in 1596 around the time when Donne circulated his own version of *Dubbi* as "*Problems*" at the Inns in manuscript. Painter is the author of the widely plagiarised, *The Palace of Pleasure*, a translation of anecdotes and stories from ancient and humanist writers.

[38] The first *Mirrour of Magistrates* and Baldwin's sequel circulated before their publication in costly manuscript form.

Orator,[39] Munday courted his readers by referring to the approval his work enjoyed with powerful patrons, even to the point of faking patronage when there was none. *The Orator* was published under the pseudonym of Lazarus Pyott,[40] and presented with the second title *The Mirror of Eloquence*. This work is a collection of highly improbable legal cases. Each one of the hundred Declamations contains a speech made in accusation and one made in reply, and the tone, as in the one in which Romulus is tried for beheading Remus, is paradoxical and full of imagination. Books were expensive, and collections such as this one were easily pirated for circulation in loose-leaf collections, along with other profitable merchandise, including broadside street ballads. This might have been the case of *Declamation 95*, the paradoxical case of "a Jew who would for his debt have a pound of the flesh of a Christian", later used by Shakespeare in the mock-judicial play *The Merchant of Venice*, which was staged at Shrovetide in 1605 for James I. *The Orator*'s addressees are the three "robes" of society identified with the secular and religious aristocracies of ecclesiastics, lawyers and knights; there is also a fourth, literate estate: the "private man", presumably the new class of "men of letters". In the *Epistle to the Reader*, as members of the *Commonweale* these potential readers are described and courted as the sole beneficiaries of the civilising effect of eloquence:

> I have thought good (in hope to advantage my selfe with the same title) to present thee with certaine Rhetoricall Declamations, the use whereof in every member in our Commonweale, is as necessary, as the abuse of wilfull ignorance is odious. [...] If thou studie law, they may helpe thy pleadings, or if divinitie (the reformer of law) they may perfect thy persuasions. In reasoning of private debates, here maiest thou find apt metaphors, in incouraging thy souldiours fit motives. [...] briefly every private man may in this be partaker of a generall profit [...]

---

[39] The full title of the work, is "*The Orator: handling a hundred several discourses, in forme of declamations; some of the arguments being drawne from Titus Livius and other ancient writers, the rest of the authors owne invention, part of which are of matters happened in our age / written in French by Alexander Silvayn, and Englished by L.P.* London Printed by Adam Islip. 1596" STC/413:02. The first page also contains the title "*The Mirrour of Eloquence: containing an hundred Historicall, or rather Tragicall Declamations*". The translation is based on "*Epitomes de cent histories tragiques, partie extraittes des Actes des Romains & autres, de l'invention de l'autheur, avecq[ue] les demandes, accusations & deffences sur la matiere d'icelles*", by Alexandre van den Busche, also called Le Sylvain (Paris, 1581). A copy of *The Defence of Poverty Against the Desire of Wordlie Riches. Dialogue wise collected by Anthonie Mundaye*, now lost, was registered on 18 November 1577 by the printer John Charlewood.

[40] On the use of pseudonyms and anonymity, see M.L. NORTH, *The Anonymous Renaissance, Cultures of Discretion in Tudor-Stuart England*, Chicago, Chicago University Press, 2003.

Munday also extols the moral and "civic" value of the work to his presumed patron, Lord John of St John, Baron of Bletsho, a stern magistrate who presided at the trial of Mary Queen of Scots, and emphasises the utility of the oratorical style for the common good and the national advancement of law, religion and military discipline. He sycophantically includes expressions of a radical Puritan view in matters of jurisprudence, and suggests that religion is above the Law of the Land ("divinitie reformer of law").[41]

----

[41] On zealous Puritanism and the bar in late 16th-century, see W. PREST, *The Rise of the Barristers, A Social History of the English Bar 1590-1640*, Oxford, Clarendon Press, 1986, p. 228.

THE ENGLISH RECEPTION OF *PARADOSSI*

> Wit's a disease, that fit employment wants
> [...] haue we worthy gifts, as Iudgement, Learning,
> Ingenious sharpnesse [...]
>
> We vent our blessing in prophane conceits,
> Or in strong Arguments against our selves,
> Foule Bawdry, and starke blindly hold it best,
> Rather to loose a soule, then loose a iest.
>
> NATHAN FIELD

ENGLISH PARADOXY

The genre of the paradoxical *joco-serio* was already known in England before the publication of *The Defence of Contraries* in 1593. Chaucer had joined "earnest and game" for moral purposes well before Erasmus wrote his *Encomium Moriae* while staying with that most eminent "morosoph", Thomas More. The texts of philosophical scepticism that had influenced Lando also circulated in England in French and English translation.[1] Two texts in which sound reasoning led to paradox, Erasmus's *Encomium*, and Agrippa von Nettesheim's *De Incertitudine*, had been translated. The sceptical doctrines of Pyrrhonism, much admired by Montaigne, were also known in the French translation of Sextus Empiricus's *Hypotyposes*, annotated by Estienne's father, Henri *le grand* (1562). Writers were also acquainted with Textor's encyclopedic *Officinae* with its mine of anecdotes and questions, often presented from contrasting points of view, which was used extensively by Lando and plundered by generations of Europeans.[2]

---

[1] On the history and forms of the English essay and paradox, in addition to R. Colie, see E.N.S. THOMPSON, *The 17th-Century English Essay*, «University of Iowa Humanistic Studies», III, 3, 1926; A.E. MALLOCH, *The Technique and Function of the Renaissance Paradox*, «Studies in Philology», 53, 1956, pp. 191-203; "morosoph" from Rabelais "*morosophe*" or "wise fool"; implicitly a follower of Erasmus' *moria* or "folly".

[2] Ravisius Textor, Joannes, ca. 1480-1524. Officinae Joannis Ravisii Textoris epitome: Tomus I [and II] Lugduni: Apud Seb. Gryphium, 1551.

The earliest known book of paradoxes in English is the anonymous *Foure paradoxes*, published in 1570. The work is modelled not on Lando's *Paradossi*, but on Cicero's *Paradoxa*.[3] It contains very little folly and is quite stern in its religious zeal. The author claims that his assertions will only appear paradoxical to a corrupt Roman Catholic, whereas they are the self-evident Truth to the reformed Christian.[4] As the epigraph on the title page suggests, the four paradoxes are inspired not by Stoicism but by the Evangelical spirit found in Lando's work. The quotation *"Quae doctrina nova hæc?"* (*Acts of the Apostles*, 17.19) evokes Paul's visit to Athens, where he meets the Stoic and Epicurean philosophers. The latter take him for a "babbler" preaching "strange gods" (Jesus and the Resurrection), and question him with subtle irony on his "new doctrine".[5] From the outset, the author means to pre-empt any accusation that he, like Paul and Socrates, is a charlatan who collects strange words and sentences quite void of meaning.

For Protestants, paradox remained a congenial way to express the reformed creed and to apply Pauline insights into ordinary Christian life. The first authoritative reference to a "religious" use of paradox is by that eminent Protestant Sir Philip Sidney in his *An Apology for Poetry* (1580). Here he discusses the uses of paradox, or more specifically ironic praise and blame, taking Agrippa and Erasmus as his models. The latter, unlike the multitude of superficial "smiling railers", wrote paradoxes that had a "foundation" of piety and simple faith in revealed religion.[6] Judgment

---

[3] The first translation of Cicero's paradoxes, *The paradox of Marcus Tullius Cicero, latelye translated out of the laten tonge by R. Whitinton* [sic.] appeared in 1534; Isocrates' speech "Ad demonicum" was translated from the original Greek, as *The Godly Advertisement or Good Counsell of the Famous Orator Isocrates*, by John Bury of the Inner Temple in 1559. Thomas Chaloner translated *The praise of folie* (1549); James Sandford translated Agrippa von Nettesheim, *Of the vanitie and vncertaintie of artes and sciences* (1569), edited by C.H. Miller, Early English Texts Society (EETS), 257 (1965). With the exception of Whittington the translators were all closely associated with the Inns of Court. These works were known by John Donne, as it appears in the *Catalogus librorum aulicorum*, of his library, see *John Donne, Paradoxes and Problems*, edited by H. Peters, Oxford, Clarendon Press, 1980 (XIV).

[4] *Anon. Foure paradoxes 1 A byshop and a minister is all one. 2 A byshoppe or deacon shoulde not bee called Grace, Lord, or exercise such authoritie. 3 A popish priest is no lawful minister of the gospel. 4 Canon chauncellours, & officials are no meete officers in the churche of God*, London, 1570; Thomas Newton translated in 1569 Cicero's works including the paradoxes, *Foure severall treatises of M. Tullius Cicero* (2nd edn., 1577); the first translation, *The Paradox of Marcus Tullius Cicero, latelye translated out of the laten tonge by R. Whitington*, appeared in 1534.

[5] The word "babbler" is taken from the King James Bible and is "spermológos" in Greek, meaning "gatherer of seeds", hence "magpie".

[6] *An Apology for Poetry*, E. Forest and G. Robinson, Indianapolis, Bobbs-Merrill, 1970, pp. 51-52.

on scepticism was not unanimous, as the author of *The prayse of nothing* (1585)[7] suggests in this mock encomium of moral, religious and political scepticism. As late as 1654, Ralph Venning, a scholar from the Protestant Emmanuel College writing in the tradition of John Donne, published a rhetorical exegesis of the Bible and an illustration of the paradoxical nature of Christian religion, *Orthodox Paradoxes*.[8] In it, Venning combines, some-what pedantically, Paul's doctrine and Donne's poetics. Scriptural para-doxes and metaphors, he says, resonate with "Truth" and only appear as "new doctrine" to "them who are lost".

By the 1590s paradox was being used less as a rhetorical device of re-formed exegesis and more as an expression of "wit", or the "power of in-tellect". When subjects traditionally associated with specialised academic study, such as logic and rhetoric, began to attract the attention of witty courtiers and the affectation of paradoxical manners became a London fashion, profit-seeking printers started to produce books of rhetoric and eloquence for the fashionable elites.[9] It was a good time for Munday to re-turn to paradoxes and to disguise them as "mirrors" of eloquence. Books of paradoxes for the entertainment of selected audiences had become so popular that in *The Prayse of the Red Herring* (1599), a mock encomium of mock encomiums, Thomas Nashe in his usual irreverent tone declared that:

Phylosophers come sneaking in with their paradoxes of povertie, imprison-ment, death sicknesse, banishment, and baldnesse [...] The posterior Italian and Germane [...] applaude and cannonize unnaturall sodomitrie, the strumpet errant, the goute, the augue [...] a fourth comes with something in prayse of nothing [...] a ninth offers sacrifice to the goddesse *Cloaca*, and disportes himselfe very schol-lerly and wittilie about the reformation of close stooles [...].[10]

---

[7] Attributed to Sir Edward Dyer (1543-1607) courtier, poet and member of the Inner Temple.

[8] *Orthodox paradoxes, or, A believer clearing truth by seeming contradictions the second part by Ralph Venning*, 1652. He also uses as epigraph a quotation from Paul's Corinthians 4.3 Ven-ning also wrote *Mysteries and revelations, or, The explication and application of several extra-es-sential and borrowed names, allusions, and metaphors in the Scripture*, 1647. On Venning, see CO-LIE, *op. cit.*, p. 31.

[9] "Wit" was a means of social distinction, but also a strategy of presentation of the self in the conflict ridden Elizabethan society. In John Donne's case, witty rhetoric veiled the workings of a mind nurtured in the Catholic faith.

[10] *Lenten Stuffe*, in *The Works of Thomas Nashe*, edited by Ronald B. McKerrow, Vol. III, 176-178; Nashe refers to, A. FLEMING's *A Paradoxe, proving by reason and example, that Bald-nesse is much better than bushie haire* (1579) translation of *Calvitii Encomium*; G. HARVEY's *A New Prayse of The Old Asse* (1593); SIR J. HARINGTON, *Praise of the water-closet* or «Metamor-phosis of Ajax» (1596), and R. BARNFIELD's *The Encomion of Lady Pecunia* (1598).

However, the *paradox epidemics* were not quite as worthless as Nashe claimed. In Hoby's popular translation of Castiglione's *Book of the Courtier*, Lady Emilia alludes to pseudo-encomium as a sophisticated rhetorical game in which both sexes practise their intellectual skills.[11] Courtiers' manners were established at the Court of Urbino and in London fashion, as well as the language of the realm, the Queen's English, was established at court. Writing in about 1599, John Hoskyns (1566-1638), a member of John Donne's circle as well as an Oxford don, Serjeant-at-law and Member of Parliament, complained that:

[...] we study according to the predominancy of courtly inclinations: whilst mathematics were in request, all our similitudes came from lines, circles and angles [...] whilst moral philosophy is now a while spoken of, it is rudeness not to be sententious.[12]

Learned paradoxy also started at court, and like all other fashions spread to the circles of talented young gentlemen at the Inns of Court, who in turn wrote "realistic" paradox, epigrams and satires to pillory courtly fashion and "common opinion".

In the late 1590s the generational gap in society had widened enormously, and "youth" had become a pole of both social aggregation and unrest.[13] With other manifestations of the conflict between the young and the old, paradoxical affectation must have been a mark of distinction among the young "wits", a term that at the time meant, "men of intellect". Ben Jonson thus described the new vogue of affecting "deformity" and "harshness":

These men erre not by chance, but knowingly, and willingly; they are like men that affect a fashion by themselves, have some singularity in a Ruffe, Cloake, or Hat-band; or their beards, specially cut to provoke beholders, and set a marke upon themselves.[14]

---

[11] *The Book of the Courtier... Done in English by Sir Thomas Hoby*, New York, AMS Press, 1967, p. 123.

[12] J. HOSKYNS, *Directions for Speech and Style*, edited by H.H. Hudson, Princeton, N.J., Princeton University Press, 1935.

[13] For generational conflict, see DONNE's *Paradox III*.

[14] BEN JONSON, *Timber: or Discoveries; Made upon Men and Matter, as they have flowed out of his daily readings, or had their reflux to his peculiar notion of the times*. VIII, p. 585, edited by C.H. Herford and P. Simpson, Oxford, Clarendon Press (1925-1952).

In *Satyre IIII* John Donne, a reader of the more licentious Roman satirists proscribed by the early humanists and himself a practitioner of epigrams and paradoxes, wrote a vitriolic description of a witty courtier as a:

> As vaine, as witlesse, and as false as they
> Which dwell at Court, for once going that way.
> Therefore I suffered this; Towards me did runne
> A thing more strange, then on Niles slime...[15]

A TIMELY DEFENCE

The meteoric first appearance of Ortensio Lando's *Paradosso V*, "*Meglio è d'esser pazzo che savio*" in English was in 1576, when James Sandford (1567-1582), a Latin and Greek scholar and translator associated with the Inns of Court, published *The Mirrour of Madnes*, allegedly translated from the French. His defence of madness, enriched with Greek and Latin maxims, is presented not as a *divertissement* on anti-intellectualism but as a moral commentary on the present "corrupte tyme".[16] The following year, a copy of *The Defence of Poverty Againste the Desire of Wordlie Riches, Dialogue wise collected by Anthonie Mundaye*, now lost, was registered on November 18 by the printer John Charlewood. Having returned from Rome in 1579, Munday began his literary career, and published belles-lettres, interspersed with some moral intent, alongside his anti-Catholic

---

[15] *Satyre IIII*, in *Donne Poetical Works*, edited by H.J.C. Grierson, Oxford, Oxford University Press, 1971.

[16] Sandford knew Italian well and translated the work of Lodovico Guicciardini (1521-1589) for the classroom: *The garden of pleasure contayninge most pleasante tales, worthy deeds and witty sayings of noble princes [et] learned philosophers, moralized. No lesse delectable, than profitable. Done out of Italian into English, by Iames Sanforde, Gent. Wherein are also set forth diuers verses and sentences in Italian, with the Englishe to the same, for the benefit of students in both tongs* (1573). He also translated's Agrippa, *Of the vanitie and vncertaintie of artes and sciences, Englished by Ia. San. Gent., Imprinted at London: By Henry Wykes dwelling in Fleete streat, at the signe of the blacke Elephant* (1569); Epictetus, *The manuell of Epictetus, translated out of Greeke into French, and now into English, conferred with two Latine translations. Herevnto are annexed annotations, and also the apothegs of the same author* (1567). Single *paradossi* kept surfacing in the same period: one small work entitled *Hygiasticon*, and not published until 1634 at Cambridge, contains a short dissertation on "A Spare Diet" translated directly from Lando's *Paradosso XXIV* and was reprinted in 1678 in *The Temperate Man* and again in *The Frugal Life*. In 1613 seven paradoxes were published in T. MILLES, *The Treasurie of Auncient and Modern Times*. Another paradox was printed in J. HALL's *Paradoxes by F. De la Salle* (1653). Six of LANDO's *Paradossi* were printed by J. DUNTON, in *Athenian Sport: Or, Two Thousand paradoxes Merrily Argued, To Amuse and Divert the Age* (1707), and included the eleven paradoxes collected in the 1633 edition of Donne's *Paradoxes and Problems*.

pamphlets. These included the *Mirror* and a second paradoxical publication, *The Paine of Pleasure* (1580) in which he examines in verse some 23 "pleasures", such as beauty, love, honour, music, study, all of which imply a countering "pain" that vitiates the pleasure.

Elizabethan hack writers were masters in coining the catchpenny titles so beloved of 16th-century printers. The title *Defence of Contraries*, with its Latinate words is meant to suggest the work's intellectual and moral weight. Titles with the term "defence" or "apology" were mostly used in books of divinity: whereas Reginald Pole had written a *Pro Ecclesiasticae unitates defensione*, both Cranmer and Jewel wrote "defences". This commanding word was also used in other contexts, as varied as Robert Greene's *The defence of conny catching* (1592), and Sidney's *The Defence of Poesy*.[17] The paratextual material of the *Defence* contains interesting information on both patronage and readership, and Munday claims it is sponsored by none other than "*Ferdinando Stanley: the great and puissant Earle of Derbie*".[18] Ferdinando Stanley (1559?-1594) was a prominent courtier generally considered the Queen's heir apparent and a literary patron and noted lover of poetry and drama to whom poets dedicated their books. His company of players, named Strange's Men, after Lord Strange, had at one point included actors and playwrights of the calibre of Edward Alleyn and William Shakespeare.[19]

The second address, "To the King", is rather puzzling: why is he addressing a "King" when "Queen" Elizabeth was still alive?"[20] As no known edition of Estienne's *Paradoxes* contains such a dedication, we can safely assume that it may allude to the continuing Catholic plot, leading to a revolt, to claim the English crown before the death of the Queen. This would have been because Ferdinando Stanley, as the great-grandson of Mary Brandon, Henry VIII's younger sister, had a claim to it. Munday was probably involved in some capacity: he knew the plotters's messenger,

---

[17] The title of William Ponsonby's 1595 edition. In the same year Henry Holney published the same text under the title of *An Apology for Poetry*.

[18] In 1602 appeared a rebinding of *The Defence* with a new title page, but with identical paratextual material; the only, defective, known copy is in the Bodleian Library.

[19] E.K. CHAMBERS, *The Elizabethan Stage*, Vol. II, Oxford, Clarendon Press, 1951, pp. 118-134; D. KATHMAN, *Stanley, Ferdinando, Fifth Earl of Derby (1559?-1594)*, *Oxford Dictionary of National Biography*, Oxford, Oxford University Press, 2004.

[20] Trevor Peach, the editor of Estienne's *Paradoxes* has assured me that none of the French editions contains any reference "to the King". I doubt that the "King" in question is James I or that the 1593 edition was reprinted after Elizabeth's death with the old date of publication. Why indeed leave the old date on a newly printed title page?

who, failing to persuade the Earl of Derby, was turned in by the earl himself and promptly executed. He was, in fact, one Richard Hesketh, like Munday a freeman of the Drapers' Company in the City of London, and an intelligence agent working for the regiment of the old Earl of Derby. In addition, Hesketh's brother had been prosecuted for sheltering the Jesuit Edmund Campion, on whose capture Munday had written his infamous *Discovery of Edmund Campion* (1581) for Leicester. As for Stanley, he died the following year, probably as a result of poisoning. Returning to literary matters, the dedication to "the King" is also interesting for its allusion to a continuing literary debate on paradox among the "gentlemen" of the court, and reminds us that at the time taste in all the arts was determined there. Munday claims that "the King", having proposed several paradoxes "and heard the censures of divers learned Gentlemen", asked him to write down his own "opinion". He has taken on the task, he argues, only because it was "imposed" by the "King" himself.

Not only gentlemen, but also courtly ladies were taken up by the *paradox epidemics*, as the 1599 English translation of Pontaymeri's *Paradoxe apologique*, addressed to "worthy Ladyes and virtuous Maydes of honour, to her royal Majesty [etc.]"[21] indicates. If we examine the biography of the main addressee, who is none other than the "Right Honourable Lady, Elizabeth, Countess of Southampton", *neé* Vernon, the Queen's First Maid of Honour, we can detect Anthony Munday lurking behind it.[22] Indeed, the title page of this book carries Munday's motto (*Patere aut abstine*), but the dedicatory epistle is signed by one Anthony Gibson, who writes that the work has been translated "by a fellow and friend of myne now absent". The "fellow" in question is not publishing the book under his own name because the lady in question had incurred the Queen's disfavour in 1599 for being pregnant and having secretly wed the androgynous courtier who was Shakespeare's literary patron, Henry Wriothesley, Third Earl of Southampton (1573-1624). Anthony Gibson is therefore another pseudonym for Anthony Munday, who not wanting to miss an opportunity with a powerful patron, but also wishing to avoid royal disapproval, devises a scheme to present the book to Wriothesley's wife, most probably on the

---

[21] *A womans woorth, defended against all the men in the world Prooving them to be more perfect, excellent, and absolute in all vertuous actions, then any man of what qualitie soeuer. Written by one that hath heard much, seene much, but knowes a great deale more. Imprinted at London: By Iohn Wolfe, and are to be solde at his shop in Popes head Alley, neere the Exchange*, 1599 STC (2nd edn.)/11831.

[22] This translation has never previously been attributed to Munday.

birth of their first daughter. Either as Catholic conspirator or as spy and double agent on the Queen's side, and as an admirer of Wriothesley, Munday, who had just obtained courtly preferment as Queen's Messenger of the Bedchamber, clearly courted all sorts of readers and patrons. He was able to secure a place for himself in that network of complex and oblique links between "books", the establishments of learning and the seats of political power.

In the 1590s Munday also began to collaborate in writing plays with dramatists such as Michael Drayton, Thomas Dekker, Henry Chettle, Thomas Middleton, Thomas Heywood, and John Webster, for whom the Inns of Court, of which some of them were members, were an important constituency. In *The Defence*, the epistle to the "friendly reader", an abridgment of Estienne's *salut au lecteur*, is addressed by Munday to the *yong wittes* at the Inns, who were the English counterpart of the Parisian *jeunes esprits/avocats* or law-apprentices. *The Defence*'s declared objective is:

[...] for him that woulde be a good Lawyer, after he hath long listened at the barre; he must adventure to defend such a cause, as they that are most imployed, refuse to maintaine: therby to make himselfe more apt and ready, against common pleaders in ordinarie causes of processe. For this intent, I have undertaken (in this book) to debate on certaine matters, which our Elders were wont to cal Paradoxes.[23]

A Lame Translation

Munday entreats his gentlemen readers, saying that:

if ye finde any harsh English in my rude Translation, or faults unwillingly escaped in the Printing: mend the one with patience, and the other with your pennes [...]

We should listen to him: to mend this work a great deal of patience and ink would indeed be required. Compared with Estienne's translation of the original Italian, or even with the anonymous English translation of *Paradosso* XXIV in Lessius's *Hygiasticon*, the *Defence* indeed appears to be both "rude" and "harsh".[24] Munday, who never went through the grammar

---

[23] The *Defence* was translated not from the first 1553 French edition addressed to the *jeunes advocats* but from a later one in which Estienne extends his audience to include the *jeunes esprits*. Munday's version may have used a 1554 edition in which to the title is added: *"Traicté non moins plein de doctrine, que de recreation pour toutes gens"* he paraphrases in the title. An index was also added and "[...] gathered for Readers More easie finding them".

[24] *Hygiasticon: Or, The right course of preserving life and health unto extream old age to-*

school apprenticeship, the backbone of Tudor translation,[25] is unconcerned with conveying the sober elegance of the original French in the English tongue; his diction expresses neither scholarship, nor freedom, nor art: he follows the French ordering and structure to the extent of being slavishly literal; French words are expressed by their English derivative, and when in dire straits he even coins words that "sound like" English, but which are false neologisms devoid of meaning.[26] The rhythm is hurried and the use of punctuation reflects the slovenliness of both author and compositor.

At the time, English was far from a definitive language: its vocabulary was unstable, its grammar imperfect and its spelling chaotic; and there were no uniform laws regarding cultural borrowing, the coining of neologisms or the use of archaisms. Munday knew some Latin, French and Italian, and styled himself as a polyglot. His "art" of translation was learnt on the job and consists, as did most commercial Elizabethan translations, of a mixing and hybridisation of modern languages and English dialects. The English he adopts does not appear to be a conscious linguistic experiment in the manner of, for instance, Thomas Nashe, who aimed at *heteroglossia* or *polyglossia*: the "interanimation" of high and low cultures and languages. Munday is unconcerned with the humanist and courtly models derived from a common European cultural language to which the prominent translators of his times aspired; nor does he try to emulate Shakespeare's continuing experimentation with language. The disputes among the academic purists of his time, who were concerned about the rather hotchpotch state of the language and dreamed of a *monoglot*, pure Anglo-Saxon, simply do not interest him. He took no part in the linguistic *agon* between the "Greeks", who favored elegant Latinisation, and those true English "Brutians" who affected the use of monosyllabics and were involved in a patriotic search for Anglo-Saxon roots, opposing the importation of foreign words.[27]

---

gether with soundnesse and integritie of the senses, judgement, and memorie. Written in Latine by Leonardus Lessius, and now done into English. Printed by Roger Daniel, printer to the Universitie of Cambridge. 1634. British Library STC/1688:03.

[25] In the 1570s he studied with the London Hugenot, CLAUDIUS HOLLYBAND author of *The French Littelton A most easy, perfect, and absolute way to learne the French tongue: Set forth by Claudius Holyband, gentil-homme Bourbonnois. Let the reader peruse the epistle to his owne instruction London 1566.* This new French dictionary was addressed to law students and included a dancing manual, written by Antoine Estienne. It went through many editions.

[26] A ridiculous example is in *Declamation* 12 where we find "rabulanes" for "rabioles" ("cabbage").

[27] M. BAKHTIN, *The Dialogical Imagination*, edited by M. Holquist, Austin, University of

Munday appears equally unconcerned with the original religious, ideological and political allusions surviving in part in Estienne's *Paradoxes*. There is no attempt to adapt the French text to the different interests and attitudes of his English audience. In Declamation XII, *"That Scarsitie is better, than aboundance"*, for instance, he makes no concessions to his readers, and for the presumed "good of the Commonwealth".[28] By contrast, Estienne subtly manipulates Lando's *"Esser miglior la caristia che l'abbondanza"*, a moral essay in political "economics" arguing that abundance generates immorality and political discord while scarcity improves men and governments. In the French translation, the original political subtext of Lando's anti-Spanish polemics is avoided and French name places are substituted for Italian ones in order to sing the praise of Gallic industry. The political issues are reduced to the simple practical question:

Je diray pour conclusion que la grande fertilité et abondance des biens de la terre ne nous sert que nous afetardir.[29]

The only attempt at a "cultural" translation is when Munday cuts the reference to More in *Declamation III*, although he had collaborated in around 1593 on the play *The Book of Sir Thomas More*:[30]

[...] le pauvre Thomas More eut la teste tranchée en Angleterre. Autant en eut le sçavant Evesque De Roffe (John Fisher).

Munday's somewhat hasty collection of paradoxes worked as a catalyst so that any writer wishing to create a stir presented his ideas in the fashionable "against common opinion" format. Political, moral, literary, military, scientific and economic paradoxes, often collected in anthologies and ad-

---

Texas Press, 1981, pp. 65 ff. The "interanimation of languages and cultures" reaches its zenith in Elizabethan England with Thomas Nashe's Rabelaisian narratives. On languages and cultures, see P. BURKE, *Languages and Communities in Early Modern Europe*, Cambridge, Cambridge University Press, 2004. On a Bakhtinian view of translation in the Renaissance, see ID., *The Renaissance Translator as Go-Between*, in *Renaissance Go-Betweens: Cultural Exchanges in Early Modern Europe*, edited by A. Höfele and W. von Koppenfels, Berlin and New York, de Gruyter, 2005, pp. 17-31.

[28] This *Declamation* is amplified in the anonymous, *The present state of England expressed in this paradox, our fathers were very rich with little, and wee poore with much* (1626).

[29] On Lando's political use of geography in this paradox, see CORSARO, *Paradossi*, cit., p. 167 n. 4. For "affetardir" = être paresseux, *Paradoxes* (154), n. 273.

[30] It only exists in manuscript in the British Library (BL, Harleian MS 7368) and was never published in Munday's lifetime, although it may well have been performed. Chettle, Dekker, Shakespeare, and Heywood all collaborated. See *The Book of Sir Thomas More*, cit., p. 14.

dressed to the general reader or to select professional clienteles, began to appear and remained a commercial commodity for printers and authors alike for more than a century. Throughout the 17th-century, authors cast their arguments in the paradoxical frame in order to stress the novelty of their arguments, using titles with catchpenny appeal to attract the attention of elite and professional audiences.[31] Even the solemn William Est, in the Preface to his translation of Willibaldus Pickheimer's *Praise of the Gout* (1617), declared that in such *encomia* many learned men had revealed great acuteness of wit and not the least of their learning.

Although aspiring to a profession based on the "law of reason", students at the Inns of Court would find this collection of paradoxes appealing. It could be used as a useful source book of highly improbable cases for their aural exercises, or moots and public disputations, which were then part of a university and legal education.[32] Mooting, and the debates in which theological and philosophical propositions were defended or impugned, were often jocular or semi-jocular. Paradoxes used as rhetorical models could stretch both "rational argument" and "common sense", law's two prerogatives, to the limit of absurdity, while arguing *a contrario* improved forensic dexterity.[33] "Writing with a double meaning", as Sir John Harington defined his epigrams, was a lawyer's specialty and a wit's delight. Paradox appealed to the legal mind: its cognitive instability reflected the misapprehension of meaning, as well as of people, in the legal process. The practice of law and the reading of classical and modern "writing with double pointing", with its ironic and comic reversals of meaning, provided students at the Inns of Court with the inspiration for the lewd

---

[31] To cite just a few: G. SILVER's *Paradoxes of Defence* (1599) an elegant little book, on fencing, arguing for the advantage of the short sword over the rapier, written for the Earl of Essex; T. DEKKER's *A paradox in praise of serjeants* (1607); *The praise of the gout, or, The gouts apologie A paradox, both pleasant and profitable* (1617); *Paradoxon de morbo Gallico libr. II, or A paradox concerning the shameful disease for a warning to all against deceitful cures* (1662); *Paradoxa hydrostatica* (1669); R. BOYLE, the founder of the Royal Society, wrote *Of the cause of attraction by suction a paradox* (1674) and *New experiments, and observations [...]: to which is annexed A chymical paradox* (1682).

[32] In *Readings and Moots at The Inns of Court in the 15th Century*, edited by S.E. Thorpe and J.H. Baker, London, Selden Society, vol. II, 1990, professor Baker discusses the preference for highly improbable cases and cites a 1552 legal manuscript: *nota bien le mysterey de cest case, quar ill est cy erudite, politique et suubtyell et nient intelligeble* (lxxiii, note 383).

[33] In the text of the 1618 *Gesta Grayorum Part II* there are 13 mock moots. "Question 11" reads: "A Burgomaster that hath passed his clymatericall yeare maryeth a young inheritrix that holds per *servicium socae*; whether this intermarriage alter the tenure into cornage *in capite*, to give the wardship of his heire; or into dotage, to give the custody of himselfe" D.S. BLAND, *Three Revels from the Inns of Court*, Averbury Publishing Company, 1984, p. 90.

farces that they, like the *avocats* of the *Basoche,* staged during the festival season. The popularity of paradox among them was such that in due course *Parradox* appeared in flesh and blood on the stage of Gray's Inn, during the Christmas revels, as "the son of a Jesuit father and an Anabaptist mother".

PART TWO

Chapter One

LAWYERS AS READERS AND WRITERS
IN ELIZABETHAN LONDON

> Such is the subject of the institute
> And universal body of the law:
> This study fittes a mercenary drudge,
> Who aimes at nothing but external trash,
> Too servile and illiberal for me.
>
> MARLOWE

> Here dwells the Sages of the worlde,
> and all the Muses nine. The Court it self,
> & Innes of court (where wit & knowledge floes),
> Haunts here as terme and time commands,
> and people comes & goes.
>
> THOMAS CHURCHYARD

> Poetry is the hunny of all flowers, the quintessence
> of all Sciences, the Marrowe of Witte, and the very
> phrase of Angels: how much better is then to have
> an elegant Lawier to plead one cause, than a stutting
> Townsman, that loseth himself in his tale.
>
> THOMAS NASHE

THE ELIZABETHAN INNS OF COURT

The Inns of Court were not founded with a datable act, but rather emerged as legal societies developed from a number of houses in Holborn that served as lodgings for the lawyers and clerks attending the London courts. The apprentices-at-law and the clerks lived in common in the lodging houses (*hospicia*), literally inns for the practising common lawyers on business in London. The *hospicia majora*, or major Inns (the Inner Temple and the Middle Temple, in Fleet Street, and Lincoln's Inn, in Chancery Lane, by the old Temple and Gray's Inn), housed those barristers who eventually gained the right of audience in the higher courts, while the *hospicia minora*, the lesser Inns of Chancery, in time came to be dominated by attorneys and other practitioners of law.

During the period ca. 1500-1700 the common lawyers became the largest and most flourishing body of legal practitioners in the three great royal courts, of Common Pleas, King's Bench and Exchequer, sitting at Westminster Hall. In stark contrast to the Parisian lawyers, who managed to set themselves apart from the mayhem of the city in a corporate order only in the 17th and 18th-centuries, the English common lawyers by the end of the 15th-century had successfully managed to consolidate their corporate identity both professionally and politically. The independently wealthy peers trained at the Inns had substituted the hitherto indispensable prelates in prestigious positions such as ambassadors and diplomats. And in addition to their purely litigious functions, practising lawyers acted as accountants, brokers, financiers, entrepreneurs and land agents. It is not surprising, therefore that during Elizabeth's reign, when litigation had mushroomed to an unprecedented degree, they amassed enormous wealth, and that critics never tired of denouncing their greed and arrogance:

> [they] refuse nothing that is offered [...] and ruffle it out in their silks, velvets and chaines of gold: they built gorgious houses [...] They keepe a Port (i.e. outward show) like mighty Potentates, they have their bands and retinues of men.[1]

Even Ben Jonson, who included several lawyers, "wity yong masters of the Innes of Court", among his literary friends, and who described the Inns of Court as "the noblest nurseries of humanity and liberty in the kingdom", on occasion endorsed the contemporary picture of the deceitful and avaricious lawyer.[2]

The professional identity of common lawyers, together with their strength and unity, did not rest on wealth alone, however, but remained firmly grounded in a distinctive and quasi-mythical pedigree stretching back into pre-Christian Britain and traced for them by the major political theorist of the 15th-century, the Lancastrian Chief Justice, Governor of Lincoln's Inn and Serjeant-at-law Sir John Fortescue. The uniqueness of their training in socially exclusive societies, with its independence from

---

[1] P. STUBBES, *The Anatomie of Abuses*, edited by M.J. Kidnie, Temple, Ariz., Arizona Center for Medieval and Renaissance Studies in conjuction with Renaissance English Text Society, 2002.

[2] See, for instance, the character of "Voltore" (volture) the lawyer in *Volpone*.

both university and church, their direct participation in the cultural and political programme of the Tudor monarchs and their cachet in international circles for their intellectual freedom and secular cast of mind set them apart.

In *De laudibus legum Angliae* (ca. 1470), a political treatise written to persuade the Lancastrian Prince Edward that the law and government of England were much superior to those of France, Fortescue discusses the role of the law and of its practitioners in government as a *dominium politicum et regale*. In such a government, the power of the king was supreme, except in areas where law and custom ruled that regal power was restrained by "political law". Fortescue praises the uniqueness and sacrality of English law and glorifies the role of trained common lawyers. They are, he says, "priests" and "sacerdotes", intermediaries between the law and the body politic. This communal solidarity was sanctioned with an oath, *sacramentum sociorum de Lyncolllysyn*, introduced late in 1439.[3] Common law, he goes on to say, rules the English polity, a dominion both political and royal; it holds together the body politic (a "body mystical"), and preserves the rights of its members. In his *On the Laws and Governance of England*,[4] we find the first literary description of a special London "academy", the four Inns of Court and the 10 "lesser" Inns of Chancery, where a distinctive body of substantive law was taught. The Inns are depicted in idyllic terms as the perfect society, both mutual and voluntary, attended not for the sake of future profit but for the acquisition of virtue and knowledge.[5] Besides being England's academy of law, the Inns were also:

> [...] a kind of public school of all manners that the nobles learn [...] to sing and exercise themselves in every kind of harmonics [...] to practice dancing and all games proper for nobles [...] this is indeed a cultivation of virtues and a banishment of all vice [...] so knights, barons, and also other magnates, and the nobles of the realm place their sons in these Inns, although they do not desire them to be trained in the science of the laws, nor live by its practice, but only by their patrimonies.[6]

---

[3] This appears from a list in the *Black Books*, see E.W. IVES, *The Common Lawyers*, in *Profession, Vocation and Culture in Late Medieval England*, edited by C.H. Clough, Liverpool, Liverpool University Press, 1982, p. 204.

[4] Sir J. FORTESCUE, *On the Laws and Governance of England, Cambridge Texts in the History of Political Thought*, edited by S. Lockwood, Cambridge, Cambridge University Press, 1997.

[5] FORTESCUE, *On the Laws and Governance of England*, cit., pp. 68-72.

[6] ID., *On the Laws and Governance of England*, cit., XLIX, 69. For references to the Inns as

The Inns had always been very exclusive centres of learning, reserved for the hereditary nobility.[7] Daily life was governed by a strict set of rules that preserved social distinction. The sons of merchants and yeomen were denied admission to these "seminaries and nurseries wherein the gentrie of this kingdome are bredd and trayned up".[8]

The 1590s, precisely the time of the great renaissance of arts and letters in England, witnessed an increasing number of entrants to higher education, both at the universities and the Inns. With the volume of litigation and the size of the bar reaching an absolute peak in the history of early modern England, the Inns of Court and the legal profession reached their maximum growth. It is not surprising, therefore, that commercial London printers began to produce, as well as legal books in English, a variety of extracurricular books unrelated to law or religion, which would appeal to the rising professions,[9] as their counterparts had done in France in the 1550s. In the Middle Ages, courtly poets and translators such as Geoffrey Chaucer and John Gower were almost certainly connected to the Inns and had careers in the public administration.[10] The former might have been a member of the Inner Temple, and a record says he was once fined two shillings for beating a Franciscan friar on Fleet Street; the latter was a court official, or even a Serjeant-at-law.[11] Two hundred years later, the

---

finishing schools, see also, J. STOW, *A Survey of London*, 1603, edited by C. Kingsford, 2 vols. Oxford, Clarendon Press, 1908, W. DUGDALE, *Origines [juridicales: or historical memorials of the English laws [...] London, Printed by F. and T. Warren, for the author, 1666*, Harvard University Library, Houghton: Br 106.80.3.

[7] One of the main sources for the history of the Inns is the Lincoln's Inn register, or *Black Books*, that start in 1422.

[8] Throughout this chapter I have used W. PREST's *The Inns of Court under Elizabeth I and the Early Stuarts 1590-1640*, London, Longman, 1972, and *The Rise of the Barristers, A Social History of the English Bar 1590-1640*, Oxford, Clarendon Press, 1986; as quoted in *The Inns of Court*, cit., p. 24.

[9] The phenomenon reached a peak at the end of Elizabeth's reign and historians refer to it as an "Educational Revolution". For classical studies on this topic, see C. HILL, *Intellectual Origins of the English Revolution*, Oxford, Oxford University Press, 1965; and L. STONE, *The Crisis of Aristocracy, 1558-1641*, Oxford, Oxford University Press, 1965. On legal literature, see E.L. EISENSTEIN, *The Printing Revolution in Early Modern Europe*, cit., Cambridge, Cambridge University Press, 1983, pp. 361-362.

[10] D.S. BLAND, *A Bibliography of the Inns of Court and Chancery*, London, Selden Society, 1965. See also, ID., *Chaucer and the Inns of Court: a Re-examination*, «English Studies», xxxiii, 1952.

[11] In his *Mirour de l'Omme* Gower says that he "wore the striped sleeve" ("ai vestu la raye mance"; *Mirour*, 1.21.774), apparently the distinctive dress of serjeants and court officials. The poems of both men indicate a sound knowledge of legal privileges and terminology.

friars had gone, but Fleet Street remained the busy centre of legal affairs, law students' brawls and London's cultural life, since the study of law and the pursuit of the liberal arts were still requirements for court preferment.

The Inns of Court had always represented a distinct cultural sphere with its own specific character. From early on, the legal citadel in Holborn enjoyed relative freedom from government control. In the Tudor era, the new legal aristocracy actively cooperated in rebuilding the religious and national identity and in fostering the patriotic and Protestant values of the state by supporting learning. The system of literary patronage among the social élites that had gained importance in government, politics and religion also involved lawyers. Increasingly conscious of themselves as an international community of professional men, lawyers were united by common goals, problems and ideals, and by an intellectual common ground that transcended political and confessional boundaries. Some of them were professional as well as intellectual writers and scholars who went on to serve the state by espousing and openly advocating the policies of the Crown. As amateurs, the cultivated aristocrats at the Inns engaged in humanistic and scientific pursuits considered beneficial to the Commonwealth. The ability to read, write and criticise English and continental "literature", with skills ranging from music and dancing to interests in science, history, philosophy, theology, the military and diplomacy were paramount for preferment in early modern courtly society.

The Inns were located close to the seat of power and were the ideal place for those ambitious and resolute young aristocrats who, despite their limited financial resources, aspired to service at Court. Some were reform-minded Catholics or Protestants, some of whom belonged to the old nobility, such as Sir Philip Sidney, who became a member of Gray's Inn at the age of 15. Others came from the ranks of the new Tudor nobility, impecunious gentlemen students who read law with a view to embarking on prestigious and lucrative careers. As a social and professional group traditionally involved in the "good governance" of the Commonweal, lawyers used textual transactions to obtain social and financial advancement. Young "wits" from the Inns of Court used "letters" to vie for patronage and gift books, in manuscript or printed form, to court influential people.

The Queen's godson Sir John Harington (1560-1612) of Lincoln's Inn (1581) distributed books widely and in a variety of formats. He wrote epigrams and Latin poems to prove his mental agility to more talented fellow Inners such as Sir John Davies and John Donne. His two translations were presented as educational allegories. The first was a sumptuous edition of his translation of Ariosto's *Orlando Furioso*, containing the allegorical interpretation of the poem. It is dedicated to his godmother, the Queen, and in it he panders to the pleasures and prejudices of the court and monarch. Then, in 1604, a year after the death of Elizabeth, he presented King James I with his revised translation of the sixth book of Virgil's *Aeneid*, for use in the instruction of Prince Henry. The translation of the prophetic sixth book, dense with religious, moral, philosophical and political teachings from the first monitory representation of Daedalus and Icarus to the concluding Sybil's good auspices, was clearly meant as an allegorical "mirror" for the young prince, to whom Harington hoped to become tutor.[12] Sir John's cultural background, his family connections with the seats of power, his use of letters to vie for patronage and public office, his disenchanted and sarcastic spirit and his tolerant outlook on religion, which allowed him to describe himself as a "protesting Catholicke Puritan",[13] all exemplify the qualities required from an Elizabethan gentleman learned in the law of the country who aspired to play a privileged role in the life of the realm.

Common lawyers in the Tudor and early Stuart period enjoyed a high level of social prestige and consequent freedom to conduct the world's activities according to principles of their own.[14] The Tudor monarchs, for instance, rarely made a direct move against them on the grounds of religion despite evidence of a conspicuous Catholic presence at the Inns. Indeed the substantial privileges and ancient customs of the legal societies included special ecclesiastical status for their chapels and exemption from Episcopal control. The Inns were often accused of being a nursery for popery but were in reality a haven of religious tolerance and nonconformity where a man was unlikely to be unduly harassed on account of his beliefs.[15] This religious freedom, combined with a humanistic bent and a unique le-

---

[12] J. SCOTT-WARREN, *Sir John Harington and the Book as Gift*, Oxford, Oxford University Press, 2001. It must be pointed out that despite gift-giving and a close relation with the Queen (his father had been imprisoned with Princess Elizabeth in the Tower), he was never appointed to high office, especially after he joined Essex in Ireland.

[13] *The Metamorphosis of Ajax or Praise of the water-closet* written with the intention to reveal his wit, learning and eligibility for office, it is at once a satire of courtly fashion and a plea for toleration of those recusants who were loyal citizens. The argument for the toleration of conforming Catholics surfaces in his legalistic work, *Tract on the Succession to the Crown*.

[14] W. BOUWSMA, *Lawyers and Early Modern Culture*, «The American Historical Review», Vol. 78, No. 2 (1973), pp. 303-327.

[15] G. DE PARMITER, *Elizabethan Popish Recusancy in the Inns of Court*, «Bulletin of the Institute of Historical Research», 1976. On Augustinianism and lawyers in the Renaissance, see W.J. BOUWSMA, *The Two Faces of Humanism*, in *Itinerarium Italicum: the Profile of the Italian Renaissance in the Mirror of its European Transformations, dedicated to Paul Oskar Kristeller on the occasion of his 70th birthday*, edited by H.A. Oberman with T.A. Brady, Jr., Leiden, Brill, 1975.

gal training based on the practical application of legal skills did not make lawyers unbelievers. On the contrary, both Catholic and Protestant lawyers shared an Augustinian view of the world and a common piety that stressed the spiritual and inward quality of faith. In their desire to organise the "city of man" in a manner most conducive to salvation, they felt safer in a secular society free from direct religious control. Unlike in the universities, which did not granted degrees to nonconforming students, in the tolerant atmosphere of the Inns members with superior judgment and experience could contribute to the Tudor goal of fostering and consolidating national identity and secularisation, despite their Catholic faith.

LAWYERS AND LETTERS

Lawyers were readers and writers of contemporary writing, as well as patrons and benefactors of it. As accounts of book purchases and library inventories illustrate, barristers were prime consumers of "literature", both ancient and modern. In addition to professional texts, they were ready purchasers of the mathematical and scientific material and books on theology, heraldry, history and genealogy that were sold within the precincts of the Temple and the nearby churchyard of Saint Paul's.[16] Contemporary satirical depiction of the "Inn-a-Court" man also suggest that in the 1590s "opinions" on "literature" were a social must for a young Templar and would-be courtier.[17] In the Elizabethan period, and into the reign of James I, the "nurseries of humanity", as Jonson called the Inns, were a vital centre of coterie writing, scholarship and patronage. The humanistic activity was supported directly by the nobility and by members of the Queen's Privy Council, who for the most part were members of Gray's Inn or the Inner

---

[16] PREST, *The Inns of Court*, cit., pp. 158-165; a French dictionary, with the catching title of *The French Littelton A most easy, perfect, and absolute way to learne the French tongue: Set forth by Claudius Holyband, gentil-homme Bourbonnois. Let the reader peruse the epistle to his owne instruction London 1566*, included a dancing manual written by Antoine Estienne and became a bestseller.

[17] Affectation of poetic disposition was also fashionable: satires on Inns-a-Court men were written among others, by John Donne and his fellow-Templar John Davies (*Epigrammes and Elegies*, 1599); descriptions can be found in in Manningham's *Diary*; see P.J. FINKELPEARL, *John Marston of the Middle Temple: an Elizabethan Dramatist in his Social Setting*, Cambridge, Harvard University Press, 1969, pp. 25-26. See also Ben Jonson's Fungoso, the law student in *Everyman out of his humour*. The young Francis Beaumont of the Inner Temple (1600) entertained his fellow-Templars with a burlesque oration *The Grammer Lecture* (c. 1601) in which the three commonest types of inns-of-court man (young students, revelers and plodders) were satirized. For the transcription of the manuscript see M. ECCLES, *Francis Beaumont's Grammar Lecture*, «The Review of English Studies», Vol. 16, No. 64 (Oct., 1940), pp. 402-414.

Temple. Any gentlemen aspiring to service at court, political appointment and government employment congregated at the Inns; from the safety of their legal citadel, barristers often used their work to make indirect political commentary, and chose Privy Councellors as patrons and protectors in order to promote their own works with the public.[18] The fashioning of a courtier was conducted largely by "discourse", and a direct witness, Jasper Heywood, the son of John Heywood, while a member of Gray's Inn described the legal citadel as a new Parnassus, and its inhabitants as followers of both Minerva and the Muses:[19]

> A pryncely place in Parnasse hill, for these there is preparde,
> Where crowne of glittryng glorie hangs, for them a ryght rewarde.
> Wheras the lappes of Ladies nyne. shall dewly them defende,
> That haue preparde the Lawrell leafe, about theyr heddis to bende.

We know that after supper the students remained in the hall, rearranged the chairs and benches and began their learning exercises, or moots; this done, they would proceed to more informal activities. Some would retire to their chambers and, quite against the rules, keep company with a young wench, or play dice and smoke. Others would cross the river to visit the theatres or the stews; the more diligent would go to their rooms and read Littleton [ref. *Treatise on Tenures*]; others would stay in hall and meet their fellow students, to spend the rest of the night in disputations on a range of matters.

[...] all Gentilmen in the house was immedyatelye after supper to assemble together [...] Where amonge other recreations, musicke and dauncynge, whiche they used contynuallye, sometyme they propounded feate questions, otherwhyle they invented certayne witty sportes and pastimes, at the devyse sometyme of one sometyme of an other, in the which under sundrye coverts, often tymes the standers bye opened subtylly theyr imaginations unto whom they thought beste. At other tymes there arose other disputations of divers matters, or else jestings with prompt inventions.[20]

---

[18] Thomas Newton's first and second editions of Cicero's works were dedicated respectively to Sir Walter Mildmay and Lord Russell, both Privy Councillors. Sir Walter Mildmay (1520?-1589) was Queen Elizabeth's Chancellor and married Mary Walsingham (the sister of Sir Francis Walsingham, Secretary of State). In both editions Newton stresses the "weale of the Country".

[19] For Heywood, see H. DE VOCHT, *Jasper Heywood and his Translations of Seneca's Troas, Thyestes and Heracules furens*, Louvain, A. Uystpruyst, etc., 1913.

[20] Sir T. HOBY, *The Book of the Courtier*, cit., p. 33.

Situated as they were outside the city's southwestern walls, alongside the river Thames, the Inns of Court were not an insular reality: they were close to the Courts of Law and to the Royal Court, and the theatres were only a short boat ride across the river. Barristers were actively involved in the rich world of ideas that emanated from both Court and the metropolis, and one, as we have said, attended the Inns of Court not merely to become a well trained barrister, but also to acquire the virtues of a "true gentleman" and future civil servant. From Elyot's *Governour* to Henry Peacham's *The Compleat gentleman* (1622), the "honourable study" of the common law continued to be considered essential to true nobility, defined as learning applied to the public good.[21] The gentlemen students at the Inns convened in "societies", or coteries of amateur authors, either formal or informal, for disputations on the extracurricular subjects that were then fashionable. These ranged from theology to science and alchemy, from drama and translation to history, education, philosophy, geography and exploration; or, as in the case of John Donne's circle, the "monarchy of wit", poetry.

A LANGUAGE FOR THE COMMONWEALTH

Before he went to Italy as a Jesuit, and quite literally lost his mind for the Catholic cause, Jasper Heywood was known for his translations of Seneca. In the Preface to *Thyestes* (1560), dedicated to his former school companion the Queen, he names the fellow barrister-translators at the Inns of Court, one by one. He presents himself and his friends as a self-conscious and compact group of learned young men, with "no heares vppon my chynne", somewhat at odds with the older and more established generation of scholars, "of grauer age, and men of greater skill", and invites the reader to go:

[...] where Minervaes men, And finest witts doe swarme:
whom she hath taught to passe with pen.
In Lyncolnes Inne and Temples twayne, Grayes Inne and othe mo,
Thou shalt them fynde whose paynfull pen thy verse shall florishe so,
That Melpomen thou wouldst well weene had taught them for to wright,
And all their woorks with stately style, and goodly grace t'endight.
There shalt thou se the selfe same *Northe*, whose woorke his witte displays,

---

[21] On barristers acquiring the status of gentlemen, irrespective of their social origins, see PREST, *The Rise of the Barristers*, cit., pp. 314-318. For a general discussion of the intellectual life of the legal profession see *John Spelman Reports*, edited by J.H. Baker, 2 vols., Selden Society, xciii-iv, 1977-8, ii, pp. 28-51, 123-135.

And *Dyall dothe of Princes* paynte, and preache abroade his prayse.
There *Sackuyldes* Sonettis sweetely [...], and featly fyned bee,
There *Nortons* ditties do delight, there *Yeluertons* doo flee
Well [illeg.] pewrde with pen: suche yong men three, as weene thou mightst
agayne,
To be begotte as Pallas was, of myghtie Ioue his brayne.
There heare thou shalt a great reporte, of *Baldwyns* worthie name,
Whose *Myrrour dothe of Magistrates*, proclayme eternall fame.
And there the gentle *Blunduille* is by name and eke by kynde,
Of whome we learne by Plutarches lore, what frute by Foes to fynde.
There *Bauande* bydes, that turnde his toyle a Commonwelthe to frame,
And greater grace in Englyshe geues, to woorthy authors name.
There *Gouge* a gratefull gaynes hath gotte, reporte that runneth ryfe,
[...] And yet great nombre more, whose names [...].[22]

These patriotic young gentlemen lawyers translated from the ancient and modern classics, either as part of the government's cultural objectives or to draw the attention of the influential figures surrounding the monarch in the hope of advancement. Their approach to learning was nonscholarly and characterised by a practical and nationalistic bent; they were patriots who took as much pride in the law of the realm as they did in their mother tongue. Even at the expense of the technical language of common law, that barbarous law-French, barristers defended and improved the English idiom and made a major contribution to the "process of civilisation".[23] Indeed, of the 54 known translators of the classics of the generation working in the period 1558-1572, 25 were members of the legal societies.[24] Irrespective of whether or not one can legitimately speak of a "translation movement" or "society" at the Inns of Court, one cannot deny that the "domestication" of *humane litterae*, was promoted by men learned in common law.

Barristers, who needed a basic knowledge of Latin and French for their profession, from the onset of New Learning contributed to translating into

---

[22] This author's italics. The translators and fellow Templars, North, Sackville, Norton, Yelverton, Baldwin, Bavand, Googe, are all named. For Heywood, see H. DE VOCHT, *Jasper Heywood and his Translations*, cit.

[23] E. ROSENBERG, *Leicester, Patron of Letters*, cit., p. 3; J.G. EBEL, *Translation and Cultural Nationalism in the Reign of Elizabeth*, «Journal of the History of Ideas», Vol. 30, No. 4, 1969, pp. 593-602; on the new gentry, see A.G. DICKENS, *The English Reformation*, New York, Schocken Books, 1964, pp. 147-166. For a general discussion of the intellectual life of the legal profession see *John Spelman Reports*, cit.

[24] C.H. CONLEY, *The First English Translators of the Classics*, cit., Chap. II.

English, and not only of legal texts but also of works by classical and modern authors. The Tudors' system of patronage of letters, meant to support their plan to encourage and direct public opinion in favour of Reformation, was essentially one of nationalist propaganda that reached its apotheosis in the representation of Britannia as the new Athens, with Queen Elizabeth the virgin Astrea at the centre of the royal solar system.[25] The *translatio imperi* to England had been achieved by the means of statesmanship and of a *translatio studi* (that is, the migration of sciences and letters from east to west) induced by the greatest English scholars, writers and patrons, identified as the descendants of Albanact, the mythical son of the Troyan Brutus, and founder of England. And it is Jasper Heywood, again, who proclaims:

And where theyr Pennis shall hang full hie, and fame that erst was hyd, Abrode in Brutus realme shall flie, as late theyr volumes dyd.

As members of a language-based profession and participants in the aristocratic literary culture of the time, gentlemen lawyers were well aware that their own language in the vernacular was in a state of formation and "that they were not only forging their own identities in language but forging for posterity a language itself".[26] The English vernacular that had supplanted first Latin progressively substituted the esoteric language of the law, law-French. This professional Anglo-Norman patois used in English courts since the time of William the Conqueror, became progressively obsolete, and by 1650 all law reports were written in English. It is not surprising, then, that the "art" of translation, that is to say the fluent domestication of foreign languages and values, was practised by men learned in the law from Chaucer onwards.[27] The courtier, prominent lawyer and eminent translator Sir Thomas Elyot, who was close to the scholarly circle of Sir Thomas More, was known not only for his *Governour* (1531) but also for his translations from the classics and for his Latin-English dictionary (1538). Many shared Elyot's belief that the time had come to discard the obscure and *barbarous* (ie.alien) law-French, and to

---

[25] On the representations of "the kingdom" from poetry to geography see, R. HELGERSON, *Forms of Nationhood: The Elizabethan Writing of England*, Chicago and London, University of Chicago Press, 1992.

[26] D. BIOW, *Doctors, Ambassadors, Secretaries*, cit., p. 12.

[27] For a discussion of "fluent domestication" as a canon of English-language translation, that unfortunately does not include the Tudor age, see L. VENUTI, *The Translator's Invisibility: A History of Translation*, London and New York, Routledge, 1995.

[...] conforme the style therof with the phrase of our English, desiringe more to make it playne to all readers than to flourishe it with over moch eloquence.[28]

Twenty years after Elyot's pronouncement in 1561, a government official called Thomas Hoby, who was well connected with both the Privy Council and the Inns of Court wrote the *Courtier*, his famous translation of Castiglione's *Cortegiano*. In his dedication to the work, he said that the translation of Latin or Greek authors:

[...] doeth not onely not hinder learning, but it furthereth it, yea, it is learning it self, and a great staye to youth to fill their minde with the morall virtues, and their body with civyll conditions [...]

He thus echoes Elyot's *Governour* and, indirectly, Thomas More's 1518 letter to the University of Oxford, and adds that only more translations of the classics would enable men in England,

[...] *not to be counted barbarous in oure tunge*, as in time out of minde we have bene in our maners [...] and become as famous as the learned men of other nations have ben and presently are.[29]

Yet, much of the "Elizabethan art of translation" from the classics achieved at the Inns was gained at second-hand. Generally speaking, neither translators nor their readers were much concerned as to whether or not a work was translated from the original language.[30] With some notable exceptions, many works in the modern vernaculars, as well as important Greek texts and some Latin works, had all been translated from the French. For instance, Sir Thomas North's (1535-1603?) "Plutarch" (*Lives of the Noble Grecians and Romans*, 1579), then considered one of the most famous Elizabethan translations, had been "Englished" from the French of Jaques Amyot. North did not embark on the translation unprepared. He must have been struck by the refined quality of Amyot's French and, as he said, he wished to do as much for his "barbarouse" native tongue:

---

[28] Sir T. ELYOT, *The Boke named the Governour*, cit., pp. 63-66.

[29] Sir T. HOBY, *The Book of the Courtier*, cit., p. 11. This author's italics.

[30] F.O. Matthiessen idealized Elisabethan translation in his *Translation: An Elizabethan Art*, Cambridge, Mass., Harvard University Press, 1931.

[...] the office of a fit translater, consisteth not onely in the faithfull expressing of his authors meaning, but also in a certain resembling and shadowing out of the forme of his style and the maner of his speaking (*Lives*, sig. *7r).

It is sufficient to recall Montaigne's words in order to understand that Amyot's objective was to endow his native idiom with a cultural and moral authority. Montaigne's personal success was the creation of a linguistic *koiné* that reflected the sense of a common cultural language shared by Latin, French, Spanish, Gascon and Italian readers. For this reason, he could declare Amyot's French the winner of an ideal linguistic contest:

I give, and it seems to me with reason, the palm to Jaques Amyot over all our French writers, and not only for the naturalness and purity of his language, in which he surpasses all others; [...] We ignoramuses would have been lost if this book had not lifted us out of the quagmire; thanks to it, we now dare to speak and write; from it the ladies give lessons to the schoolmasters; it is our breviary [...] [31]

In the course of the 17th-century, it was the idiom and style of the *Essais* that took the place of Latin in the worldly, cosmopolitan, French-reading Republic of Letters.[32] Just as Montaigne had appreciated Amyot's "naturalness and purity of language", North and Hoby recognised in the modern classics "playnenes, withoute counterfaite eloquence [and] inkehorne termes". After Florio's translation of Montaigne, the following pronouncement on style became a rule:

Le parler que j'ayme, c'est un parler simple et naïf, tel sur le papier qu'a la bouche; un parler succulent et nerveux, court et serré, non tant delicat et peigné comme vehement et brusque. [...] plutost difficile qu'ennuieux [...] non pedantesque, fratesque, non pleideresque, mais plutost soldatesque [...] naïf et meprisant.[33]

To the many well educated and cosmopolitan Elizabethan translators at the Inns of Court, "naturalness and purity of language", that is to say "fluency", was more than a mere question of style. Lawyers with a foot

---

[31] *The Complete Essays of Montaigne*, translated by Donald Frame, Stanford, Stanford University Press, 1979 (II, 4), pp. 262-263.

[32] W. BOUTCHER, *Vernacular Humanism in the 16th Century*, edited by J. Kraye, *The Cambridge Companion to Renaissance Humanism*, Cambridge, Cambridge University Press, 2003, p. 196. On the persistence of Latin to transmit significant scholarly and scientific findings, see EISENSTEIN, *The Printing Revolution in Early Modern Europe*, cit., I, p. 138.

[33] MONTAIGNE, *Essais* (I, xxvi), Paris, Garnier.

in diplomacy and policy were well aware of the need to raise their native language to the level of French or Italian. They felt that "fidelity" to the writer, or the literal meaning of a foreign text, was not enough, and that it was necessary to "naturalise" a language, thus imbuing it with a sense of "civilisation".[34] The "fluent" domestication of ancient and modern classics in translation and the construction of a linguistic identity was one of the ways in which the new Tudor patriotic zeal and nationalism asserted itself against the rival courts of Europe. Under Elizabeth, London came to rival Paris as the capital of civilisation, and in 1592 Nashe could proudly proclaim:

> The poets of our time [...] haue cleansed our language from barbarisme, and made the vulgar sort, here in London [...] to aspire to a richer purity of speech than is communicated with the Comminality of any Nation under heauen.[35]

THE STUDY OF HISTORY

In 1557, the young Thomas North in *The Diall of Princes* (1557), his translation of Bishop Antonio de Guevara's work, in the dedication to Queen Mary addressed his "beloved compaignyons, and fellow students of our house of Lyncolnes Inne" as the beneficiaries of a book meant to provide instruction on how to "serve to hygh estates for counsell, to curious serchers of antiquityes, for knowledge".

These "curious serchers of antiquityes", who were also part of the translation movement at the Inns, formed a coterie of young scholars who saw the study of the past as an ennobling extracurricular activity pursued under royal patronage for the improvement of English and the representation and consolidation of the monarchy. From early on, lawyers' interest in antiquarianism, custom and the evolution of the Common Law for the sake of political instruction and patriotism upheld their vocation to counsel, which included all aspects of experience.

Since the Dissolution, London had become the centre of writing and printing of historical works. After the dispersal of the monastic libraries, manuscripts of antiquities ended up in London, where citizens of middling rank became the main practitioners of vernacular chronicle writing. The

---

[34] On the method of *domestication* vs. the *foreignizing* methods of translation, see VENUTI, *The Translator's Invisibility*, cit., p. 20.

[35] T. NASHE, *Pierce Penilesse*, cit., R.B. McKerrow, Vol. I, p. 195.

wealthy London merchants had an active interest in the preservation of the medieval heritage. By the 1530s, the production of civic historical scholarship in London, which had been quite vital in the preceding century, was appropriated by gentry and used by Cromwell for his campaign to consolidate the Reformation. The London printers who published works of historical nature were Protestants well connected to the seats of power. Richard Grafton, publisher of the English Bible, was a protégé of Cromwell and Crammer, while Reyner Wolfe, the Protestant immigrant who became King's Printer in Greek and Latin and promoted the publication of Raphael Holinshed's *Chronicles* under Elizabeth, became the most affluent printer on Saint Paul's Churchyard. Among them, Edmund Whitchurch played a key role in assembling the team of learned barristers, including William Baldwin, George Ferrers, Thomas Phaer, John Higgins and Thomas Blenerhasset, that produced the collective *Mirrour for Magistrates* (1559-1610).[36]

In the Middle Ages, "history", factual or legendary, had been a literary pursuit functional to moral exemplarity. The narratives of the past were broken down into moral *casus* and *exempla* to be collected in manuals of *ars predicandi* and edificatory texts such as Vincent of Beuvais's *Speculum historiale* or Boccaccio's *De casibus virorum illustrium*, and in England John Gower's *Mirour de l'omme*. In the early Tudor period, the historiographic model of *specula* was still used by the humanist lawyers involved in both education and policy, who like the Florentine historiographers believed in the proximity of sound learning and sound government. Systematic tracts, on the continental model of the "mirror for princes" outlining in detail the type of training to be given to young aristocrats involved in the business of government began to appear in print.[37] From Thomas More's *History of King Richard Third*, composed in Latin and English (1513-1522), to the collective *Mirror for Magistrates*, from Camden's *Britannia* (1586) to Francis Bacon's "politic" *History of the Reign of King Henry VII*, to the Inns drama, which often bore the titles of *Gesta* and *Chronicle*,

---

[36] O. HARRIS, *Stow and the Contemporary Antiquarian Network*, in *John Stow (1525-1605) and the Making of the English Past*, edited by I. Gadd and A. Gillespie, London, British Library, 2004, pp. 27-36. For the essential bibliography on early modern historical writing in Britain see D.R. WOOLF, *The Shapes of History. A companion to Shakespeare*, edited by D. Scott Kastan, Oxford, Blackwell Publishers Ltd, 1999, pp. 186-205. Woolf underestimates the role of common law lawyers in the early Society of Antiquaries.

[37] D. QUAGLIONI, *Il Modello del Principe Cristiano gli* specula principum *fra Medio Evo e prima età moderna*, in *Modelli della Storia del Pensiero Politico*, edited by V.I. Comparato, Florence, Olschki, 1987, pp. 103-122.

6

historical discourse in verse, prose narratives or plays written for intramural revels was aimed at counsel.

The ideas that knowledge ought to be "for use" and that the highest form of *ars historica* was "civil history" were later developed by the polihistorian and lawyer Sir Francis Bacon, who followed narrative techniques perfected, and made to serve didactic purposes by Machiavelli and Guicciardini. In *The Advancement of Learning*[38] he indirectly clarifies the Pauline implications of the medieval notion of *"speculum historiale"*:

> But contrariwise, in the governors toward the governed, all things ought, as far as the frailty of men permitteth, to be manifested and revealed. For so it is expressed in the Scriptures touching the government of God, that this globe, which seemeth to us a dark and shady body, is the view of God as crystal: *Et in conspectus sedis tamquam mare vitreum simile crystallo.*[39]

The close relationship between learning and government remained, from Francis Bacon to Samuel Jonson, who wrote *Rasselas* at Staple's Inn in 1759. To these pragmatic "commonwealths men", the propagation of knowledge among the professions and the literate middling ranks of population was a powerful tool for breaking through traditional ignorance.

As prospective civil servants and courtiers, lawyers clearly saw the continuity existing between law, history, education and policy, and participated in a variety of activities, as amateur translators, dramatists, teachers and poets. In the early Tudor period, the publishing career of the Oxford-educated physician and lawyer Thomas Phaer (1510-1560) of Lincoln's Inn exemplifies lawyers' attitudes towards the propagation of knowledge. He was part of the translation movement at the Inns and, like his fellow lawyers, upheld the worthiness of English on patriotic grounds. He published two legal treatises in English as well as Virgil's first seven books of the *Aeneid*, collaborated in the *Mirrour*, and with Baldwin and Ferrers was involved in writing plays; as a physician he translated French work on childhood health and diseases into English. Similarly George Ferrers, an eminent practising lawyer and well known political figure, was involved in writing, policy and entertainment. His non-professional activities involved both the royal Court and the Inns. He acted as *dominus festi*, or Lord of Misrule, in 1551/1553 for Edward VI; and as a member of Lin-

---

[38] G.W. KITCHIN, ed., *The Advancement of Learning*, London, Dent & Sons Ltd., 1973, p. 206.

[39] *Revelation* 4. 6.

coln's Inn and author of tragedies, he wrote tragic histories of retribution for the 1559 *Mirrour for Magistrates*.

In its various extensions, the *Mirror for Magistrates* was a typical product of the culture of the Inns and the result of lawyers' interest in history and exemplarity for the sake of law and policy.[40] The representation in verse of native tragedy, in which the two themes of ambition and revenge came to possess outstanding popularity and importance, were made to join with and support self-improvement and the fashioning of the Prince for the good of the Commonwealth. It had originated in the adaptation of British and local history to the medieval tragic, non-dramatic historical genre of *De casibus virorum illustrium*, first translated by John Lydgate as the *Fall of Princes*. The meaning of the history and "mutability" represented in the *Mirrour* was not unfolded, as in the past, by the mysterious motions of Fortune's wheel, or by divine plan, but for the first time by the dramatic progress from cause to effect. The ghosts' narratives centred on the catastrophic consequences of imperfect humanity, rather than on those of Fortune, and on tragic retribution. As Jack Cade laments:

> Shal I cal it Fortune or my forward folly
> That lifted me, and layed me downe belowe [...]?
> (Folio xliiii)

From the 1559 original collection, dedicated by William Baldwin to "the Nobilitye and all other in office", to its later issues, the subject of the *Mirrour* was feebleness, sins or the faults that foil men, and tragic retribution. In this plan, Justice was the grand virtue, while Goddess Fortuna in the looking glass of history represented a mystery no longer. The *Mirrour* showed that "mutability" was actually only "retribution" or reward according to deserts: men may avoid "mutability" by virtuous living. In words that echo Machiavelli's secular and pragmatic perspective on man's destiny, Francis Bacon thus refined the Mirror's view on fortune:

The way of Fortune is like the milken way in the sky; which is a meeting or knot of a number of small stars, not seen asunder, but giving light together. So there are a number of little and scarce discerned virtues, or rather faculties and customs, that make men fortunate.[41]

---

[40] Collaborators, among others included, at various stages, George Ferrers, Thomas Churchyard, Thomas Sackville, Thomas Norton, John Higgins, Thomas Lodge and Michael Drayton.

[41] Essay *XL. Of Fortune* (121).

The writing of the *Mirrour* was preceded by a process of consultations and discussions not unlike the aural learning exercises, or moots, and as such it was also a natural product of a common-law education based on discussion of precedents and collaboration. In the espistle "To the Reader", Baldwin describes how the consultation was conducted among the contributors gathered in a discussion group, and how George Ferrers was elected to "usurpe Bochas rowme", receive the ghosts' complaints and begin the discussion. The *Mirrour*'s review form – that is to say, a simple sequence of separate tragic speeches in which a set number of characters in turn deliver a self-characterising monologue – is an intrinsically judicial and penitential form. The dramatic effectiveness with which in the *Mirrour*, unlike in the work of Boccaccio or Lydgate, the ghosts conjured from the past, as in a court of justice, tell their own stories in the form of complaints to a selected audience presided over by an elected "receiver", was amplified by the amateur dramatists at the Inns in fully fledged plays for intramural performance.[42]

By the 1580s, the practice of meeting in a discussion group on historical matters became consolidated when Sir Robert Cotton of the Middle Temple joined with his former teacher William Camden, John Selden, Sir John Davies and other lawyers to institute the "Society of Antiquaries" at Lincoln's Inn.[43] Throughout the 1590s, with a brief interruption in the plague years and until its demise in 1607, the Society kept records of contributions to "discourses" (discussions), as well as of exchanges of manuscripts among the fellow antiquarians. The intense book exchange among members, who must have felt the need for a library, generated the writing of a petition to the Crown for a permanent historical academy and the foundation of a national library for those interested in public affairs. This proposal was primarily intended to stimulate research and publications, but did not meet with royal approval. Politicians distrusted antiquarianism, and realised that the growing potential of antiquarian research would cause them political difficulties, especially in a parliament where debate to decide questions of the day was dominated by the use of precedent; and lawyers considered antiquarianism an essential part of the search for precedent and

---

[42] The structure of the *Mirrour* is similar to that of early liturgical drama, usually static. It also recalls the precursor of German judicial plays, the strophic *Reihenspiel* or revue.

[43] The activity of John Speed, Merchant Taylor, historian, cartographer, genealogist, numismatist, author of the atlas volume The *Theatre of the Empire of Great Britaine* exemplifies the wide range of antiquarianism. With Sir Walter Raleigh (M.T.) the powerful common law magistrates Sir Henry Spelman (L.I.) Sir Edward Coke (I.T.), the herald William Dethick and William Lambarde (L.I.) all belonged to the original Society of which John Stowe was the only non-gentleman member.

authority in all aspects of life and thought. To make analogies and parallels between the shape of the past and the shape of the present was, in fact, a habit of mind of men learned in the law of the land.

THE THEATRE OF COUNSEL

The lawyer's patriotic pursuit, definition and direction of historical studies during the Tudor age found expression in the writing of moral and historical drama for intramural performance. Relaxation of rules and carnival license during the revels season gave the amateur playwrights freedom for indirect political commentary on delicate issues. On occasions, lawyers stressed in their plays their qualification for the role of royal counsellors, but their political advice was not always welcomed. A morality play staged for the 1526 Christmas celebrations at Gray's Inn aroused the ire of Cardinal Wolsey, who saw in the play allusions to his own administration. The allegorical representation, devised at least 20 years before, must have contained farcical elements: it staged *Lord Governance* ruled by *Dissipation* and *Neglicence*, which caused *Rumor Populi, Inward Grudge* and *Disdain of Wanton Sovreignty* to rise with a great multitude to expel both *Neglicence* and *Dissipation* and to restore *Lady Publike Wele* again to her state. Wolsey retaliated against its author, Master John Roo, a member of Gray's and Sergeant-at-Law-to-be; author and actors were rebuked, and Master Roo was decoiffed and sent to the Fleet prison, from where influential friends rescued him. Simon Fish, who had acted a part of the cardinal in the play, had to flee the country. Farcical representations of political import at the Inns must have occasionally chagrined also the "Ancients". In 1550, for instance, all "comedies called enterludes, except during times of solemn Christmas" were banned by an order of the Bench. But the show went on, and it was in the Hall of the Inner Temple during the Christmas revels of the 1561-1562 that the first historical tragedy in blank verse, *Gorboduc, or Ferrer and Porrex*, was acted by amateurs actors from the Inns of Court.

Thomas Norton (1532-1584) and Thomas Sackville (1536-1608), a distinguished collaborator of the *Mirrour*, were members of the Inner Temple and translators of the classics. They wrote the play in five acts, attempting unity of action and place. They used a chorus, a messenger and other Senecan techniques, along with dumb shows, blank verse and a close interworking of law and rhetoric.[44] Drawn from of a story in Geoffrey of Mon-

---

[44] As was often the case at the Inns, Norton and Sackville united by common humanistic

mouth's *Histories of the Kings of Britain*, *Gorboduc* is now famous mainly
for having introduced to drama the blank verse that Surrey had adapted
from an Italian metre only a few years earlier. Written at the time when
the Crown lawyers, assembled at Serjeant's Inn had all agreed that "[...]
the King has in him two Bodies, viz., a Body natural, and a Body politic",
the play, conceived as a historical, legal and political drama, must have
been considered a sophisticated attempt at native classical drama.[45] It preserved the *Mirrour*'s outlook on tragedy as the outcome of freely willed human acts. The chorus of "ancient and sage men of Britain" in fact presents
the tragic action as:

> A myrrour shall become to Princes all
> To learne to shunne the cause of suche a fall.
> (I, ii 392-93)

It was first acted for the Christmas revels of the Inner Temple in 1561-
1562, and on 18 January 1562 at Whitehall, before the Queen. Deeming
marriage and succession her prerogatives, Elizabeth resisted discussion in
Parliament, and on this occasion took no offence from the fact that the sovereign in person was being warned of the dangers involved for the state
when it lacks a definite successor.[46]

The question of Elizabeth's succession surfaced in other plays written
for the Inns' revels. George Gascoine and Francis Kinwelmarsh of Gray's
Inn, for the 1566-67 festivities, wrote and staged the domestic tragedy *Jocasta*.[47] The following year, five Inner Templars produced and performed
before the Queen the four-act tragedy *Gismond of Salerne*, another domestic tale of love thwarted by a sovereign who will not allow her daughter to
marry a worthy man.[48] Despite an order of the Bench in 1585 forbidding
the election of a "lord" of revels for the Christmas revels of 1587-88, the

---

ideals were otherwise very different. Norton was a Puritan, Cranmer's son-in-law, translator of
Calvin and parliamentarian, whereas the higher born Sackville was a committed royalist with
more authentic literary credentials, moved in loftier literary circles and became a powerful magistrate. He wrote the prefatory verses to Hoby's *Courtier*. On *Gorboduc* and the question of
succession, see M. AXTON, *The Queen's Two Bodies Drama and the Elizabethan Succession*,
London, Historical Society, 1977, pp. 39-56.

[45] For the mystic fiction of the "King's two bodies" as divulged by English jurists of the
Tudor period, see E.H. KANTOROWICZ, *The King's Two Bodies: A Study in Medieval Political
Theology*, Princeton, N.J., Princeton University Press, 1957.

[46] On the public discussion on succession an official ban was issued at the time.

[47] A blank-verse translation of Lodovico Dolce's *Giocasta* (1549), itself an adaptation of the
Phoenissae of Euripides.

[48] Axton (56-57).

Grayans elected a *Prince of Purpoole*. On this occasion, Francis Bacon collaborated with Christopher Everton and six other prominent lawyers, five of whom were in the House of Commons and only one of whom had not yet been called to the Bar of Gray's Inn, in the Shrovetide production of *Certaine Devices and shewes* to celebrate Elizabeth's 30 years on the throne.[49] *The Misfortunes of Arthur*, acted during the revels, a blank-verse tragedy on the attempted usurpation of Arthur's kingdom by his nephew Mordred, was acted before the Queen at Greenwich and presented guarded advice on the subject of preservation of the realm; it contained allusions to the political uncertainties facing England under the threat of the Spanish Armada, the recent execution of Mary, Queen of Scots, and the question of James Stuart's loyalty to Protestantism.

Inns' drama, with its potentially subversive implications, was in general tolerated by the Benchers and the Privy Council: this, we must remember, was not the popular stage but an elitist intramural theatre not subject to the strict censorship of the anti-theatrical London government. Coterie drama at the Inns, supported by the Privy Council and often attended by the Queen in person, was free of censorship and immune from municipal control over sedition and heresy. It can even be argued that amateur dramatists at the Inns shared the same anti-theatrical prejudices of the government. The tragedy of Sackville and Norton, for instance, was not intended for publication. In 1565, the play was pirated and printed without the authorisation of its authors, as often happened. In the authorised 1570, second Quarto edition of *Gordboduc or Ferrex and Porrex*, the pirating of the text is described by the authors, in the letter to the reader, in terms of *villany*, rape and disfigurement against a *fair maid*. The tragedy, having being restored to her pristine state, is offered to the "good readers", who are urged to "gently entertain her in favour of the house from whence she is descended".[50]

---

[49] T. HUGHES, *Certaine deu[is]es and shewes presented to her Maiestie by the gentlemen of Grayes-Inne at her Highnesse court in Greenewich, the twenty eighth day of Februarie in the thirtieth yeare of her Maiesties most happy raigne*, London, R. Robinson, 1587; Early *English Classical Tragedies (Gorboduc. Jocasta. Gismond of Salerne. The Misfortunes of Arthur)*. Edited with introduction and notes by J.W. Cunliffe, Oxford, Clarendon Press, 1912. For a new discussion of the political aspects of the play, see P. RAFFIELD, *Images and Cultures of Law in Early modern England*, Cambridge, Cambridge University Press, 2004, pp. 124-138; AXTON, *op. cit.*, pp. 76-79.

[50] On coterie theatre see the classic study by A. HARBAGE, *Shakespeare and the Rival Tradition*, Bloomington and London, Indiana University Press, 1952; on the various and complex ideological aspects of anti-theatrical sentiments and Jonson, see J. BARISH, *The Antitheatrical Prejudice*, Berkeley, Ca. University of California Press Berkeley, 1981, pp. 80-15; L.S. MARCUS, *The Politics of Mirth*, Chicago and London, University of Chicago Press, 1986, pp. 24-63.

Around the end of the 16th-century, historical and dramatic writing could still seem an alternative and complementary means of recovering the lessons of the past for the sake of moral and political instruction of the present. Both Ben Jonson and William Shakespeare, two authors well connected to the Inns of Court, knew this well and appropriated the spirit of the *Mirror*'s reflection on British history to re-canvass history and legend for indirect political commentary. Jonson, in particular, was closely connected to the old Society of Antiquaries, and with its founding members, John Selden and William Camden, belonged to that *convivium philosophicum* that met in places as diverse as the London house of Sir Robert Cotton, the Temple, the house of the herald, William Dethick, and perhaps the mythical Mitre and the Mermaid Taverns.[51] In Jonson's surviving tragedies, *Sejanus His Fall* (1604) and *Catiline His Conspiracy* (1611), both laden with subtle allusions to real courtiers and advisors of the monarch, the writer consciously acts as historian, dramatist and poet.[52] In the address to the readers of *Sejanus*, his "understanding auditory", he alludes to a continuing philosophical debate on truth and history among the gentlemen lawyers at the Inns of Court, and answers the demands of Renaissance critical theory, which argued that tragedy is most authentic when it represents historical truth before a knowing audience. Historians had to be tactful in an age when rulers expected men of letters to endorse the legitimacy of royal power. Jonson's declared use of written, factual history, and the apparatus of marginal notes appended to the printed text of his Roman tragedies, were not there to parade his scholarship: they were meant to back up the accuracy of his detail, and to protect him from detractors and authorities. In *Sejanus*, Jonson claims to have discharged the offices of a tragic writer in "truth of argument, dignity of persons, gravity and height of elocution, fullness and frequence of sentence". But only Jonson's "fellowship of friends" would have been able to grasp the allusion and see that "truth of argument", in this particular context, was meant as accurate, historical truth intended to correct the hazy Elizabethan notion "mutability".

---

[51] Tavern meetings appear to have been an invention of nineteenth century historians; see I.A. SHAPIRO, *The Mermaid Club*, «Modern Language Review», 45, pp. 6-17.

[52] In the summer of 1605 he was imprisoned for the third time for having aroused the anger of the James I by mocking his Scottish manners and favourites in the play *Eastward Hoe!* written with George Chapman and John Marston of the Middle Temple. B. WORDEN, *Ben Jonson among the Historians*, in *Culture and Politics in Early Stuart England*, edited by K. Sharpe and P. Lake, London, Macmillan, 1994, pp. 67-89. Chapman was connected with the Inns of Court, although there is no direct evidence for this other than his dramatic associations with John Marston, and his poetic dedications to Matthew Roydon, who studied at Thavies Inn.

CHAPTER TWO

RHETORIC AND PARADOX AT THE INNS OF COURT

> Sweete Analutikes tis thou hast ravisht me,
> Bene disserere est finis logicis,
> Is, to dispute well, Logickes chiefest end
> Affoords this Art no greater miracle?
>
> MARLOWE

RHETORIC AND THE TEACHING OF LAW

The teaching of common law at the Inns of Court and Chancery was based on a system of aural learning exercises spanning the legal year. The legal calendar was divided into four terms, during which time the Westminster courts were in session and legal business was conducted. Despite the Protestant reform of the legal calendar and the official abolition of the cult of the saints, the former kept its old notations. The Michaelmas term (October and November), Hilary (January and February), Easter (April and May) and Trinity (May and June) referred to both fixed and movable feast days of the old ecclesiastical calendar.[1] All Sundays and certain saints' days, including papist celebrations such as Corpus Christi, were in fact *dies non juridici*. In addition, the three religious seasons of Christmas (with Advent and Epiphany), Lent (with Easter) and Trinity (with Whitsun and Corpus Christi) were kept free. These were therefore "vacations", in which the common-law courts and the Inns closed down and the "apprentices" at the Inns of Courts learned the law (hence "learning vacations").

The main academic elements in order to qualify for a call at the bar were attendance at either four or six "learning vacations" immediately before the call and participation in a given number of moots. The reading was the most ceremonious and sophisticated learning exercise, and the equiva-

---

[1] D. CRESSY, *Bonfires and Bells National Memory and the Protestant Calendar in Elizabethan and Stuart England*, London, Weindenfeld & Nicolson, 1989.

lent of a university lecture. It was devoted to the exposition of a statute or part of a statute. The form of the reading was modelled on the scholastic *quaestiones* and, unlike the theological disputation, was not abstract. In the law schools, there was the added refinement of a "case" – a specific problem with hypothetical facts – with no disputation or solution attached.

Readings took place in the autumn and Lent vacations, and were delivered by two different readers, who addressed a mixed audience of young, talented students and seasoned practitioners. Unlike university lecturers, they did not impose their views on the audience but instead encouraged open disagreement and discussion on given points of law. Legal education was thus "less a cramming course in ancient precedent than an endeavor in developing forensic agility".[2] The process of graduation from inner barrister to utter barrister was inseparable from the performance of moots. These were pleading exercises conducted in "homely law-French" and held after supper in the halls of the Inns for the inner, and junior utter, barristers. The earliest descriptions of mooting date to the time of Henry VIII, but the most detailed come from Dugdale's *Origines Juridiciales*, a description of the customs of the Middle Temple, which were quite probably still performed by the newly summoned barristers in 1660.[3] Mooting took the form of a mock trial, with three or two utter barristers or benchers sitting as judges and two students or barristers acting as opposing counsellors:

> [...] whensoever any of the said moots be brought in before any of the said benchers, then two of the said inner barristers, sitting on the said form with the utter barrister, do for their exercise recite by heart the pleading of the same moot-case, in law-French, which pleading is the declaration at large of the said moot case, the one of them taking the part of the plaintiff and the other the part of the defendant [...] after this done, the utter barristers argue some questions as be disputable within the case – as there must be always one at least – and, this ended, the benchers do likewise declare their opinions how they think the law to be in the same questions. And this manner of exercise of mooting is daily used during the said vacations [...] The moot being ended, all parties return to the cupboard, where the mootmen present the benchers with a cup of beer and a slice of bread...

Other exercises, probably included "bolts", probably moots for junior students, and "keeping a case", where a junior at each mess would ex-

---

[2] E.W. IVES, *The Common Law Lawyers of Pre-Reformation England*, Cambridge, Cambridge University Press, 1983, p. 32; M. McGLYNN, *The Royal Prerogative and the Learning of the Inns of Court*, Cambridge, Cambridge University Press, 2003, pp. 17-24.

[3] W. DUGDALE, *Origines Juridiciales*, cit., pp. 205*b*-206*a*.

pound a point and be followed by the rest of the table in order of seniority. But what was the whole system of collective learning designed to teach and test? Rather than mere rules, Professor Baker tells us that:[4]

> [...] what was taught was a method, and a cast of mind [...] some of the questions were clearly designed more to stretch the mind than to establish any principles which might be of practical utility [...] The cases in the moot books also betoken a love for the improbable...the participants were less concerned to discover any right answer than to know whether a point was good and arguable or mootable: a true moot point.

The method of aural instruction at the Inns suffered a progressive decline from at least the reign of Henry VIII onwards until it disappeared altogether during the Civil War. A series of concurrent events changed the significance of the old system of aural exercises within the context of legal education. The great expansion of membership in the second half of the century in turn increased the demand for a systematic and simplified body of common law and for a more rational approach to its educational system. This need, which had already generated a new kind of manuscript collection of problem ("mootable") cases or "moot books", was answered by the printing press.[5] By the mid-1480s, the monopolistic trade in printed law books, which had supplied the professionals since 1484 or thereabouts with yearbooks, as well as rare texts from previous generations and different sorts of practical literature, increased the volume of publication. Primers and books of case law intended to help the student wade through the innumerable cases, statutes and writs that had to be read and digested all sold well at the printers' shops conveniently situated close to the Inns of Court and in St Paul's churchyard. Unlike in the past, these were not intended solely for reference purposes but for sustained private study, in what was to prove a new and lasting trend in English education.

The printing press did not, however, entirely replace the old learning exercises. Like the pulpit before it, it helped create a more atomised and individuated reading public, even in these tight-knit centres of communal learning.[6] John Donne, who in May 1592, like his famous relative Thomas

---

[4] *Readings and Moots at The Inns of Court in the Fifteenth Century*, eds. S.E. Thorpe and J.H. Baker, London, Selden Society, 2 vols., 1990, p. LXXII.

[5] See J.H. BAKER, *The Books of the Common Law*, in *The Cambridge History of the Book in Britain*, edited by L. Hellinga and J.B. Trapp, Vol. III, Cambridge, Cambridge University Press, 1999, pp. 411-432.

[6] It remains an open question as to whether or not such changes in the educational programme of the Inns of Court, no longer based only on discussion and debate but more on private

More, was admitted at Lincoln's Inn after a spell at Oxford, vividly echoes his solitary reading and dreaming of the law when he says: "One of our Giant Statutes ope his jaw, To sucke me in [...]".[7]

MOOTS, WIT AND METHOD

One key event that helped bring about the transformation of the system of legal education in England, as well as the composition of membership, was the progressive influx of university-trained men into the Inns of Court. During the reign of Henry VIII, instead of attendance at one of the lesser Inns of Chancery, a period of residence at Oxford or Cambridge was starting to gain favour as the best introduction to the study of law. At the same time, the progressive collapse of the university system, still based on medieval curricula for undergraduates, and heavily theological for resident graduates, determined a steady migration of young wits to London in search of government employment and court preferment. With Oxford's demand that all students over the age of 16 should accept the supremacy of the monarch over that of the church, and growing anti-papism at Cambridge, Roman Catholics were practically excluded from graduation. John Donne, for instance, completed his higher education at the Inns of Court, where many Roman Catholics had found an atmosphere of relative religious tolerance.

With the sons of peers, baronets, knights, and esquires entering the Inns of Court, either as professionals or as amateurs, after a brief spell of college and travel on the continent, the education of common lawyers became less strictly and severely professional than in the past. The entrance of these young men, some of whom had studied at Padua and Bologna, who knew classical languages and were familiar with both civil law and *mos gallicus*, was like that of the Trojan horse, and led to a subtle introduction of educational reform.[8] From Richard Morison's *Discourse touching the Reformation*

---

reading, affected collective identity and encouraged the emergence and competition of new forms of groups identities. See EISENSTEIN, *The Printing Revolution in Early Modern Europe*, Vol. I, Cambridge, Cambridge University Press, 1983, p. 132.

[7] *Satyre IIII* (pp. 131-133), in *Donne Poetical Works*, edited by H.J.C. Grierson, Oxford, Oxford University Press, 1971.

[8] On the question, raised by F.W. Maitland in the famous Rede Lecture *English Law and the Renaissance* (Cambridge, 1901), that in the second quarter of the 16th-century the continuity of English law was seriously endangered by a threatened, but failed, reception of Roman Law, see S.E. THORNE, *Essays in English Legal History*, London, Hambledon Press, 1985, pp. 187-195. For a critique of the idea that common lawyers were isolated from the major currents of their

of the laws of England (ca. 1540) to Sir Thomas Wilson's *Arte of Rhetoricke* (1553), *The Lawiers Logike* (1588),[9] by the future Queen's solicitor Abraham Fraunce, and Henry Finch's *Nomotechnia* (1613), humanist common lawyers of Elyot's and More's mettle repeatedly suggested formal, that is to say logical and rhetorical, improvements of common law on the model of Justinian's *Corpus Juris*, as well as the need to pursue the unity of learning and style with morality and a sense of citizenship.

In his book of princely counsel *The Boke named the Governour*, Sir Thomas Elyot, who was part of Cromwell's inner circle, based his representation of the ideal lawyer and orator on Sir Thomas More, whose *cursus studiorum*, from Oxford to New Inn and Lincoln's Inn, and professional life he regarded as exemplary. Elyot, the son of a judge and himself a prominent lawyer, advised parents against setting children of 14 or 15 to the study of law with out some knowledge of the liberal arts and the "right studie of very philosophy". They should be aware, he said, that knowledge of government and rule in the Commonwealth could not be achieved without the study of the classical languages, philosophy, poetry and eloquence.[10] Of the liberal arts, rhetoric had always appealed to the cultivated lawyer, but the New Learning brought classical rhetoric to bear on legal training and gave common lawyers the awareness that the pleading exercises had a classical dignity of their own. Sir Thomas Elyot described moots, for him unfortunately still conducted in the "barbaric" law-French, in terms of rhetorical division. He also instructed the reader how to make legal pleas according to *Invention*, *Disposition* and *Memorie*.[11]

The rationalising trends of continental pedagogical and legal humanism advocated by the first generation of Tudor lawyers such as Starkey, Morison and Elyot were in part realised during the last quarter of the century,

---

age, see W. PREST, *The Rise of the Barristers*, cit., Chap. VI. See also, J.H. BAKER's position in *The Legal Profession and the Common Law: Historical Essays*, London and Ronceverte, Hambledon Press, 1986, pp. 461-476. On the question of the defence of English law against Roman Law within a larger literary context see HELGERSON, *Forms of Nationhood*, cit., pp. 21-103; D.R. KELLY, *Juriconsultus Perfectus: The Lawyer as a Renaissance Man*, «Journal of the Warburg and Courtauld Institutes», Vol. 51 (1988), pp. 84-102. On English students in Padua see J. WOOLFSON, *Padua and the Tudors English Students*, cit., pp. 10-38.

[9] The full title is *The Lawiers Logike, exemplifying the praecepts of Logike by the practice of the Common Lawe.*

[10] See *The Boke named the Governour*, Chap. XIV, *On the Study of Law*, cit.

[11] Sir T. ELYOT, *The Boke*, cit., pp. 63-66. On the dissemination of classical rhetoric at the Inns of Court, see R.J. SCHOECK, *Rhetoric and Law in 16th-century England*, «Studies in Philology», 50 (1953), pp. 110-127.

when the "modern" and logical method of knowledge inspired by the French dialectician and reformer of educational methods the Protestant Pierre de la Ramé (1515?-1572) was introduced to England.[12] Ramism, galvanised by the printing press, had met with great success at the major European establishments of learning. It enjoyed much success among Cambridge dons and would-be courtiers such as Gabriel Harvey (1550-1631) owing to the fact that they saw in the Ramist use of logic the key to excellence in the use of the liberal arts for a successful public life.

As has been noted, Ramus's simplification of the traditional curricula of higher education was admirably suited to the rising bourgeoisie and "attracted those who regarded education as a means to social position rather than a preparation for a life of scholarship [...]".[13] Ramus's utilitarian approach to knowledge, championed by Sir Philip Sydney reached its apotheosis in the works of Francis Bacon, that *jureconsultus perfectus* who, it has been said, "cut short the dilemma of counsel, whether involving oneself actively in the business of government, posed by the humanists of the previous generation".[14] In general, barristers acquainted with continental, pedagogical and legal humanism, who were averse to the subtleties of scholastic logic, were attracted by this "new logic". To a prospective lawyer determined to embark on a diplomatic or political career, the essentially pragmatic, Ramist view of the "perfect orator", with its simple idea that *ars disserendi* could offer a route to high government office without any "moral underpinning" must have been very appealing.[15] Abraham Fraunce's *Lawiers Logike* (1588),[16] published when he was called to the bar of the Temple, is an acknowledged translation of Ramus's *Dialecticae Libri Duo*. Here one finds the same emphasis on the separation of logic and rhetoric and on the practical applications of logic and rhetoric in busi-

---

[12] W. ONG, *Ramus, Method and the Decay of Dialogue*, Cambridge Mass., Harvard University Press Cambridge, 1958; F.A. YATES, *The Art of Memory*, Chicago, University of Chicago Press, 1966, pp. 231-242; M. FEINGOLD, *English Ramism: A Reinterpretation"*, in *The Influence of Petrus Ramus*, edited by M. Feingold, J.S. Freedman and W. Rother, Basel, Schwabe & Co AG-Verlag, 2001, pp. 127-176.

[13] A. GRAFTON and L. JARDINE, *From Humanism to the Humanities: Education and the Liberal Arts in 15th and 16th-Century Europe*, London, Duckworth, 1986, pp. 167-168.

[14] Q. SKINNER, *The Foundation of Modern Political Thought*, Vol. 1, *The Renaissance*, Cambridge, Cambridge University Press, 1978, Chap. 8.

[15] On Ramism and the "perfect orator", see D.R. KELLY, *Juriconsultus Perfectus: The Lawyer as a Renaissance Man*, «Journal of the Warburg and Courtauld Institutes», Vol. 51 (1988), pp. 84-102.

[16] The full title is The *Lawier's Logike, exemplifying the precepts of Logike by the practice of the common Lawe*.

ness and the professions.[17] Fraunce also followed Ramus in the practice of enlivening his logic by quoting poetry of the day, such as *Shepherd's Calendar*. The neat, diagrammatic analysis in dichotomised outline form, and the emphasis on dexterity in disputes of Ramist method, greatly facilitated the learning of law and reduced the oft-lamented inadequacy of the legal process. The new textbooks gave the apprentices-at-law a shortcut to specialised knowledge previously attained only through an extended course of aural instruction.

The printing press was ready to meet the needs of such prospective lawyers, and those of scholars, professionals and scientists who sought to reorganise the arts and sciences according to new rules of "method". In the late 1580s we witness a proliferation of books of logic and rhetoric on the bookstalls of Saint Paul's churchyard and around the Inns. Indeed, anything vaguely logical or rhetorical that could be exploited by a young opportunist with an eye on a career in the public service, sold well.[18] By the 1590s, Ramus's logic, not unlike Machiavelli's political philosophy, had been misused and vulgarised. If, on the one hand, the mechanical extremes of Ramistry, not unlike Machiavellianism, were perceived as a threat to sound morality, on the other hand affectation of "logical" disposition, political "subtlety" and poetic paradoxy and "wit" became a matter of courtly fashion. In his representations of Machiavelli's ghost, of the well deserved death of Ramus and of Doctor Faust raging against logic and law, Marlowe was not moralising but was instead playing tongue-in-cheek with his audience, which, as we know, included many learned lawyers.[19] Among them there was the young John Donne, described by a contemporary as "not dissolute, but very neat, a great visiter of ladies, a great frequenter of plays, a great writer of conceited Verses",[20] who while at Lincoln's

---

[17] R.J. Schoeck, *Rhetoric and Law in 16th-Century England*, «Studies in Philology», Vol. 50, 1953.

[18] R. Dallington, who always angled for patronage, clothed his travel book, *A method for trauell Shewed by taking the view of France. As it stoode in the yeare of our Lord 1598*, in Ramist garb, with tables and diagrams.

[19] See *"Dr. Faust"* (I, 6-9), in *The Complete Works of Christopher Marlowe*, edited by R. Gill, Vol. II, Oxford, Clarendon Press, 1990. Ramism was by no means unanimously accepted; both Elizabeth's tutor, Roger Ascham, and the judge, John Selden, pointed out the potential risks posed to education by abridgments and tables; the Anglican theologian, Edward Hooker, deplored its mechanical extremes as "Ramystry". Marlowe had him stabbed in scene IX, 29 of *The Massacre of Paris. The Complete Works of Christopher Marlowe*, edited by R. Gill, Vol. V, Oxford, Clarendon Press, 1998.

[20] *The most elegant and witty epigrams of Sir Iohn Harrington, Knight* (1618). STC (2nd ed.)/12776. Harvard University Library.

Inn, where the Roman art of "writing with double pointing", in epigrams and paradoxes, was being revivived, was spoken of as

> the king that ruled as he thought fit
> The universal monarchy of wit.[21]

JOHN DONNE'S STRUGGLE OF CONTRARIES

Before he became the most eminent divine of his day and author of the politico-theological treatise *Pseudo-Martyr* in his early 20s, John Donne was known as the witty gallant "Jack". He was a Catholic student at the Inns of Court who aspired to a position worthy of his gifts in the body politic. He sported a moustache, long hair, fashionable clothes and a sword, affected a melancholic disposition and endeavoured in various ways to set a "mark" upon himself.[22] He did not spend all his time studying law, as he pleads in *Satyre* I:

> Away thou fondling motley humorist,
> Leave mee, and in this standing wooden chest,
> Consorted with these few bookes, let me lye
> In prison, and here be coffin'd, when I dye (1-4).

The late 1590s and the earlier years of the reign of James I were the "giddy days", when the fashionable *flâneur* "of study and play made strange hermaphrodites". He read much, saw plays and wrote ephemeral poetry. *Songs* and *Sonnets, Elegies Satyres, Letters, Paradoxes* and *Epigrams* circulated in manuscript at Thavies and Lincoln's Inn, where he ruled over his own "fellowship of friends" as the "monarch of wit".[23] Member of the Inns were courtiers of high status who had gained a reputation as writers, such as Sir Philip Sidney, Joint Master of Ordnance, who enrolled at Gray's Inn at the age of 15. In the late 1590s, besides Donne we find other impressive practitioners of both statesmanship and literature, among them

---

[21] T. CAREW, *An Elegie upon the death of Doctor Donne, Deane of Pauls.*

[22] The 1595 portrait of Donne, bequeathed by the poet himself to his friend Sir Robert Ker and now owned by the Marquis of Lothian, represents him as a victim of "Lover's Melancholy." The other portrait, in the collection of Queen Elizabeth II, was probably painted by Nicholas Hilliard (ca. 1591) and represents him as a soldier.

[23] *The Complete Poetry of John Donne*, edited by J.T. Showcross, Garden City, New York, Anchor Books, 1967; on Donne's circle see J.B. LEISHMAN, *The monarch of wit: an analytical and comparative study of the poetry of John Donne*, London, Hutchinson University Library, 1967.

Sir Francis Bacon (Gray's Inn 1576), future Viscount of St Albans and Lord Chancellor, and Sir Walter Raleigh, Privy Councillor, Sir John Davies, Lord Chief Justice, and Sir Henry Wotton, Ambassador.

Both Davies and Wotton were part of Donne's inner circle and amateur poets themselves. This coterie of young courtiers of both higher and lower status was an intellectual elite composed of men who after a spell at one of the universities had gone to London to study law. It included the lawyer-poets John Hoskyns, John Harington, Richard Baker, Robert Ker, Benjamin Rudyers and William Herbert. As wits, they wrote licentious epigrams and satires, and their models were Horace, Martial, Juvenal and, above all, Persius.[24] Only this very select group was able to decipher Donne's riddle-like poetry, understand the complex web of literary, personal and cultural allusions, and laugh at the jokes. Indeed, as has been noted, all the basic features of Donne's oral and "performative" art come from its coterie character:

> His creation of a sense of familiarity and intimacy, his fondness for dialectic, intellectual complexity, paradox and irony, the appeals to shared attitudes and group interests [...] all relate to the coterie circumstance of his verse.[25]

With the exclusion of seven poems printed with his cooperation, Donne circulated his occasional, manuscript poetry among his intimate friends at the Inns, who in turn copied them for other friends and probably also memorised them. At a time of growing literacy, expansion of the market for printed books and the rise of a profession of letters, Donne distrusted the printing press and resisted publication; only on rare occasions did he "descend" to this kind of writing.[26] As a non-professional poet writing for a select circle of "understanders", he always affected a gentlemanly disdain for belles-lettres, considered then unworthy of a mature man of status.[27] He was critical of the triviality of contemporary literary tastes, and

---

[24] See FINKELPEARL, *John Marston of the Middle Temple*, cit., pp. 71-75.

[25] A. MAROTTI, *Manuscript, Print and the English Lyric*, Ithaca and London, Cornell University Press, 1995.

[26] For the moral and social stigma devaluing any kind of professional, printed poetry, see P. SHEAVYN, *The Literary Profession in Elizabethan England*, cit., pp. 162-163, a subject also developed by J.W. Saunders. On the question of the modes of transmission of Donne's manuscript works see the introduction to the *Variorum Edition of the Poetry of John Donne*, Bloomington, Indiana University Press, 1995-2005. On manuscript poetry of the English Renaissance, see H. LOVE, *Scribal Publication in 17th-Century England*, Oxford, Clarendon Press, 1993, and A. MAROTTI, *Manuscript*, cit.

7

vilified the fashionable poetic conventions as well as the senseless affectation of wit. In one of his own *Paradoxes*, he condemns the "dejection" and
"deformity" of the paradox epidemics that infected the Court:

> [...] civility of manners is become but mutuall tickling flattery of one an-
> other, allmost every man effects a humor of jeasting, and is content to deject,
> and deforme himself, yea to become foole, to none other end that I can spy,
> but to give his wise companions occasion to laughe, and to shew themselves wise
> [...].[28]

However, despite his repeated disavowals of and disdain for "literature", his early poetry shows that he wished to set himself apart from
the professional poets writing for the city's *nouveaux riches*, and the poe-
tasters who fed the "corrupted" courtly taste.

Speaking with the distinctive passions of the Roman satirists in *Satyre* II
Donne denounces the mercenary poets:

> [...] who write to Lords, reward to get,
> Are they not like singers at doores for meat?
> And they who write, because all write, have still
> That excuse for writing, and for writing ill;

Here he introduces us to a different type of amateur lawyer-poet, Coscus, whom he pillories as a pox corrupting society. Metaphors of disease,
sickness copulation, anality, food and excrement are all linked to images of
clothing and fashion to express, as is the case in Rabelais, a sense of greed
and waste.[29] This mercenary barrister, says the poet, uses:

> Law practice for mere gaine, bold soule, repute
> Worse then imbrothel'd strumpets prostitute [...]
> (62-63).

---

[27] On the "understanders", see A. ALVAREZ, *The School of Donne*, London, Chatto &
Windus, 1961, p. 39.

[28] J. DONNE, in *Paradoxes and Problems*, edited by H. Peters, Oxford, Clarendon Press,
1980, pp. 55-60. They were published under the title *Juvenilia* with the date 1633 on the title
page; in 1652 his son edited them in a volume containing also *Epigrams* and *Ignatius His Con-
clave*, all considered works worthier of the dead Dean of St. Paul. John Manningham of the Middle Temple copied in his *Diary* extracts of four *Paradoxes* which circulated already among Inns of
Court students some thirty years before. See *The Diary of John Manningham of the Middle Temple*, 1602-1603: edited with an introduction by R. Parker Solien, Hanover, N.H.: Published for
the University of Rhode Island by the University Press of New England, 1976, p. 382.

[29] For scatological metaphors in Rabelais, see M. HOLQUIST, *The Rabelaisian Chronotope*, in
The Dialogical Imagination, cit., pp. 167-258.

Indignation turns to disgust when this scarce poet, who "wooes in language of the Pleas and Bench", is denounced in a scatological metaphor as a plagiarist. For Donne, the lawyer-poet's satire is a pretext for a deeper and paradoxical reflection on time and "mutability". "Time rots all," says the poet, and *Poëtry* and *Law*, as Coscus's career proves, in time become "pestilence" and "prostitution".[30]

In the dedicatory epistle to his mentor, Lando had said that *Paradossi* had been written not for fame's sake, but "sol per fuggire la molestia del caldo" (as a distraction from the summer's heat). Using a similar exordium, the future Dean of Saint Paul's defends his *nugae* in a letter accompanying his 10 paradoxes sent to his lifelong friend the civil lawyer and courtier Sir Henry Wotton (1568-1639):

Only in obedience I send you some of my paradoxes; I love you and myself and them too well to send them willingly for they carry with them a confession of their lightness, and your trouble and my shame. But indeed they were made rather to deceave tyme then her daughter truth: although they have been written in an age when any thing is strong enough to overthrow her: if they make you to find better reasons against them they do there office: for they are but swaggerers: quiet enough if you resist them. If pe[r]chance they be pretyly guilt, that is there best for they are not hatcht: they are rather alaru[m]s to truth to arme her then enemies: they have only this advantage to scape fro[m] being caled ill things th[a]t they are nothings: therefore take heed of allowing any of them least you make another.[31]

This is not a simple *excusatio*: Donne says more on the subject than Lando ever did in his epistles and later in the tongue-in-cheek *Confutation* of his own *Paradossi*.[32] He presents *Paradoxes* as typically Ciceronian in that they state a "truth" that the present time has "overthrown"; but they are also described in the Aristotelian terms of the functioning of metaphor. In the *"Art" of Rhetoric* we read that ænigmas, and the "most successful smart sayings" (such as proverbs and jokes), are derived from proportional metaphors; Aristotle also says that metaphors *par excellence* are those "no-

---

[30] See C.D. LEIN, *Theme and Structure in Donne's Satyre II*, «Comparative Literature», Vol. 32, 1980, pp. 130-150.

[31] *Paradoxes and Problems*, edited by H. Peters, Oxford, Clarendon Press, 1980. Regarding the identification of Wotton as Donne's addressee, see PETERS, *op. cit.*, p. XXV. Donne's original definition of paradox goes well beyond that given by contemporary rethoricians such as George Puttenham who classed it among the tropes of "wonder", in *The Arte of English Poesie* (1589).

[32] *Confutazione del Libro de' Paradossi* (1544); on the confutation see GRENDEL, *Critics of the Italian World*, cit., pp. 30-31.

vel expressions" that arise "when what follows is paradoxical [...] and not in accordance with our previous expectation." (1412 a. 6). Because such metaphors have a surplus of "energy" and "movement", he adds, "there is something youthful" in them "for they show vehemence" (1413 a. 16). Donne, who knew his Aristotle well, describes his paradoxes "dramatically"; they are swaggerers that transgress and provoke meaning; nevertheless, they can be easily kept at bay by stronger paradoxes; they are not contrary to Truth but "alarms" and aides in her defence; morally they are not evil because they are "nothings"; that is to say, they exist only within the realm of the name; therefore they defy "actualisation" and paraphrase inasmuch as any description of paradox (as well as of metaphor) is bound to be paradoxical, as Donne's own description proves and modern linguists believe. Paradoxes are described as being both generative and interpretive: if you "allow" one, that is to say, if you understand it and enter the paradoxical game, you will make another paradox.

Donne's paradoxes are variations and amplifications on themes selected from and inspired by Lando's original work in the Italian.[33] Written to outsmart and even to contradict Lando, from a paradoxical perspective, they are: "That all things kill themselves", "That women ought to paint themselves", "That old Men are more Fantastique then younge", "That Nature is our worst Guide", "That only Cowards dare dye", "That the guifts of the body are better then those of the mind or Fortune", "That a wise man is known by much Laughing", "That good is more common then evill", "That by Discord things increase", and "That it is possible to find some vertue in some women". If we, for instance, compare Donne's first paradox, a variation on *Meglio morire che lungamente campare* (XIV), we see that Lando's meditative and anti-Aristotelian praise of death is turned into a rhetorically and linguistically tight-knit, philosophical paradox arguing that self-destruction and not self-preservation is the law of life. In his middle age, Donne developed it into *Biothanatos*, a controversial prose work on suicide addressed, as he remarks in the accompanying letter to Sir Robert Ker, "onely to some particular friends".

Donne's *Paradoxes* are neither conventional exercises in rhetorical agility nor wanton mockery of Elizabethan "aesthetics." The subtle art of syllogistic misdirections and the dialectical sleight-of-hand reroute every argument to paradox solely for the sake of wit; it is rather for a linguistic exploration of the human awareness that each truth has its equal and op-

---

[33] For the complex textual problems of Donne's *Paradoxes* see the Introduction by Peters.

posite truth.[34] The horizon of paradox, perfected throughout his life, spans from the philosophical love riddles of youth to the theological writings of maturity. *Paradoxes* are *hors d'oeuvre* that express the same half-serious, half-ribald mood of the *Songs and Sonnets*, *Elegies* and *Satyres*, with that outrageous coupling of apparent irreconcilables (in the contemporary idiom, "conceits").

Aristotle had said that "to metaforize well, is to see resemblance". Such was Donne's supreme art, in which all the *artes liberales*, with their specialised and apparently incompatible languages, concur with the *discordia concors* typical of his poetics. In his profane poetry, which he later abjured as "the mistress of my youth" for theological speculation, "the wife of mine age, Divinity", Donne inverts the hierarchical structure of the universe, so that the secular becomes metaphysical and the metaphysical secular. The languages of science, religion and metaphysics, law and theology serve his relentless argument on Eros; his paradoxical, polyphonic imagery unites in a witty "conceit", what has become separated. However his redescription of the World as Logos, conducted in terms of opposition, unity and reintegration, rests on a fine and precarious balance.

With Pico della Mirandola in his *Princeps Concordiae*, Donne sees in the incongruence of paradox a cognitive instrument and the key to a reformed Christian language. In observing and handling "mutability", however, the poet's coolness and philosophical detachment are closer to Montaigne's deep awareness and blunt pronouncements on the world. When Donne took Holy Orders in January 1615, becoming the following year Reader of Divinity at Lincoln's Inn, he was accepted by the Church of England as the penitent he claimed to be; and, as Kermode noted, his audience would remember St Augustine.[35] It was in these and subsequent years that the poet, most famous of preachers, found his true genre. Moreover, he began to "fashion himself", or rather "re-fashion" his identity, on Augustine's doctrine of salvation. He began to look upon his previous experience in terms of "conversion" from the Platonic way of salvation Eros, to Agape, or Christian love. He forswore poetry, the mistress of his youth, for the "wife of mine age, Divinity". In Donne, the juvenile taste for amorous conceits derived from religion and bordering on obscenity, the inclination for the *gusto espagnol*, or witty preaching, gave way to the exploration

---

[34] See F. KERMODE, *Shakespeare, Spenser, Donne: Renaissance Studies*, New York, Viking Press, 1971, pp. 116-148.

[35] KERMODE, *Shakespeare, Spenser, Donne*, cit., p. 118.

of the paradox of God's love, the Incarnation.[36] The "swaggerer" or *flâneur*, who like a "fencer" moved among the London crowd, dealing verbal blows in order to open a path of "distinction" for himself, becomes the "penitent". Retrospectively, then, the Dean of St Paul's cast his early biography on Augustine's spiritual process: it had begun with the ascent on the ladder of the philosophical Eros, from the beauty of the corporeal world, through the world of the soul and reason, to the eternal and immutable Being. From Augustine, Donne learned that the fault in Eros that must be corrected is *superbia*, that is, pride, which is always bound up with Platonic Eros; and he learned that the incomprehensibility of God's love is its humility.[37]

---

[36] But Donne's use of paradox in his sermons may be seen as subtle parody of both Jesuit casuistry and mannerism and Puritan Ramism in preaching.

[37] On the "Eros" motif in Augustine's religious development see A. NYGREN, *Agape and Eros*, translated by S. Watson, Chicago, University of Chicago Press, 1982, pp. 449-459.

CHAPTER THREE

REVELS AND PARADOXICAL KINGDOMS
AT THE INNS OF COURT

> But it is not good to stay too long in the theatre.
>
> FRANCIS BACON

FESTIVE MISRULE

The English observance of Christmas and winter festivals honouring the nativity of Christ, with its attendant "twelve days madness", had been scarcely affected by the Reformation. With the rest of the English people, the gentlemen of the Inns of Court celebrated the old liturgical holidays as well as the new national festivals of secular and dynastic calendar centring on the anniversary of the Protestant monarch.[1] The holy days of the Roman calendar, from the feast of All Saints, or All Hallows, to the long Christmas season to Shrovetide, continued to be celebrated in town, as in the country, with a variety of activities – sports, games, interludes and "mummings" – that enacted the cosmic *combat* between Carnival and Lent.[2] In a long sequel of celebrations, interrupted at time by bursts of the plague, during the festival season the law students exercised their skills

---

[1] D. CRESSY, *Bonfires and Bells: National Memory*, cit., on the consolidation of the Tudor dynasty and revels see the classic study by S. ANGLO, *Spectacle Pageantry and Early Tudor Policy*, Oxford Warburg Studies, Clarendon Press Oxford, 2nd edition, 1992. Anglo does not, however, discuss the role played by the gentlemen at the Inns in the celebrations and commemorations of Tudor festivities.

[2] The English word for Carnival is Shrovetide, whose usage, according to the OED, is attested remarkably late (15th century). The first element, "shrove", is undoubtedly related to the Old English word "shrive", whose primary meanings are "to impose a penance", "to make one's confession and receive absolution and penance", and "to confess". Shriving refers to the spiritual preparation for receiving in purity the ashes on the first day of Lent. At the time of the Celtic churches, when the Lenten period had been irregularly increased by pushing its period back from Sunday to Ash Wednesday, Shrovetide or Shrove Tuesday, the climax of modern Carnival festivities, became the day of confession and absolution Other early names, such as *Fastingong* and *Fastens-een*, carrying the same sense as the Latin word *carniprivium*, were also used with reference to Lenten fasting.

as organisers, amateur dramatists and actors of intramural revels[3] and drama. Revelry at the Inns was organised by the junior members, and involved, from Christmas to Shrovetide,[4] monastic and academic licensed misrule, with rituals of status reversal that played upon the themes of power, jurisdiction, youth and gender. Given the strictly hierarchical organisation of monastic and academic institutions, the theme of jurisdiction was always the first to be played out in games such as the old schoolboy game *bar out the Master*. Here the students deposed and expelled for three days the schoolmaster and barricaded themselves within the school, as in a citadel; at the end of the three days, terms of capitulation were proposed to the master, who had to grant cock fighting and football matches.[5]

The mimetic, musical and ceremonial activities organised by the sons of the nobility at the Inns of Court remained closely connected to "popular" carnival traditions, at least until the 17th-century, when French and Venetian taste dominated at court.[6] The law students, not unlike the 12th-century *pueri* of London, who celebrated Shrovetide with violent games of football (*lusum pilae celebrem diae quae dicitur Carnilevaria*), engaged themselves in the «devilish pastimes» of bachelors' football games, cock-fighting, cock-trashing, hunting of cats and foxes and rope-pulling, and all sorts of violent faction-fights were common as well as around the city.[7] The 1517 election at the Inner Temple, of Jack Straw, the mock traitor and anti-king, who caused great turmoil and was therefore banished by an order of the Bench, is one testimony to the interplay of high and low festive

---

[3] "Revel" derives from the French *reveler*, to make merry, and ultimately from the Latin *rebellare*, to rebel.

[4] D.S. BLAND, *Interludes in Fifteenth-Century Revels at Furnivall's Inn*, «Review of English Studies», 3 (1952), pp. 263-268.

[5] H.W.C. HAZLITT, *Popular Antiquities of Great Britain*, London, 1870, pp. 37-57.

[6] The traditional continuity between Court and the Inns increased with Queen Elizabeth, who relied on the Inns, and Gray's in particular, for entertainment.

[7] J. STRUTT, *The Sports and Pastimes of the People of England*, pp. 201-282, London, Methuen, 1903; E.K. CHAMBERS, *The Medieval Stage*, Dover Publications. New York, Inc. Mineola, 1996 (reprint of 1903 Oxford edition), pp. 114-182; T.F. THISELTON DYER, *Folklore of Shakespeare*, New York, 1884; R. HUTTON, *The rise and Fall of Merry England The Ritual Year 1400-1700*, Oxford, Oxford University Press, 1994; *The Stations of the Sun A History of the Ritual Year in Britain*, Oxford, Oxford University Press, 1996 pp. 151-178; M.D. BRISTOL, *Carnival and Theatre, Plebeian Culture and the Structure of Authority in Renaissance England*, New York and London, Methuen, 1985, pp. 59-88; S. BILLINGTON, *Mock Kings in Medieval Society and Renaissance Drama*, Oxford, Clarendon Press, 1991; L.M. CLOPPER, *Drama Play and Game*, Chicago, The University of Chicago Press, 2001; Mimetic hunts by "green men" were performed at the Inns; for a description of London Carnival in the 12th century see *Vita S. Thomae*, by William Fitz Stephen, in «*Memorials for the History of Thomas Becket, Archibishop of Canterbury*», edited by J.C. Robertson and J.B. Sheppard. Rolls Series, no. 67. London, 1875-1885, Vol. 3, pp. 1-154.

customs. Jack Straw is in fact an ancient popular Shrovetide icon that burnt in effigy on the public square on Fat Tuesday.[8] The New Year popular custom of youths setting out on a ritual hunt of small animals was not disdained by the students of the Inner Temple, who at one point during Christmas chased a cat and a fox around the Hall.[9]

Law students, like the London apprentices outside Holborn, were not alien to rough and indecent carnival play, and revelry could degenerate into violence and rebellion. From the 1530s onwards, with the expansion of membership, the Inns were no longer the perfect functioning society and havens of peace and tranquillity depicted by Fortescue. The problems faced by the Inns were those of Tudor and Stuart society at large. The benchers, often guided by self-interest, made for a disunited and factional governing body and were blamed for being absentee and ineffective in policy-making and administration and indifferent to the entire study programme. Despite strict regulations and a set of sumptuary laws regulating expenditure on dress, food, use of servants and outward appearance, the Inns faced serious internal problems. In 1533 a group of Inner Templars defied their elders' supremacy with secession, a tactic used at Lincoln's Inn in 1555 to challenge an order against the wearing of beards. Bans against showy apparel, carrying weapons, women visitors, drunkenness, gaming and casual violence, masques and revels would often cause disorder among the junior members of the Inns, who were notorious for their violent behaviour outside their societies.

The growing number of dishonest servants, the rising level of casual violence among the students, and the failure to police and discipline the lives of the junior members both inside and outside the Inns all seriously threatened the unity and functioning of the societies.[10] Some 1590s ac-

---

[8] E.K CHAMBERS, *The Medieval Stage* (414); T. PETTITT, *Here comes I, Jack Straw: English Folk Drama and Social Revolt*, «Folklore», vol. 95: i, 1984 (3-20). On the banishment of the anti-kingdom of Jack Straw from Lincoln's Inn see A.W. GREEN, *The Inns of Court and Early English Drama*, by A. Wigfall Green, with a preface by Roscoe Pound, New Haven, Yale University Press; London, H. Milford, Oxford University Press, 1931 (56).

[9] T.F. THISELTON DYER, *Folk-lore of Shakespeare*, New York, 1884, p. 161.

[10] PREST, *The Inns of Court*, cit., pp. 50-114; E.K. CHAMBERS, *The Elizabethan Stage*, Vol. IV, p. 273 cites a document of control in which we read of "eavell practizes of incontinencye in greate Innes [...] alleurynge of maides, speciallye orphanes [...] to previe and un mete Contractes [...]". In *The chronicles of England from Brute vnto this present yeare of Christ. 1580 Collected by Iohn Stow citizen of London*, London, 1580 we read: "In the moneth of August was a great fray in *Fleetstreete*, betwéene the yong Studentes of the Innes of Courte, and the inhabitauntes of the same stréete, whiche Fray began in the night, and so continued the assaultes and bickeryngs till the next day, in whiche season muche people of the Cytie was thyther gathered, and diuerse men

counts represent the Inns as a crowded and chaotic place; the young, non-reading members, with their quarrels, drinking, whoring and gaming, attracted the censure of both the benchers and the Puritans. In the same period, violent Shrovetide rioting broke out in the courts and slums of London, a city where destitution was pervasive and society was always teetering on the brink of chaos. During the early Stuarts, from 1603 to 1641, there were in London 24 Shrove Tuesday riots, led by the young, unmarried apprentices who took the city by storm; people and property were abused in a manner unprecedented in Elizabethan times.[11] But not everyone at the Inns followed the rake's progress of Jack Falstaff, whose old fellow student Robert Shallow, described by Shakespeare as a mad, scrawny and lecherous youth at Clement's Inn, might even go on to become justices of the peace; these, having read law seriously, also pursued a non-vocational, liberal education, cultivated circles of prestigious friends and went on to occupy key positions in government, or moved on to other professions.[12]

Carnival misrule at the Inns, as in academic and monastic institutions, was mostly controlled, and, as appears from a 1526 record, high-standing courtiers and Benchers were involved in its organisation. In the Tudor period, the attitude of rulers and ruled, old and young, towards festive licence was not at great variance; it was only later, under the early Stuarts, when the swelling of membership generated deep institutional changes and widened the age gap, that rough and indecent carnival foolery shifted to outright rioting.[13] At "meeting nights", the entertainments the two Temple Societies offered to honour each other at Christmas, things could get out

---

on both partes slaine and many hurte, but lastly, by the presence of the Maior and Sherifes, this Fray was appeased, of whiche was chiefe occasioner one of *Cliffords Inne* named *Herbotel*".

[11] J. STOW, *Survery of the Cities of London and Westminster*, ed. J. Strype (2 vols.; 1720), ii 332-3. R.B. MANNING, *Village revolts Social Protest and Popular Disturbances in England, 1509-1640*, Oxford, Clarendon Press, 1988 (193); D. UNDERDOWN, *Revel, Riot, and Rebellion. Popular Politics and Culture in England 1603-1660*, Oxford Clarendon Press, 1985, pp. 99-103. G.B. HARRISON, *The Elizabethan Journals being a record of those things most talked of During the years 1591-1603*, Ann Arbor, The University of Michigan Press, 1955; T. CORYATE, *Coryats Crudities 1611*, With an introduction by W.M. Schutte, London, Scholar Press, F. LAROQUE, *Shakespeare's Festive World. Elizabethan Seasonal Entertainment and the Professional Stage*, Cambridge, Cambridge University Press, 1993, pp. 93-107.

[12] See *Henry IV*, III, ii, pp. 13-26; 298-328. On Davies' epigrams, see PHILIP J. FINKELPEARL, *John Marston of the Middle Temple*, pp. 12-15. On law students pursuing different careers, and becoming physicians and astronomers, see PREST, *The Rise of the Barristers*, cit., pp. 114-115.

[13] PREST, *Inns*, cit., p. 112, on the student revolt in 1630 against a Bench order to close the Hall during the Christmas period, see G. GODWIN, *The Middle Temple: The Society The Fellowship*, London, Staples Press, 1954, p. 76 ff.

of hand; students decided to take the law into their own hands, to settle old grudges and rivalries. Ceremonial encounters between Templarians and Grayans at one point degenerated in gang warfare.[14] The legal citadel was turned by rampaging youths into a stage for not-so-fictitious affrays and "wars" not unlike those among the Montagues and Capulets in *Romeo and Juliet* or the Greeks and the Trojans in *Troilus and Cressida*.[15]

Each of the Inns had, like the medieval abbeys with their "boy bishop" and King of the *Kitchen Boys* in charge of the Shrovetide revelry, its own kingdom with a mock king prince or emperor, and a complete staff of advisors, and a privy council. These activities were viewed as an integral part of the life of all of the Inns of Court, and were conducted, as at Oxford and Cambridge, with the consent and advice of the Benchers. The election of mock ruler and officers for the organisation of the grand Christmas festivals was always held in the great Hall, the place for instruction and recreation, tribunal and theatre. This practice is recorded early on in an announcement in the *Black Book* of Lincoln's Inn (1422):[16]

Ceux sont les nouns de ceux que fuerunt assignes de continuer yci le nowel [...]

Besides mentions of revels in Sir Fortescue's *De Laudibus* (1463 ca.),[17] the earliest known reference to a Christmas "king" at the Inns has been found in a student notebook:

Treshonure et tresreverent seignorur le Roy de Nowell et seignor de toutz solaces par my le mounde.[18]

In 1505, an Inner Temple record shows that a *magister jocorum* presided over the organisation; another 1519 record refers to the custom of electing a fellow student "king", who appointed a court and gave orders that on Innocents' Day the "King of Cokneys" should "sytt and have due service".[19] Festive kingdoms at the Inns were, as at the royal court,

---

[14] Godwin (74).

[15] Both plays have been connected to the Inns of Court. See in particular W.R. ELTON, *Shakespeare's Troilus & Cressida and the Inns of Court Revels*, Ashgate, Aldershot, 2000. Shakespeare's source for *Romeo and Juliet* was a poem by a young Inner Templar, Arthur Broke (I.T.1561) a protege of Sackville. The poem, entitled *Romeus and Juliet*, was printed by the printer of law books Tottel on November 19 1562. Broke had a part in the Pallaphilos revels of the Inner Temple that same year. See Axton (55).

[16] CHAMBERS, *The Medieval Stage*, p. 413.

[17] Chap. xlviii.

[18] BAKER, *Readings and Moots*, cit., p. xxxv.

[19] Baker, John Hamilton, An Inner Temple miscellany: papers repinted from the Inner

a permanent ludic institution with a specially appointed Master of Revels, usually an utter barrister, and officers to supervise the organisation of the festivities and keep the accounts in imitation of the government at Whitehall. Christmas officers, as in the *Royaume de la Basoche*, the mock kingdom of the French law clerks,[20] included the Marshal (*Marescallus*), the butler (*Pincerna*), the Constable Marshal, the server and the cup-bearer. At the Inner Temple, a clerk of the kitchen (*Clericus Coquine*), a Master of the game, and a constable of the tower (*Constabularius Turris*) were appointed in addition to the officers in imitation of court. The assignment of such roles to students lasted until the Restoration, and was viewed by the elders as necessary to the education of the junior members in preparation for life at court:[21]

which officers for the most part are such as are exercised in the king's highness house and other noble men, and this is done onely to the intent that they should in time come to know how to use themselves they have all manner of pastimes, as singing and dancing, and in some of the houses ordinarily they have some interlude or tragedy played.[22]

During the festival season Gray's Inn became the land of *Portpulia*, ruled by the crowned *Prince of Purpoole*. Named after the Manor in which it lay, it had authority over the lesser *Stapulia* and *Bernardia*, the two Inns of Chancery Staple's and Barnard's.[23] At one point Lincoln's Inn had the

---

Temple Yearbook / Sir John Baker. [London?]: Masters of the Bench of the Honourable Society of the Inner Temple, c2004. H.J. BAKER, *Christmas in the Inns of Court and Chancery*, «An Inner Temple Miscellany», (2004), p. 42; CHAMBERS, *The Medieval Stage*, p. 414. See also W.C. RICHARDSON, *A History of the Inns of Court: With Special Reference to the Period of the Renaissance*, Baton Rouge, Claitor's Pubblishing Division (1978), Chap. 7; F. COWPER, *A Prospect of Gray's Inn*, London, Graya, 1985, pp. 39-49; GODWIN, pp. 71-84.

[20] English law students certainly knew about the *Basoches* and must even have seen their productions in France. In C. HOLLYBAND, *Dictionarie of the French...*, cit., we find the following entry for "Basoche": f. The whole troupe, or companie of Lawyers Clearks in the palace of Paris, hauing among them a king, and their peculiar lawes; hence also, reuell, misrule (for these fellowes are none of the soberest) also, a certaine baudie Court, wherein wiues that beat their husbands, are censured. Fief de la Basoche. Il tient du fief de la B. He is a pratling, or iangling Lawyer; or (as a Lawyers Clerke) an vnruly copesmate; or, his wife is his master. Roy de la Basoche. The Master of Misrule, or chiefe man among the Clerkes, when they make their shewes". This and the following entries on the subject indicate first-hand knowledge.

[21] A general account of "Grand Christmasses" at the Inner Temple is given by Sir William Dugdale, who says that the Master of Revels ceased to be elected soon after 1554, pp. 153-155.

[22] *The Bacon Report*, Appendix IV (A), p. 418 as quoted in PREST, *Inns*, p. 105.

[23] It was chiefly through the educational system that the Inns of Chancery were linked with the particular Inn of Court to which they were appurtenant. Thus both Staple and Barnard Inn looked for their Readers to Gray's Inn.

Prince de la Grange,[24] at the Inner Temple ruled the *Prince of Sophie*, and at the Middle Temple held sway the *Prince d'Amour* with his knights of the Quiver. The Prince, King or Emperor was elected yearly to rule over his mock court of gentlemen students, who enthusiastically involved themselves with all sorts of mimetic activities. The "monarch" was solemnly enthroned in Hall, on a stage and scaffolds built for the occasion; and like the Carnival king of folklore, he was attended by a large retinue of mock officers of state, ecclesiastical, legal and military; he received foreign potentates, declared war and made peace; his brief reign was a celebration of worldly possessions – food, money, sex, confusion and "errors" – that ended with his "death" at the end of the festival season, on Shrove Tuesday, the day before Ash Wednesday.[25]

The revels of 1561-62 at the Inner Temple remained memorable for their grandeur, as well as for the not-so-oblique allusions to the succession debate and for the political metaphors of contemporary significance in both play and masques. The best extant description of that grand Christmas is by Gerard Legh, probably himself a member of the Temple.[26] The Christmas Prince *Pallaphilos*, and second Perseus, was Lord Robert Dudley, who was at the time Master of the Queen's horse, Elizabeth's favourite and, after the Earl of Leicester (1564), the greatest patron of letters and the most powerful man in England.[27] He ruled, in the name of his mistress, Pallas, with the help of mock officers, or "knights of the order of Pegasus", who were the actual governors of the Temple, and future powerful men in government.[28] In his role of "*The mighty Palaphilos, Prince of Sophie, High*

---

[24] In "The Masque at the Marriage of the Earl of Southampton", presented by the gentlemen of Lincoln's Inn during Shrovetide 1565-66, can be found the earliest reference to a Christmas Prince of Lincossos, Lincoln's Inn, named Troposonte. See *The Copye of an oration made & pronounced By Mr Pownde of Lyncolnes Inne with a brave maske owt of the same* [...], verbatim reprint Cambridge, Privately Printed, 1975.

[25] The character of Jack Falstaff, an Inn of Court man, with his mock court of vagabond and ruffians deserves to be studied within this context.

[26] G. LEGH, *The Accedens of Armory. R. Tottil*, London, 1562, British Library, 605b, fol. 213r-v; 214v-215r; Portions of this description were reproduced by Dugdale in his *Origines* and have been reprinted in W. GREEN (67 ff.) and J. NICHOLS, *The Progresses and Public processions of Queen Elizabeth*, Vol. I, 1823 (131); S. IRELAND, *Picturesque Views of the Inns of Court A facsimile edition of 1800*, London, Kudos & Godine, 1982, pp. 46-68; D.S. BLAND, *Three Revels from the Inns of Court*, England, Averbury Publishing Company, 1984, p. 116 ff.

[27] A great lover of the theatre, Leicester became the patron of the acting company led by James Burbage, the builder of the first permanent theatre in London.

[28] He was elected to rule over the mock kingdom for having mediated, through the Queen, in a quarrel over Lyon's Inn with the Middle Temple. The Revels' "Chancellor", Richard Onslow, was later named speaker of the House of Commons, in 1566; Roger Manwood, mock "Chief Baron of the Exchequer", was raised to that same office in Elizabeth's government in

constable, Marshall of the Knights Templars, and Patron of the Honorable Order of Pegasus", Dudley reigned for several days, entertaining lavishly the court, ambassadors and dignitaries with the tilt, tourney and masque performed consecutively.

Following Legh's description, the order of events at the Inner Temple would have been: [29]

> The masque of *Desire* and *Beauty*
> The fest of the Prince Pallaphilos
> Receptions of the "ambassadors of foreign nations" (i.e. the other Inns)
> Presentation of twenty-four knights to the Prince
> Presentation of the Prince's Coat of Arms
> Investiture of the knights of the order of Pallaphilos
> Procession to the "Temple" church
> Return to the Hall for the final proceedings and concluding dance.

The entertainments included the performance of *Gorboduc*, acted by the law students, and addressed, as we have seen, the succession question through the representation of the destruction of a realm by a doting father. The subject of royal descent was reiterated in the wedding *masque* centring on the myth of Pallas, the patroness of lawyers, and her enemy, Medusa, and was performed for the Queen at Whitehall Palace.[30] Such close continuity between the Inns and the royal court, culture and governance, had not been seen since George Ferrers, lawyer and royal Master of Revels, had staged a triumphal progress through London for the 1551-52 Christmas season.

LAW SPORTS AT GRAY's INN

The 1561-62 revels at the Inner Temple marked the decline of intra-mural *engagé* drama. As the century neared the end, "law sports" less concerned with the common good became a means to curry the monarch's favour, and flattery took the place of sober and sound political advice. For

---

1578; the "Master of the Game", Christopher Hatton, most admired by the Queen for his dancing skills, became Chancellor of England in 1577. Pegasus, the mythical winged horse borne from the blood of Medusa, is to this day the device of the Inner Temple. For the description of grand parade of the Christmas "Lord of Mysrull" of 1561 see *The Diary of Henry Machyn, citizen and merchant-taylor of London, from A.D. 1550 to A.D. 1563*, edited by J.G. Nichols, New York, Jonson Reprint Corp., 1968, p. 275.

[29] See BLAND, *Three Revels*, cit., p. 20.

[30] M. AXTON, *Robert Dudley and the Inner Temple Revels*, «The Historical Journal», Vol. 13, No. 3 (Sep., 1970), pp. 365-378.

the wealthy, careerist lawyers and courtiers, Christmas revels were an occasion to show off their largesse and extracurricular skills in hope of preferment. Whereas Tudor interludes and masques were performed as an insertion of nonverbal theatre into a play, and were staged in the Inn's hall and at court, early Stuart masques and antimasques were fully fledged courtly representations comprising an independent sequel of elaborate and spectacular effects. Such productions required the joint effort and collaboration of a variety of artists, and great sums of money.

When Lady Anne Bacon wrote on the December 5 1593 to her son Anthony, then at Gray's Inn, saying: "I trust they will not mum nor mask nor sinfully revel at Gray's Inn [...]",[31] her other son, Francis, was already planning the next season of revels, the *Gesta Grayorum*. Francis Bacon, who entered Gray's Inn in 1576 at the age of 15, must be credited for some of the theatrical innovations, and perhaps for calling William Shakespeare to perform at Gray's Inn in 1594. Dubbed by his contemporaries the "chief contriever", he had a hand, as deviser and patron, in several Inns of Court shows for over 20 years: from the 1588 *Misfortunes of Arthur*, for which he devised dumb-show, to the 1594-95 *Gesta Grayorum*, which he masterminded, to the consecutive *Masque of the Inner Temple and Gray's Inn* (1612- 1613) and *The Masque of Flowers* (January 6 1614), a grandiose performances staged at Whitehall that put Gray's in great debt.[32] The 1616-17 festivities at Gray's were instead staged to honor "Sir" Francis Bacon himself, who had at last been ordered Lord Chancellor, and who was soon to be Lord Verulam and Viscount of St Alban.

Whereas Templarians, and students of Lincoln's Inn were known for their achievements in poetry, history and other noble studies, the reputation of Gray's, the most aristocratic of the Inns, traditionally rested on its theatrical productions and masques in particular. The young Grayans were notorious for their revels, which could be as wicked and as pleasurable as the ungodly *ludi* of May. A coterie of young playwrights had always been active at Gray's. From the early Tudor interludes to the great series of Stuart and early Caroline court masques, from Shakespeare's *Comedy of*

---

[31] As quoted in Basil Brown (pseud. of Isabelle Kittson, 1860-1928), *Law Sports at Gray's Inn (1594)*, New York, 1921, p. 92.

[32] On July 23 1603, Bacon was knighted; on June 25 he became Solicitor-General, on October 27 1613, Attorney General, in March 1617, Lord Keeper, and on January 7 1618, Lord Chancellor. The masque was staged for the marriage of the Earl of Somerset, favourite of James I, who had helped Bacon to rise to the Attorney-Generalship. See *A Book of Masques in Honour of Allardyce Nicoll*, edited by G.E. Bentley, Cambridge University Press, 1967, pp. 151-157.

Errors to Ben Jonson's and Inigo Jones' masques and antimasques, and William Davenant's final production of *Salmacida Spolia*, Gray's Inn was the place to be for those who loved plays staged even during the solemn professional feasts of Readers and Serjeants, when:

divers Noblemen have been mixed with them, and solemnly invited as Guests to the Dinner [...] to be entertained with Post Revels, performed by the better sort of young Gentlemen of the Society with Galliards, Corrantos, and other Dances; or else with Stage-plays [...] [33]

Passion for the theatre was for Grayans a mark of distinction, and one that brought Shakespeare and Bacon into close contact when in 1594-1595, on the occasion of the society's magnificent Christmas kingdom, *The Comedy of Errors* was performed in the Hall in the course of its law sports, the so called *Gesta Grayorum*.[34] At that time Gray's was the largest legal society, with approximately 155 Inner Barristers in residence during the Christmas vacation; it was richly endowed, and the only one with special privileges granted by Elizabeth.[35] The *Gesta* was a costly enterprise, conceived not for a small coterie but for a large number of participants that included, as we learn from the impressive list of guests of honor, the most powerful courtiers of the time.[36] Revels, conducted with the collaboration of the Inner Temple, began on December 20 (St Thomas' Eve) and extended through Shrovetide, ending on Shrove Tuesday, March 4 1595. Masterminded by Francis Bacon under the auspices of Robert Devereux, second earl of Essex (1565-1601), the *Gesta* was conceived with the aim of attracting a general

---

[33] Sir W. DUGDALE, *Origines juridiciales*, pp. 205, ff.

[34] The contemporary manuscript description of the Carnival kingdom of 1594-95 at Gray's was transcribed by a William Canning as *Gesta Grayorum, or The history of the high and mighty Prince, Henry Prince of Purpoole... who reigned and died, A.D. 1594: together with a masque, as it was presented (by His Highness's command) for the entertainment of Q. Elizabeth, who, with the nobels of both courts, was present thereat.* He assures the reader that he did not "clip any thing; which, though it may seem odd", from the original copy. (Houghton Library and Bodleian Library). It was reprinted as *Gesta Grayorum 168* by the Malone Society Reprints, Oxford University Press, 1914; also in *Law Sports at Gray's Inn* (1594), cit.; and in D.S. BLAND, *Three Revels*, cit.

[35] "Her Majesty gave them her Hand to kiss, with most gracious Words of Commendations to them; pa[...]ticularly, and in general, of Grays-Inn, as an House that she was much beholden unto, for that it did always study for some Sports to present unto her". *Gesta*, p. 68.

[36] "On the 3d. of Ianuary at Night, there was a most honourable Presence of Great and Noble Personages, that came as invited to our Prince; as namely, the Right Honourable the Lord Keeper, the Earls of Shrewsbury, Cumberland, Northumberland, Southampton and Essex, the Lords Buckhurst, Windsor, Mountjoy, Sheffield, Compton, Rich, Burleygh, Mounteagle, and the Lord Thomas Howard; Sir Thomas Henneage, Sir Robert Cecill; with a great number of Knights, Ladies and very worshipful Personages".

political consensus around Essex's faction against Sir Walter Raleigh's. Bacon at the time was bidding to become solicitor-general, while Essex, the queen's favorite and self-styled flower of chivalry, needed royal support for his military exploits more than ever.[37] Performed as they were before the Queen and an audience comprising the most powerful men at court, the *Gesta* represented a fully fledged "political" act, meant to serve one political faction against another while soliciting patronage and cementing alliances. In front of an audience that comprised none other than William Cecil, Lord Burghley, the Grayans carried out many and elaborate law sports. After the coronation, an additional series of "Grand Nights" spent in reveling was arranged for the entertainment of "strangers"; the first one, held on Innocents Day, was only the beginning of a larger collective fiction that lasted for two months. On this particular night, since remembered as "the night of errors" a company of "base" players was invited to perform *The Comedy of Errors* by William Shakespeare.[38]

The "youths" of Gray's, after "many consultations" and with the "consent and assistance of the Readers and Ancients" on the December 12, as was customary elected the youngest student, a Henry Helmes (or Holmes)

Prince of *Purpoole* and "Arch-Duke of *Stapulia* and *Bernardia* [...]very proper Man of Personage, and very active in Dancing and Revelling. [...]

The mock coronation, attended by 120 officials, was followed, in imitation of the ancient inaugural rituals of the British monarchy, by the homage to a mock general pardon by the Prince of *Purpoole* in person. The political and financial functioning of the kindom was ensured by the organisation of a privy council to advice the Prince on all governmental affairs, by the levying of a general subsidy on all Inn members for the state treasury and by the assigning of adequate revenues to officers of the household with gentlemen pensioners and bodyguards. The Prince proceeded to institute the "most honourable Order of Knighthood of the *Helmet*", which in-

---

[37] The producers and writers of the *Gesta*, besides Bacon and Davison were with the guests of honour of Essex's faction, including Henry Wriothesley, Earl of Southampton, for whom the year before Shakespeare had written the discreetly erotic poem *Venus and Adonis*. At the time Bacon, who had consistently relied on the patronage of Essex, needed Burghley's backing in order to overcome Elizabeth's lingering doubts about him and secure for himself high legal office. Later Bacon was instrumental in securing a guilty verdict against his former patron, who rebelled against the Queen in 1601.

[38] The disparaging term must have been used in jest, the performance of *The Comedy of Errors* at Gray's is the first recorded association of Shakespeare with the prestigious Lord Chamberlain's Players. Before 1594, Shakespeare's plays had appeared anonymously.

8

cluded, as the long list of officers and attendants reveals, a number of pro-minent Inner Templars, whose ensign, the shield of Pegasus, was displayed together with the shield of the Griffin, of Grays Inn, and the great shield of the Prince's Arms. The rules governing the chivalric order included a read-ing a list suggestive of the literary taste of the time:

> Every Knight of this Order shall endeavour to add Conference and Experience by Reading; and therefore shall not only read and peruse *Guizo*, the *French Aca* [...], *Galiat* [...]o the Courtier, *Plutarch*, the *Arcadia*, and the Neoterical Writers, from time to time; but also frequ[...]nt the Theatre, and such like places of Experi-ence; and resort to the better sort of Ord'naries for Conference, whereby they may not only become accomplished with Civil Conversations, and able to govern a Ta-ble with Discourse; but also sufficient, if n[...]ed be, to make Epigrams, Emblems, and other Devices appertaining to His Honour's learned Revels.[39]

In the imaginary kingdom of Graya, day after day, the exercise of power alternated play and ceremonies with banqueting and consort music, the staging of devices and masques with dicing, gambling and occasional debauchery. Besides reception of "foreign" diplomats from the Inner Tem-ple, the Prince's time was taken up with an imaginary voyage to visit "the great and mighty emperor of Russia", which included mock exchanges of missives and a mock royal progress around London.[40] Mockery of govern-ment affairs extended also to the proceedings of Privy Council:

> [...] there was a Table set in the midst of the Stage, before the Prince's Seat; and there sate six of the Lords of his Privy Council, which at that time were ap-pointed to attend, in Council, the Prince's Leisure.

The six speeches, attributed to Francis Bacon, are serious and well ar-gued set pieces in the high-flown Elizabethan oratorical style. However, each piece of advice to the Prince stands in complete contradiction to the next, and in such a way that the overall result is paradoxical and utterly ludicrous. The Privy Council, called by the Prince "our Ship of Govern-ment", must have appeared to the real Privy Counsellors in the audience a veritable *Narren Shiff*.[41]

---

[39] *Gesta*, p. 30.

[40] The imaginary voyage of Helms to Russia is a direct reference to the close relationship between Elizabeth and the tsar of Russia. Mark Ridley (1560-1624), associate at the college of physicians and a Grayan, in 1594 had just been appointed by Queen Elizabeth to serve as phy-sician to the tsar Feodor Ivanovich, *Theodore Evanwhich*, in the *Gesta*.

[41] The speeches advise in turn on the "Exercise of War; Study of Philosophy; Eternizement

The 1594-95 law sports at Gray's Inn are known to literary historians because of Shakespeare's staging of *The Comedy of Errors* and the *Masque of Proteus*, considered the first antecedent of the spectacular Stuart and Caroline masques.[42] The history of the masque may be said to coincide with the involvement in it of the Inns of Court; and its transformations reflect the changing tastes of the producers, the Inns members, as well as of the Tudor, Stuart and Caroline audiences. The magnificent Jacobean and Caroline masques the Inns of Court produced for the royal court were no longer expression of the artistic, moral and political concerns of lawyers, as in the past: they reflected the taste of the court, and were, in Ben Jonson's words, "spectacles of state" and "court hieroglyphics".[43] However, the more careful reader will discover in the *Gesta Grayorum* an intricate web of moral, mythological, scientific, economic, political, geographical and military allusions and metaphors meant to reflect the conflicting interests and aspirations of the "great and noble personages" involved in it as both actors and spectators.[44]

Under the Tudors, Inns drama, variously centring on historical, political and moral issues, had traditionally represented a "higher", cultured vision of the combat between Carnival and Lent, in which comedy was kept at bay and bawdry banished from their stage. By contrast, under the early Stuarts, the fame of Inn's drama and masques endured at court not so much for the display of literary skills, moral virtues and sound advice on "civil government" as for the show of uninhibited wit and ability in spectacular productions. The grand *Gesta Grayorum* was conceived as a deliciously entertaining and not entirely mock-heroic "epic". The comic elements in it, including Shakespeare's play, are mannered and controlled. The expressions of guarded wit, and saucy innuendos are addressed to

---

and Fame, by Buildings and Foundations; Absoluteness of State and Treasure; Vertue, and a Gracious Government; Pass-times and Sports". *Gesta* (32-42). Spedding, viii. 342; For a list of manuscripts containing Bacon's dramatic writings see CHAMBERS, *The Elizabethan Stage*, cit., III, pp. 211-214.

[42] The classic studies on the tradition of the masque, from the early Tudor disguisings to the Jacobean spectacles and choreographs of Ben Jonson and Inigo Jones, are by E. WELSFORD, *The Court Masque*, Cambridge, Cambridge University Press, 1927; and by S. ORGEL, *The Jonsonian Masque*, New York and London, Columbia University Press, 1965. Much has been published on this topic since Miss Welsford's seminal study.

[43] Still, it may be said that Stuart and Caroline masques may be regarded as representing a new and modern conception of theatre that challenged the Tudor view of drama as a vehicle for political and moral advice, as well as Jonson's own austere ideal of art.

[44] I discuss this at length in my forthcoming essay "The Magnetic *Gesta Grayorum*: Chivalry and Science at Gray's Inn 1594-1595".

the Inn's audience, for intramural enjoyment only. This is the case of the paradoxical "articles of the orders", read by by the King of Arms to the Knights of the Helmet and regular frequenters of the Land of the Amazons and the Cape of Good Hope" (i.e. the London brothels or stews), on which the Prince had full title. Another instance is the letter of "intelligence concerning the State", written by John Puttanemico (sic), who describes the "traffick to Clerkenwell" (read: whore-mongering), in keeping with the overseas *Gesta* of the Prince, in terms of maritime warfare:[45]

I have discovered an huge Armado of French Amazons, to the number of seven hundred Caracts, Galeasses, great Galeasses, and tall Ships; besides Pinnaces, Frigots, Carvels, Shallops, and such small Vessels innumerable; which being dispersed into sundry Creeks, work daily much damage to all sorts of People, and Adventurers hold in durance; not suffering one Man to escape, till he have turned French (i.e. syphilitic).

THE MIDDLE TEMPLE REVELS

The 1597-98 season of revels at the Middle Temple and the staging of *Le Prince d'Amour or the Prince of Love* and *the Knights of the Quiver*[46] set a lasting trend. It had been devised quite casually by a group of distinguished lawyers and generally admired wits "of the age", writers of epigrams, paradoxes and love poetry who moved in the literary and speculative circle of Sir Walter Raleigh.[47] The leading spirits were two lawyers-

[45] The "ship" and seafaring served as the vehicle for various types of sexual metaphors in Greek and Latin, see J.N. ADAMS, *The Latin Sexual Vocabulary*, Baltimore, The Johns Hopkins University Press, 1982, pp. 25-26.

[46] "Quiver", Lat. *Scrautum*, like all words for containers, bags and the like, is a basic obscenity for *scrotum*; see J.N. ADAMS, *op. cit.*, p. 74. The "Articles of the Order" read by the Herald contain saucy allusions to the various types and uses of "arrows", p. 43; article 28 has a pun on "intestate": "if any knight dye a maid, he shall not make any Will, or declare any heir, but shall be accounted to dye *intesticulate*, and his goods and revenues shall be taken [...], p. 46.

[47] With John Hoskins, lawyer, poet, rhetorician and parliamentarian, they were John Donne's close friends: John Owen, the literary epigrammatist; Henry Wotton, ambassador, educator and poet; Thomas Bastard, clergyman and epigrammatist; and John Davies, poet lawyer and judge. A partial account of the revels was written, around 1599 by Benjamin Rudyerd, Oxford friend, poet and future parlamentarian. See "*Noctes Templariae*", in *Memoirs of Sir Benjamin Rudyerd*, edited by J.A. Manning of the Inner Temple (London, 1841), pp. 9-18; a nearly identical account was published in 1660 as *Le Prince d'Amour or the Prince of Love With a collection of several ingenious poems and songs by the wits of the age*. BL. E. 1836 [1], the volume contains DONNE's *A Paradox of a Painted Face*, p. 99; for the calendar of events see FINKELPEARL, *op. cit.* (43-60).

wits, Richard Martin (the Prince) and John Hoskyns (Clerk of the Council), who when students at Oxford were notorious for their unleashed wit and violent bravado. The mock kingdom of the Middle Templars and of their "noble confederates" in revelry, the gentlemen of Lincoln's Inn, with its *ad personam* jokes and allusions, mirrors the "clamorous frie of Innes of court"[48] described also by Thomas Lodge's[49] (Lincolns Inn 1575), in his censorious *Wits miserie*, and Francis Beaumont (Middle Temple 1600). Beaumont's *Grammer Lecture*, a burlesque oration on the "uses" and the "varieties" of learned language, made of paradoxes, puns, mock grammatical and stylistic prohibitions, precepts and rhetorical speeches, presented in Temple Hall, contains a delicious portrait of the festive world of the Inns.

In *The Prince d'Amour* the system of turnovers and travesties is that of popular Carnival, the spirit and the language libertine and aristocratic; the atmosphere is that of the city, *urbem pagina nostra sapit*, with its hidden and mysterious streets and neighborhoods. The "popular" Shrovetide *topoi* – the penitential, judicial, agonistic, temporal and biological (food, drink, tobacco, sex) – are dramatised and made to converge in the representation of one single "Milesius Stradilax".[50] An hybridisation of the *miles gloriousus* with the fop, Stradilax is a gay monster and incarnates, not unlike that other Inn-of court man Falstaff, the spirit of Carnival: he recites "three confessions, serves as the commissioner in "the arraignment of the discontented lover", delivers for the Prince an oration and the obscene poem "comparison of pork", gives a "soldier's speech", and stirs enmity between the Prince and the Lincolnians.[51] Such is the world of this *roi pour rire*

High and Mighty Prince, Lucius Elius Pulcher &c. knight of the Honorable Order f the Quiver [...] Palgrave of *Hartsbroken*, Duke of *Suspiria*, Marquess of *Braineswound*, Governor of *Florida* and *Exultantia* Great Commander of all the

---

[48] Sir J. DAVIES, *Epigrams and Elegies*, London, 1599 STC 6350; 3.

[49] LODGE's *Wits miserie, and the worlds madnesse discouering the deuils incarnat of this age*, 1596, is a satirical treatment of the (contemporary) seven deadly sins.

[50] Stradilax has been identified with John Davies: the name refers to Davies' waddling gait, described coarsely by Manningham in his diary, see J.L. SANDERSON, *Epigrames p[er] B[enjamin] R[udyerd] and Some More 'Stolen Feathers' of Henry Parrot*, «The Review of English Studies», New Series, Vol. 17, No. 67 (Aug., 1966), pp. 241-255. Stradilax, "puft up with a poore-witted ambition", demands to be called "Exophilus, in sawcy imitation of the great Earle of the tyme" (that is, the Earl of Essex). Davis, was an epigrammatist, a lawyer and author of a poetic work entitled *Orchestra, or, A Poeme of Dancing*, the earliest extant edition of which is dated 1596 and dedicated to Richard Martin, the same "Sur Martino Prince" of the 1597 Middle Temple revels.

[51] A "prognostication" is read in which are "foretold things past".

Seas from the Streights of *Genua* to the Bay of *Porto desiderato*, and chief General of all *Venus* forces, from *Lapanto* to *Quevera* by the West, and from *Rio des Amazones* to *Lapland* by the North; in all people and nations that understand the language of Deeing and Feeling.

In this topsy-turvy legal utopia the rules of "love" and "law", of "lovers" and "lawyers" are mixed and subverted. The champion of the monarch of the "Temple of Love" laments that the descendants of the Knights Templars have forsaken chivalry and love: none has sighed, none has forsaken public shows and none has courted the door of his mistress on a cold winter's night, but all have led lives of ease and venery. Some have even attempted to study law, an abuse listed among the "offences inquirable by the jury":

If any man bring into his Excellencies Dominions, any Book, Case, Moot point, or flat cap, with an intent to utter the same [...] or to give council in any suite, title or conveyance of Law [...] this is Premunire.

In this legalistic Carnival of love, paradox reigns supreme, the melancholy lover is arraigned; Jelousy is charged with sedition and sentenced, as in Donne's first paradox, woman's inconstancy is commended, and class bigotry, both legal and academic is parodied in the "Tufftaffata Speech" and the "Fustian Answer", prompted by Sir Walter Raleigh himself.[52] "Linguistic conduct" becomes the object of humour and outrageousness; legal language is carnivalised and takes the form of lewd jokes, euphemisms, metaphors, puns and paradoxes for selected ears only.[53] Petrarchan love vocabulary is turned into the sexual language of *Atellana*; dramatic action, featuring verbal combats by the "troops of Tropes", has a fast and disordered pace; and the leading characters are those of Latin urban satire and *Comedia dell'Arte*.

The Inn-of-Court wits, like the Roman satirists, enjoyed blatant sexual language; and like Martial in his literary epigrams, they found the contrast of *gravitas* with *nequitia* particularly amusing, and used direct terminology in order to provoke laughter among their sophisticated audience. The intellectually self-assertive, Rabelaisian "knights of the quiver" were lawyers

---

[52] The clerk of council was John Hoskins (Middle Temple 1593), "wit of the age", close friend of Raleigh and Davies; and the author of an elaborate treatise on rhetoric, *Directions for Speech and Stile*.

[53] One rule reads: "that all Knights of this order be able to speak ill of Innes-a-Court-Commons", p. 44.

and coterie writers inclined to seek sensation in language and in ideas challenging established beliefs. They were also writers and clients, and lived, like Martial in Domitian's Rome, in a gilded and ferocious age of fear and adulation. Sir Walter Raleigh and "Jack" Donne, like Aretine, were debunkers, sceptics, Epicureans and naturalists. They expressed "the pathos of radical change" and the firm belief in the need and possibility of a complete *exit* from the commonly accepted order of life.[54] The Templar "knights of the quiver" more than Cupid's darts shoot Wit's pointed arrows dipped in the bittersweet juice of Menippean satire; they direct the *pointe assassine* of libertinism and impropriety against false humanism hardened into dogma and academicism. Their ephemeral war was an intellectual game in which epigrams and paradoxes freed language from the constraint of *doxa*, or "common opinion".

After a series of mock ritual combats, in the concluding description of the Prince's death "common opinion", is at last revealed as the true antagonist:

the Prince dyed of a common infectious disease called Opinion, upon the sixth month of *Candlemas* day, and may be buried in oblivion with his ancestors if tongues dig him not up.[55]

It is clear that the "knights of the quiver", throughout the festival season, have not been fighting against the material stringencies of Lent, just passed or about to follow, but against Lenten language: *vox populi, vox Dei*, pious and authoritarian truth. On the day before Ash Wednesday, the unhinibited, fearless, muckraking, paradoxical Prince of the Templars is infected and killed by paltry speech.[56] However, the parody of adulation

---

[54] M. BAKHTIN, *Rabelais and His World*, Cambridge, The M.I.T. Press, 1968, p. 274. It is still an open question whether or not Donne was an actor in the revels, like his friends; see P.J. FIN-KELPEARL, *Donne and Everard Gilpin: Additions, Corrections, and Conjectures*, «The Review of English Studies», New Series, Vol. 14, No. 54 (May, 1963), pp. 164-167.

[55] *Le Prince d'Amour*, cit., p. 90.

[56] The *Prince d'Amour*'s fight against "common opinion", reflects the critical role of both Templars and the Lincolnians in the cultural changes at the turn of the century. In the late nineties a distinction was clearly made between the educated taste for satire ("the learned ears" and the uneducated taste for story and respect for decorum (citizen auditors). Public opinion was opposed to the satirical school and the motives of the satirists were questioned from the beginning; a common charge was that they were themselves guilty of the vices they portrayed – as in *A woman is a weather-cocke A new comedy*, [...] (1612) by Nathan Field, who also acted in plays by Jonson and Beaumont. Young John Donne, Thomas Lodge, Ben Jonson and Marston were social satirists known as iconoclasts and debunkers in philosophy and religion, in poetry and drama.

and popular moralising, of amorous and martial strains and rants, does not die with the Prince: freethinking men of "ingenious sharpness", wits from both the Inns and universities and heirs to the classical tradition of disdain, continue their war against the *profanum vulgus*, against the "taffety fools" and authoritarian public opinion. With John Marston, a *mécontent de profession*, they can say:

> The more I learned the more I learnt to doubt,
> Knowledge and wit, faith's foe, turn faith about.[57]

PARADOX: A VILLAN ON STAGE

For the 1617-18 Christmas season, the students of Gray's Inn resurrected Henry, the gay Prince of Purpoole, and revived the fabulous 1594 *Gesta Grayorum*. In those 23 years the great and noble personalities involved in the old *Gesta* had all died: Elizabeth, Essex, and the Cecils, both father and son; Henry Percy IX, Earl of Northumberland, was in the Tower, and Sir Walter Raleigh was on his way to the block. The only surviver in a world greatly altered was Sir Francis Bacon, the "great contriver", who, on January 7 1618, reaping the coveted fruit of his labors, was ordered Lord Chancellor. A month later, on Candlemas day, the students of Gray's Inn celebrated their powerful *alumnus* with the staging of the The *First Antimask of Mountebankes* and a "song for the entertainment of the Lord Chancellor".[58]

The 1618 sequel of the *Gesta Grayorum* differs significantly from its original: no known contemporary poet or dramatist appears to be connected with it; besides Francis Bacon to whom the masque was dedicated, no leading personality is mentioned.[59] The literary quality and the moral tone of the revels are definitely "low"; the language is gnomic, and dramatic action is turned into pantomime. Henry, second Prince of Purpoole,

---

The *Prince d'Amour* revels may be seen as an early expression of the so-called *Poetomachia*, or "war of the theatres", of the early Jacobean period. See HARBAGE, *op. cit.*, pp. 90-119.

[57] *What You Will*, II. This play, about the failure of social satire, was presented in 1601, the year of Nashe's *Summer's Last Will and Testament*, in which the "vulgar voice" and the "taffety fools" are insulted by the unruly chorus, see NASHE, *op. cit.*, Vol. III, p. 278.

[58] Reprinted in *Three Revels from the Inns of Court*, cit., p. 72 as *Gesta Grayorum Part Two*.

[59] Both Bland and Finkelpearl, reject the suggestion, first advanced by J.P. Collier, that Marston wrote it.

has acquired new and more ridiculous titles fit for a monarch of perennially insolvent knights:

General of the invincible Forces against the savage and barbarous incursions of the Volturines Ballives, and treacherous ambushments of the Harpian Catchpoles, Mainpernor and Grand Protector of the distressed Christians, against the Jewish Inquisition of usurious, corrupt Chevisance, and Sovraigne Founder of the most noble Order of the Cressent.

The order of the "Cressent" recalls the *insegne* of Henry I *"In the Bark of a Cedar-tree, the Character E engraven. Crescetis"*.[60] But in this new context, the image of the crescent moon, used as in heraldry to signify a second son, is used as a euphemism for, and leitmotif of, the growing of a woman's belly, and the male sexual organ,

Willfull desire, knowne bayly of the Honour of the Ladyes, claimes suite service of all the Knights of the Cressent, as of common right, that every one of them may beare a man in her moone, and by the swelling of her gown be known as a cressent Lady.

The exploits of the Knights of the *Crescent* take the noble audience to the heart of London's Suburbia, where Ferdinando Fartwell, Paxnell Lotrix[61] and Humphry Alechops move from the boroughs of *Cunnilania* and *Futulania* to the *North-East Passage*, through the *Amazonian Forest of Clerkenwell*.[62] The infectious lists of *Articles of the Order, Claimes of Common Persons* and mock mootable cases or

incertentyes which have lately arisen concerninge his Highnes Prerogative in his Wards, Ideotts, Widowes, Lunaticks

are filled with pert allusions to the wild way of student life, that is, to sex and money. The new *Gesta* evoke not the mythical and exotic world and heroic personages of the Tudor Inns of Court revels, but rather the mon-

---

[60] A recurrent emblem that appears on the stage of *The Masque of the Inner Temple and Gray's Inn*, see *A Book of Masques*, cit., p. 140.

[61] Such alliterative double names can be found in all Tudor stock comedies. Lotrix, or washerwoman, with a pun on "lotium" (urine, used for washing clothes) is only one of those relating to bodily functions. Hollyband in his *Dictionarie*, 1593, gives «Lauender, washer, or lawndere, lotrix». The pun in this contect is topical since young, women servants were harassed by the students of Inns. In DUGDALE, *Origines Juridiciales*, cit., fo. 286 we read that at Gray's "[i]n 23 Eliz. (Jan 30) there was an Order made, that no Laundresses, nor women called Victuallers, should thenceforth come into the Gentlemens Chambers of this Society, unless they were fully fourty years of age [...]".

[62] With word play on *cunnus* and *futuo*, as in *cunyborowe*.

strous world of contemporary professions, from whores to humanists, described by Tomaso Garzoni in the 155 *Discorsi* of *La Piazza Universale*.[63]

In the foreword that opens the printed text of one of Jonson's earliest and best masques, *Hymenaei*, danced at court on January 5 1606, the poet makes an explicit assertion of his lofty conception of the masque and complaining about the rapidly changing tastes, alludes to royal condescension to low comedy:[64]

For these men's palates, let not me answer, O Muses. It is not my fault if I fill them out nectar, and they run to metheglin.

The Grayans' *Antimasque of Mountebanks*, staged at court on February 16, 1618, was a spicy and intoxicating mead concocted especially for the royal palate.[65] After the *Montebankes* "of severall nations" have sung and danced their antimasque of *musical charmes* and *familiar receipts* for the *infinite* diseases they can cure, they introduce a professional of a different trade, whom they hold in casual contempt for his tricks of novelty. His name is *Paradox*.

I have heard of a mad fellow, who stiles himself a merry Greeke, and goes abroad by the name of Paradox, who, with frisking and dauncing, and new broadhced doctrine, hath stolen himselfe this festival-time of Christmas into favour at the Court of *Purpoole*, and, haveinge there gotten some approbation for

---

[63] In the "claims" land tenure (*soccage*) is mocked; the mock *questiones* are about: *nonage*, *seisin* and the Statute of Merton, which among other things dealt with illegitimacy and women, two subjects the gentlemen students had to account for in person often. *The Universal Marketplace for all Professions in the World* had an immediate reception in England. GARZONI's *Hospidale de' li pazzi incurabili* (1586), an anti-Erasmian treatise on folly as mere illness, was translated by Thomas Nashe and published in 1600 as *The hospitall of incurable fooles: erected in English, as neer the first Italian modell and platforme, as the vnskilfull hand of an ignorant architect could deuise*.

[64] BEN JONSON, *op. cit.*, VII, pp. 209-210; *The Masque of the Inner Temple and Gray's Inn*, by Francis Beaumont, danced on February 20, 1613 (Shrove Tuesday) as part of the celebrations for the wedding of Princess Elizabeth and the Count Palatine, featured in the second antimasque a cast of low-comedy characters and even "He and She-Baboons". At the representations of *The Masque of Flowers*, also devised by Bacon, the King emphatically expressed his approval and let the comedians kiss the royal hands. This same privilege was granted to the gentleman actors of the *Masque of Mountebankes*, see BLAND, *Three Revels*, cit., p. 76.

[65] It is possible that the "medical" subject of the antimasque was intended as a mockery of the running metaphor of magnetism of the 1594 *Gesta*, used to ridicule Essex's rival, Sir Walter Raleigh, and his "physician" friend William Gilbert of Colchester (1544-1603) the author of the first classic of modern physics, *De magnete*, published in 1600 in London, in which he experimented with friction, electricity and magnetism while practising as physician-in-ordinary to Queen Elizabeth. BACON, in *The Advancement of Learning*, cit. p. 35, says: "Gilbertus our countryman hath made a philosophy out of the observations of a loadstone". See note 44 above.

a smale performance, is growne soe audacious as to intrude himself into this honored presence. To prevent whose further growinge fame [...].[66]

At this point Paradox barges in and presents himself thus,

Health and jouisaunce to this faire assembly. Now the thrice-three-learned sisters forsake me, if ever I beheld such bewtyes in Athens! You aske, perhaps, who I am, that thus conceitedly salute you? I am a merry Greeke, and a Sophister of Athens, who, by fame of certaine novill and rare presentiments undertaken and premised by the gallant spirits of *Graia* drawne hither, have intruded myselfe, sophister-like, in at the backe-doore, to be a spectator, or rather a censor, of ther undertakinge. The muses grant they may satisfie our expectations. Oh, the shewes, and the songs, and the speeches, and the plays, and the comedyes, and the actings I have seen at Athens! The Universe never saw the like. But let that passe. Ther was another ende of my cominge; and that was, to gett some of these bewtyes to be my disciples, for I teach them rare doctrine, but delightfull; and if you be true Athenians (that is, true lovers of novaltyes, as I hope you ar all) you will give my hopes ther looked-for expectations. Know then, my name is Paradox; a strange name, but proper to my discent, for I blush not to tell you truth, I am a slip of darkness, my father a Jesuite, my mother an Anabaptist; and as my name is strange, soe is my profession; and the art which I teach, myselfe being the first that reduced it to rules and methode, bears my own name Parradoxe.

I pray you what is a parradox? It is a *quod libet*, or straine of witt and invention, scrued above the vulgar conceipt, to beget admiration. And because Methode is the mother of Discipline, I divide my Parradox into these three heads, masculine, feminine, and Neuter [...]

A "merry Greek", a Sophister of Athens and a Ramist, Paradox is the quintessential Plautine parasite who creeps to his patron's feast and tickles his jaded palate with Attic salt and adulation.[67] He has little part in the main action of the masque; and like the semi-professional funny-men of the Roman stage or their counterparts in the Greek "new comedy" of Menander, he is a character developed merely for his witty speeches and clowning. Paradox, like Saturio, who compares himself to the poor philosopher (*cynicum esse egentem oportet parasitum probe*), studies books of jokes to supplement his extemporaneous wit.[68] He is a professional of

---

[66] BLAND, *Three Revels*, cit., p. 91.

[67] "Mathew Merygreeke" is the name of the Plautine parasite in N. UDALL's *Ralph Roister Doister*, the first English comedy. Parasites later became stock figures of the 16th-century English stage.

[68] *Persa* III, 3 and 1.

the word, and he reads a total of 79 "paradoxes". His parasitic word game is made of joke reversals and formulaic inversions, which in their unearned "novelty" are as trite as the cliches they batten upon. He is a teacher of a "strange doctrine" he himself has devised and reduced to "rules and methode". Paradox, the impossible son of a Jesuite and an Anabaptist, makes equations of things manifestly unlike; he embodies the obsessive and self-referential verbal effervescence of carnivalised language. In the Shrovetide *agon*, Paradox plays the part of the challenger of Lenten bowdlerisation and logophobia. Most of all, Paradox, who has come to Graya "to gett some of these bewtyes to be my disciples", is represented, like Jack Falstaff, as the false teacher and corruptor of youths. As soon as comedy relents and "jouisaunce" gives place to sobriety, the mask of Paradox reveals the face of the parasitic villain, both panderer and existential punster.

As Paradox leaves the stage, a choreographed presentation to music, or interlude, begins:

> four Pages [...] entering with torch lights burning, bewailing the losse of their masters, and sing this dialogue-wise.
> [...]
> What cruel Charmes berefte
> The patrons of our youthe?
> Wee must now begge for ruth.

It follows a melodramatic interlude about the deliverance of the Grayan youths, held prisoners by *Obscurity*,

the ever youthfull knights, by spells inchainde in a dark cave under a huge craggy rock.

The subject of the deliverance of youth from vice, followed by repentance and a new start under the tutelage of wiser masters was a favourite at Gray's Inn. It had originated in the homiletic tradition from the fifteenth century morality and subsequently was inherited by the Tudor authors of allegorical plays who concentrated upon youth and voiced the major preoccupation with education found in many later interludes.[69] and it had been used already in two performances masterminded by Francis Bacon. In *The Misfortunes of Arthur* (1588), a group of young law students were held captives by the Muses, who demanded that the choice wits and followers of Queen Astræa (i.e. Elizabeth as the embodiment of

---

[69] See for instance *A Preaty Interlude Called, Nice Wanton*, in J.M. MANLY, *Specimens of the pre-Shakesperean Drama*, Vol. I, Boston Ginn, The Athenaeum Press Series, 1897, pp. 459-479.

Law) put aside the barbarous law-French and pay due service "to the noble skills of language and art". In *The Masque of Proteus*[70] the *Prince of Purpoole* and his Knights of the Helmet had been held hostages inside Proteus's lodestone and freed by the superior attractive force of the Queen's love, the true "Adamant of Hearts".

When the opening song is over, a "courtain falls down", disclosing *Obscurity* lying at the mouth of a dark cave. Addressing *Light*, she bows to the superior power of *Love* and *Fate* and invites the torch-bearing pages to search for the prisoners and set them free:

> Loe hear tender yeares kinde-harted squires,
> Mourning there masters' losse;
> [...] But heare they went
> From shade to shade, and give theyr toile no end.
> [...]

As the pages seek for the knights, and *Obscurity* sings, the Grayan knights come out of the cave in couples and take out the ladies to dance. The interlude ends with *Obscurity*, who with a pun on "measure" invites the knights to observe moderation

> [...]
> To View, talke and touch, but all in measure.
> Far, far from hence be roughness, far a frowne'
> Your fair deportment this faire night shall crowne.

In the last song in four parts and lute, the identity of the antagonists of *Obscurity, Light, Fate* and *Love*, all characters with no speaking roles, is revealed. They are Francis Bacon, the King and the Queen, sitting on stage and directly addressed by the Grayans,

> [...] Love hath obtaind for us: to him be bowe,
> And to this gentler Powre, who soe contrived
> That wee from sullen shades are now depriv'd,
> And hither brought, where Favour, Love, and Light,
> So glorious shine, they banish Night

---

[70] The full title in the text is: *The Masque of Proteus* in three parts: "*the story of Proteus' transformations, The wonders of the Adamantine Rock and a Speech to her Majesty*. It concluded the 1594-1595 *Gesta Grayorum* and was acted by the lawyers at Greenwich before the Queen on Shrove Tuesday, 1595.

The music ends and Paradox comes back on stage with his four "disciples". After few priapic pranks with a dancing maypole, he is challenged to a mock tournament by the "Mountebancke and four of his disciples like Swizzers with another maypole". This Shrovetide combat between the two charlatans, a mockery of the Tudor tilts, concludes with a few obscenities the *Antimask of Mountebankes*. *Obscurity* appears on stage, followed by the knights, and sings her last songs: one in praise of *Love* (ie the King) and the other "for the entertainment of the Lord Chancellor", Sir Francis Bacon (*Light*), before whom the Grayans are

> as men with too much light,
> Dazzled, yet not blinded quite [...]

If we consider the staging of a "dark cave under a huge craggy rock", *Obscurity* lying at its mouth and conceding to the power of Light, the torch-bearing pages moving nearby and bewailing the loss of the masters, and the final release of the knights from their dark bondage, the interlude appears to be nothing less than the enactment of Plato's myth of the cave, in the seventh book of the *Republic*, cited by Bacon in the *Advancement of Learning* (XIV, 10)

Let us consider again the false appearances imposed upon us by every man's own individual nature and custom in that feigned supposition that Plato maketh of the cave; for certainly if a child were continued in a grot or cave under the earth until maturity of age, and came suddenly abroad, he would have strange and absurd imaginations. So, in like manner, although our persons live in the view of heaven, yet our spirits are included in the caves of our own complexions and customs, which minister unto us infinite errors and vain opinions if they be not recalled to examination.

If we use this as the interpretive key, it appears clearer that the *Antimask of Mountebankes*, meant to honor and please Sir Francis Bacon is about the corrupting effects of bad education. This question, vital to the *Republic*, as it had been to the Tudor monarchs, was treated by Bacon in his "general and faithful perambulation of learning", in particular in the chapters against "professory learning":

Amongst so many great foundations of colleges in Europe, I find strange that they are all dedicated to professions, and none left free to arts and sciences at large. So if any man think philosophy and universality to be idle studies, he doth not consider that all professions are from thence served and supplied. And this I take to be a great cause that hath hindered the progression of learning, because these fundamental knowledges have been studied but in passage. Neither is it to be forgotten, that this dedicating of foundations and dotations to professory learning hath not only had a malign aspect and influence upon the growth of sciences, but hath also been prejudicial to states, and governments.

Bacon, who followed closely that passage in the sixth book of the *Republic*[71] criticising Sophists and private "educators" working for pay, wrote that the greatest error of all,

is the mistaking or misplacing of the last or furthest end of knowledge. For men have entered into a desire of learning and knowledge, sometimes upon a natural curiosity and inquisitive appetite; sometimes to entertain their minds with variety and delight; sometimes for ornament and reputation; and sometimes to enable them to victory of wit and contradiction; and most times for lucre and profession; and seldom sincerely to give a true account of their gift of reason to the benefit and use of men [...][72]

The *Mountebankes* represent therefore Bacon's "empirical and dogmatical sects of physicians" who exercise their profession for lucre.[73] Whereas, Paradox, the embodiment of the false "teacher" and the Sophist, exercises it for mere "victory of wit". As "equivocation or ambiguity of words and phrase"[74] and the great sophism of all sophisms Paradox represents the arch-villain. This ephemeral Shrovetide monster as the embodiment of *Vice, as* in the old Moralities is the antagonist of *Wisdom* and the corruptor of *Youth*. He is a professional of the word with no claim to truth; and, like Jago, he does not overturn the opinions of the multitude, but inculcates them and perverts the judgment:

the false appearances that are imposed upon us by words, which are framed and applied according to the conceit and capacities of the vulgar sort; and although we think we govern our words, and prescribe it well *loquendum ut vulgus sentiendum ut sapientes*, yet certain it is that words, as a Tartar's bow, do shoot back upon the understanding of the wisest, and mightily entangle and pervert the judgment.[75]

---

[71] The *Republic* VI, 493 ff.
[72] *Advancement of Learning*, cit., I, V, 11.
[73] *Ivi*, XIII, 2.
[74] *Ivi*, II, XIV, 7.
[75] *Ivi*, II, XIV, 11.

APPENDIX

The Defence of
Contraries.

Paradoxes againſt common opinion, de-
bated in forme of declamations in place
of publike cenſure : only to exerciſe yong
wittes in difficult matters.

Wherein is no offence to Gods honour, the
eſtate of Princes, or priuate mens honeſt
actions : but pleaſant recreation to be-
guile the iniquity of time.

Tranſlated out of French by *A. M.* one of *A. Munday*
the Meſſengers of her Maieſties
Chamber.

Patere aut abſtine.

Imprinted at London by Iohn Winder
for Simon Waterſon.
1593.

THE DEFENCE OF
CONTRARIES

Paradoxes against common opinion, de-
bated in forme of declamations in place
of publike censure: only to exercise yong wittes in
difficult matters.

Wherein is no offence to Gods honour, the
Estate of Princes, or private mens
actions: but pleasant recreation to be-guile the
iniquity of time.

Translated out of French by A.M. one of
the Messengers of her Maiesties
Chamber.

Patere aut abstine.

Imprint at London by John Windet
for Simon Waterson.
1593.

The Defence of Contraries, facsimile by Windet, 1593, Cambridge University Library. The text has been reproduced here verbatim, expansions having been made on occasion for ease of reading, and the letters u and v and i and j are generally distinguished according to modern practice.

TO THE RIGHT NOBLE, VERTUOUS,
AND WORTHY MINDED LORD, FERDINANDO STANLEY:
THE GREAT AND PUISSANT EARLE OF DERBIE, C.

Most noble Lord, if your just conceived greefe, for losse of so worthy a father, may vouchsafe but a looke on a poore mans humble affection: then suffer this testimony of my unfeined zeale, the gratious aspect of your everknowne honourable countenance: wherewith I likewise give my selfe, and my very uttermost habilitie to your Honors Service, my oath and duty reserved, to my most gratious Queene and Mistreße: whome heaven blesse, and your Honor, the true heire and succeeder, in your fathers noblenesse and vertues.

Your Honours in all duty
A. Mundy.

TO THE KING.

Sir, after you had heard the censures of divers learned Gentlemen, on the severall Paradoxes which you pleased to propound, and were therein (as I imagined) fully satisfied: yet you would needes make triall of my meane judgement in such matters, and thereupon commanded me to set down mine opinion. How simple soever they be, doone they are, and now in all humblenes presented to your Maiestie: who doubtlesse will allow them gratious countenance, because it was a taske imposed by your selfe, and beside, requireth labour and good witt to defend such contraries. Let no manne thinke then, that I or any other would be so senselesse, as to holde directly any of these vaine reasons: but what (for argumentes sake) may be said, that set I downe, and no other.

TO THE READER

Were wont to cal Paradoxes: that is to say, things contrary to most mens present opinions: to the end, that by such discourse as is helde in them, opposed truth might appeare more cleere and apparent. Likewise, to exercise thy witte in proofe of such occasions, as shall enforce thee to seeke diligentlie and laboriously, for sound reasons, proofes, authorities, histories, and very darke or hidden memories. Notwithstanding, in the conceits, I would not have thee so much deceived, as that eyther my sayings or conclusions, should make thee credit otherwise, then common and sensible judgement requireth: and yet withall remember, that diversities of things, doth more comfort mens spirites, then daily and continually to behold, whatsoever is common and frequent to our judgements.

Farewell.

I

FOR POVERTIE.

DECLAMATION, 1
THAT IT IS BETTER TO BE POORE THAN RICH.

Considering for what, and against whome I am to speake in your presence, I have great occasion to feare, and withal to request, that credit and
favour shoulde have no more meanes, to blemish and obscure truth on
your partes; then may innocencie and simplicitie on my behalfe, by bringing and conducting ye into the apparent light; for minding to commend
such things, as are blamed and hated by most part of men, it will be almost
impossible for me to escape displeasure in the matters themselves, which of
each one, and at all times have beene loved, esteemed and cherished above
all other things. But one thing that heerin giveth me some comfort, is, that
among the wise and vertuous, the number whereof are dailye without comparison farre lesse (albeit much more esteemed) then the bad and ignorant;
I shall escape unblamed. Wherefore I need not be dismaied, if I find few
protectors and friends, for praising matters so good and honest, when my
adversarie findeth greater advantage, for extoling such things as are evil
and pernitious.

Nowe because the principall point of my cause consisteth in letting ye
understand, the estate and level of such matters, as I stand for: I desire ye
to wish him, who would turne ye from the knowledge heerof (as pretend-
ing not to know, that the well skilde in letters, have (for the most part)
been poore and needie persons:) To cal to memorie the life of *Valerius
Pubicola, Menenius Agrippa*, as also the good *Aristides,* who died so poore,
as they were faine by almes to be buried. Hee may remember likewise, *Epaminondas* king of *Thebes*, in whose rich houses & Pallaces (after so many
faire victories and noble deedes of armes by him perfourmed) was found
but one poore straw-bed or base matresse, for to put in his Inventory.
He may bee mindfull also of *Paulus Aemillius, Attillius Regulus, Quintus
Cincinnatus, Cato Elius* and *Marcus Manlius*: whose noble hartes were

more comanded by want; then the height of worldly fortunes. And who knows not, that love of povertie had such power over good *Abdolominus*, that to be ruled thereby, hee refused the most riche and abounding kindgome of *Sydonia,* he being elected by the people of the Countrey, to be governor thereof?

Heerein appeareth sufficiently, the great number of molestations and travailes, hidden under the vaine splendour of riches, and the aboundance of honours hidden in the beautiful bosome of povertie: honors well knowne and understood by the Poet *Anacreon*, to whom it happened, that having been two whole nights togither without any rest, troubled with continuall devisings, how he might keepe from theeves, and imploy the five talents of golde which *Polycrates* had given him: at length, to deliver himselfe from this perpetuall molestation, and returne to his former happinesse, he brought backe the faire Talentes to the Tyrant, with such wordes as one of his sorte might very well use, and notwithstanding hee was poore and indigent, yet he refused those thinges so highly accounted on. It is certaine, that hee whoe hath alwaies lived poor in this world, hath no greefe or sorrowe when he departeth from it: for it is to bee considered, that hee leaveth this earthlie life more contented and joyfullie, then he that by the meanes of riches, hath therin endured long time of pleasure.

As for my selfe, I never saw one that was poore indeed, who at his death desired to be better stored. O chaste and humble povertie, wheron, as on a most firme rocke, was builded (of olde) the Churche of God. Povertie, architectrix of great citties & towns: inventresse of all artes and faire sciences, alone without any fault or reproch: Triumphant in very great excellence, and worthy of all honour and commendation. By these was the Philosopher *Plato* esteemed so devine: *Socrates* so wise, and good *Homer* so eloquent. By they meanes was erected the Empire of the great *Romaine* people, and to be briefe; how much for other things thou art to be loved singularlie: yet for this one respect art thou highlie to be praised, because apparantlie thou makest knowne, who (among friends) are the feigned and counterfeit. Wherefore I say, that such as forsake and reject thee, ought to be shunned as a savage beast, & chased from every one: considering that in refusing thee, he repulseth the mistresse of all goods, & excellence of the spirit of man.

That this is true, howe many persons have beene seene (by the meanes of honest want) to be brought to all modesty, humility, chastitie, providence, and lastlie to joy in that, which false phylosophy, by long time and continuall studie, could hardly at any time bring to memorie. If mine oath might urge yet to beleefe, I durst affirme before ye, that I have seen some in their worldly felicities, more furious, than ever was *Orestes*, more proud, then *Athamantis*, more voluptuous & libidinous then *Verres* or *Clodius*: who soone after by some inconveniences being brought to poverty, became in one instant, chast, courteous and so debonaire, as not so much as the very shadow of their bodies, but appeared to be affable and gratious. And never did so much the gainsaiers of this vertue, no not in the honesties of morall philosophy, for it is a thing very certaine, that shee could never performe likeworthy deedes, as our good povertie hath doone; I beseech ye consider, what a mistresse in her house she hath alwaies beene, to forbid, that (where she sojourneth) sloth, prodigalitie, gouttinesse, luxurie, with such like mishapen and detestable matrones should have any harbour. Whersoever she sheweth her selfe, it behoveth pride to bee gone with all diligence; never must envy have any place there, such trumperies and abuses she scattereth from her aboades.

But may it please ye to understand Gentlemen whereon they so much affected to riches and covetousnesse of money, doe ground themselves, which in all seasons hath beene held for the greatest ruine and destruction of men. They say, that such is the inclination of our spirit. I would demand of them, what societie have the spirits of men, being of their owne nature divine and celestial, with earthly superfluities, because nothing else is gold or silver, then the very excrement of the earth? Where finde they, that any one of them who were highly wise, would ever place riches in the number of those thinges, that truly ought to bee called goods: Unhappy thornes, which brings ye such greefe in the gathering, which with so many warme teares and over-bitter sighs, ye leave lost and dissipated: and with such paines and anguishes, ye cause to be guarded and tended.

Seneca, author of great reputation, saide: That the man is greatly to be commended, whoe prizeth earthen vessels as much as if they were of silver: but much more praise deserveth he, that esteemeth veselles of golde or silver no more then if they were of earth. So in truth, if we consider well the condition of these so highly beloved riches, we shall find them naturally to be such; as in dispending or employing them, they cause nothing else but trouble and torment. And thinking to keepe them safe and sure under key, never the more easie benefite is received thereby: but oppressions of such care, as we cannot but repute our selves simple subjects, and servants to them.

For this it is, that our God, of infinite wisdom and bountie, calleth the poore most blessed: & who ever gave so much favor to povertie as he? In imitation of whom, many (I thinke by him inspired) have buried their goods, fearing least themselves shoulde be buried in them.

And brieflye to discover the pleasure of these riches. If we desire them, to have a sumptuous stable of horses, double and single, Courtals, ambling and trotting Geldings, Iennets, *Hungarian*, *Barbarian*, *Turkish*, and other horsses of excellence: let us consider, that the horsse by nature is a fantasticall beaste, night and day eating the goods of his maisster, yet for all that never satisfied; a lofty and a couragious beast, bread and nourished uppe for warre, to whom sometimes their needs but a wispe of strawe, to affright him with a shadow, which endangers the overthrow of his maister. A beast, that oft times will not obey the bridle or the spurre, and without the meanes of well ordering and managing, will fall into a thousand bogges or quag-mires. How many daungerous alarmes, and spoile of Countries (caused by the unhappie incursions of the *Gotthique*, *Vandalian*, *Hunnes*, & *Danish* hordes) have the noble kingdoms of *France*, *Italie* and *Spaine* received: whoe but for this helpe, had never been enterprized uppon by those barbarous Nations? What damage yeerely doe the poste horses, not only to riders for offices and benefices: but likewise to Princes and Lords, who sometime (for their pleasure) desire to winne ground in hast? I never looke on them, that so boldly place their affection in horses; and who without any reasonable cause, so affect and keepe them, but I say to my selfe: betweene him that loveth, and the thing beloved, it behoveth there should be some similitude and resemblance, otherwise such an appetite should never bee ingendered, nor could these two so well agree togyther. Seeing then that rich men are so immesurably affected to their horsses, as they can thinke on no other pastimes in the world, but to send to buy them at *Naples*, in *Turkie*, in *Almaigne* and *Spaine*: it must needes be esteemed, that they holde some disposition agreeing with the horsses, participating with some strange and brutish nature. And not to be silent in other discommodities which horsses bringeth, as well in the field as the Citty: first of all, if they trot, they will breake their reynes: and if they amble, they are ready to stumble and fall, hazarding thy overthrow, or perishing some member of thy body. Beside this, as faith the great *Alfirtocus*, and many good Authors of Escuyrie: the horsse is subject to more diseases then a man. So let me leave ye, to bethinke on such other greefes and vexations, which horsses daily bring unto ye.

If we see into the pleasure of the rich, concerning the beautie of their Cabinets, garnished (amonge other iewels) with pointed diamonds, Rubies, Topazses, Emeraldes, or other beautifull stones: wee may at this day perceive by proofe, that the price and valew of pretious stones, consisteth only in the affection of very wealthy persons, or in the smooth language of the abusers that sell them, the reputation and esteem of them, being subject to the incertitude and variety of opinions. That is so, the *Agath* which now is of so slender prize, was of olde had in great reputation with *Pyrrhus*, who kept one as most deere and pretious. The Saphire, because it resembled the faire colour of Heaven, was wont to bee in very high account: nowe it is of little esteeme, and helde as a slender iewell. The Diamond was never by our elders greatly prized: now ye see howe it is reckoned and valued. The To-paze was in good credit with Ladies, but now at this present (for what occasion I know not) it is reputed the simplest iewell one can weare. And who knowes not in what dignitie the Emerald should be? Now ye see how it lies complaining on Fortune.

Thou wilt tell me, that it were good for one to be rich, that he may bee decked in faire and sumptuous garments, finely cut and framed after divers fashions. Thou art very sottish and simple if thou perceiveth not, that such braveries bring thee perpetuall sollytude and molestation; for having gotten garmentes of these sorts, thou must so often rubbe, ripe, brush, fold, un-folde, alter, amend, ayre, and such like qualitie else beside, to keepe them from spots & moaths, wherein thou maiest apparantly note and expresse deepe vanity, that thou wilt cover thy body, which is made of nothing but dirt and slime, with purple, silke, gold, and other curiosities.

Some good drinker, would desire money, to see his sellers full of the best and most delciate wines, as of Balme, Arbois, wine of Orleance, Ro-setta, Muscadels, Bastardes, Malmesies, Corfa, Greeke wine, Vernacula, Romania, and others, which are not heer to be nominated. These were good for thee; were it not that thou forgettest the discommodities which drinke bringeth, and to be drunke. For wine (according as *Plato* holdeth) was in manner sent down here beneath by the Gods, to inflict punishments uppon men, and to take vengeance on their offenses, making them (after they be become drunke) to kill & murder one another. For this cause *Androcides* advertised *Alexander,* that wine was the bloud of the earth, and he ought to guard himselfe well in the use thereof. This counsell beeing not well observed by that great Emperour; in his intemperance he slewe his most deere *Clitus*, burned the Citty of *Persepolis*, stabbed his Phisitian, committing many other filthie and infamous deedes of excesse. Wherefore was it, but for this, that the *Carthaginians* forbad wine to theyr souldiors and houshold servants, and to such likwise as held any estate of govern-ment in their Common wealth, especially during the time of their authoritie and office in the Citty.

Leotichus being desired to tel the reason, wherefore the *Spartanes* (by his commandement) were so sober in drinking wine: answered, that he did it to deliver them from trouble, in consulting with other nations touching their owne affaires. *Cyneas*, Ambassador to *Pyrrhus*, whose sweet tongue was so much esteemed by every one, and of so great profit to his Prince, being one daye in *Auara*, beholding the exceeding height of the countrey vines; in smiling merely, thus spake. Good right had such a mother, to be hanged on so highe a Crosse or Iibbet, because she brought forth such a dangerous childe as wine was. Should one with riches, to have great troopes of fat cattell, store of wooll or corne? To see his court ful of fowles, his dove-cotes well bred and haunted, Turtle doves in cages, Peacocks, Phesants, Turky hens, with other kindes of excellent fowle choisly kept uppe? I thinke that the great number of these severall kindes, serves but for venison to the Fox or Wolfe, or else their rapine, that have not the meane to compasse the like: the pleasure whereof may be called somewhat beastlie, because it is nourished among beasts.

And as for fowles, what are they (if not kept as a pray for foxes, Cats, and Weasels) then are they viands for hunters, the spoile of gardens, and destruction of Garners? Can one imagine like vexation to this beastly delight? For one paultry egge, what cry, what cackling and noise heare we for so smal a thing: albeit it were good, as some doubt it is not. For who knowes not by experience, cheefly by the testimony of Phisitians, that the new laide egge subverteth the stomach, and when it is not new, it corrupteth and hurteth it? What shal I say of the Turtledove, whose sorrowfull note brings such griefe to the hearer, and to the eater, such appetite to fleshy concupiscence? What likewise shall I say of the Pigeon? Whose noise never ceaseth day or night, which breakes her maysters head, and beside, fileth the fairest houses? And as for her hoarse note, I finde it nothing inferiour to that of the Peacock, in matter of annoying and bad sound: saving that the Peacock crie is more mighty in terrour, even as it were to affright the devils. I beleeve the man that brought them into this countrey, had much more regard to his belly, than to the quarels and disturbing of neighbours, to disgrace the coverture of houses, and spoile of so many well manured and pleasant gardens.

Some good supposer may say, that riches serve for a pleasant & recreative life. Because I have wealth, I can make good cheere, I can my selfe merilie, and entertaine companies of most excellent Musitians, that shall make me pastime, and take from me all offending irkesomeneses. Let mee advertise thee, that in musicke is not to be received one onely good or honest pleasure; because it is naturally vaine and dissolute. That it is so, Saint *Athanasius* Bishop of *Alexandria*, a man of very profounde knowledge, to the reading of whose bookes, Saint *Ierom* moste instantlie exhorteth vs: chased musicke forth of the christian Church, because it too much weakened and softened mens spirits, making them inclined and disposed to all worldlie pleasures and lasciviousnes: beside this, it increased melancholie in him, that was first by nature surprized therewith. Saint *Augustine* had never any will at all to prove it: the *Egyptians* blamed it, not so much for being unprofitable, as dangerous and damnable. *Aristotle* most highly hated it, when it hapned him to say: that *Jupiter* never could find or play on the harpe. *Phillip* of *Madecon* very much blamed his sonne *Alexander,* because he saw him given too much to musicke, and sawe him (one time among other) take too great pleasure in singing melodiously: who would then with great store of goods, to employ them in such a fantasticall studie?

Who would desire riches, for the pastime of hunting, hawking, and other manner of chasing sportes? The chase is no recreation at all, that a studious or a vertuous spirit should followe: for whosoever will well resolve himselfe thereof, shall find it an exercise of crueltie, a sport for desperate people, and (if I durst say so) for mad men. This pastime was first invented by the *Thebanes,* a nation beyond other most cruell and beastlie: nor was it had in any use, but among the most barbarous, such as were the *Idumeans, Ismaelites* and *Philistines.* For the truth heereof, looke in holy writ, if any one of the good Patriarches was ever a hunter? We read somewhat of *Caine, Esau* and *Nemrod:* but this was the cause why *Saint Augustine* held, that the said *Esau* was reckoned among the number of sinners. According to which opinion, the chase was forbidden to Preests in the *Mileuitane* councel, albeit that decree at this day is little accoumpted of.

Wherefore thinke ye the fabulists feigned *Acleon,* to be turned into a Hart as hee was chasing? But only to let us understand, that the over-earnest & immeasureable love borne to that exercise, with the consuming of goods bestowed thereon: makes the hunters in the ende not onely beastly, but even horned altogither likewise. For proofe and example of this daungerous pleasure, I am to tell ye, that not manie daies past, a marvellous faire yong Gentlewoman, accoumpted of greatest trust where she dwelt, so soon as her husband was risen early in the morning to goe on hunting: received the injurious companie of hir secret friend, with whom she had greater pastime, not forsaking her bedde, then the hunter could have in midst of the fieldes, where he pursuing some horned beast, himselfe (without thinking thereon) was at home turned into a masque of the same fashion. Poor and miserable huntsmen, let me in curtesie tell ye, to what end serves this great affection ye beare to savage beasts, but to make ye continuallie haunt the woods and forrests, where likewise become savage and brutish, ready oftentimes to breake your neckes in bushes or ditches. Take example I pray ye by *Virtus*, he that by his prowesse conquered the kingdom of Portugall, and consider, how of a shepheard, hee became a huntsman, and from a huntsman, to bee a robber and theefe in the woods.

The youths that are tearmed nice-wantons, will never yeeld to mee, but that riches will serve to feast their Ladies, to banquet, daunse, vault, brave it, revel all the night, and use a thousand idle tricks of lovers, wherein we see the wealthy youthes of these daies, most commonly to place their pleasure. Heereto I woulde not willinglie agree, were it not I imagine, what is doone in secret to Ladies: so that the love of the very fairest, or most queint and finest Gentlewoman, is nothing else than a secret hidden death, a close contrived poison, incident to the spirit of the most sensible person that is. And for this cause, the *Egyptians* (willing to shewe love portraied in every part) were wont to paint a snare of halter: signifying thereby (as I thinke) the miserable ende and condition, whereto poore lovers are daily led, a passion too bitter to feele, that suddenlie making his entrie into the harts of men, departs againe very slow and slacklie: whence springeth afterward infinite fountaines of teares, sighes too piersing, anguishes and travailes insupportable.

This was in that moved *Alcesimarchus Plautinus* to maintaine, that love was the first inventer of begging and the wallet, by reason (I thinke) of the incredible molestings and torments, which he loades his poore beggars withal, being as often present with him as absent & absent as well as present: by means whereof he sends them in the end (if they be not wel grounded) the bagge for their first salutation, and with a newe shirt of sheet on their shoulder, to the hospitall, by foure horses or bearers. And that love is (of all torments) the most cruell in the worlde, it appeareth by the answere which *Apolonius Thianeus* made to the king of *Babilon;* concerning the paine he desired to be invented for punishing of an Eunuche, who was found with a gentlewoman his affected favorite. Ye need not bethinke any greater persecution for him (quoth the Philosopher) then to let him live: for I make no doubt (mighty king) if the fire of love go forwarde in him, according as already it hath begun: ye cannot make him feele and endure a more cruell passion, nor may he be so tormented with what else ye can devise. He shall finde himselfe (by his own procurement) even like the foolish fly, shall burne and consume in this flame: he shall burne when he is as cold as yee: he shall request and refuse in in one selfe-same instant, and desire as much to die as to live. In these wordes *Thianeus* erred not a jot, if we could consider, how greevously *Salomon* was toiled and tormented with this love, till men beheld him transported from all natural sense, and made a meere prevaricatour of the holy law.

If we should seeke after this wicked money, to take pleasure in many farmes, countrey houses, environed with trim gardens and buildings, beset with cleere fountaines, Thickets, Arbours, Vineyardes, Meadowes, arable land, and other singularities: I say, such things make us often poore by slothfulnes, and undoeth us by over-lavishnesse, inducing us to greevous offenses, thorow many by-places, and behaviours that are over secret. That it is not unlikely, let us remember what *Cicero* wrote to his friend *Verres*, and we shall finde, that when he would well discipher and portrait to life (as it were) the libidinous acts of a Gentleman: that first of all he painted forth, the walks and pleasures of countrey houses and faire places, which accustomably he frequented, as if such things were the ministers and helps, of his very chiefest faults and misbehaviors.

For conclusion, riches have ever beene in so bad reputation; that they have been called brambles, flames, and burning coales. See how they make insolent people arrogant, spightfull, beastly, negligent, disdainfull, fooles, melancholie, solitary and hateful: yee shall not finde one alone, but doubt-eth of their service, as being baits and nourishments to al unhappie works. Hence it came that *Pliny* saide, treasures hid by nature for our profit, doe commonly stifle us, and plunge us in the deapth of all mischances. So was *Zeno* wont to say, that the goodes of the world did more hurt then helpe: which was the cause that made *Crates* the *Thebane*, passing one day from his countrey of *Athens*, to followe the studie of Philosophy, to throw all the golde and silver he had about him into the sea, imagining, that vertue and riches coulde never partake togither: the same speeches were likewise con-firmed by *Bias, Plato,* and manie other wise Philosophers.

But what need I spend time producing so many witnesses: when the holy mouth of the Creatour hath said: that sooner shall the cable of a shippe enter the eie of a needle to sow withal, then can a rich man into the kingdome of heaven. He spake it, who (all his lifetime) distributed and spent his faculties on the poore. But the Pagan that invented the fiction (in truth very inge-nious) how *Jupiter* surprized with the marvellous and exceeding beauty of *Danae,* converted himselfe into a shower of golde, falling into the bosome and lap of the Lady, by this meane to have jouissance with his so long desired and purchased pray: dooth he not plainely enough give us to understand, that gold is the most proper and convenable thing, wherewith to oppugne and overthrowe the chastitie of innocent maidens? Yet thinke not, that gold serveth only as a custome, to persecute the modesty of women withall; but assure your selves beside, that it is daily the cause of monstrous treasons, slaughter, and many other deedes of vile excesse, which the brevity of time, and feare of offending ye, will not permit me to rehearse.

Wherefore I will conclude with the good Phylosopher *Posidonius*, that riches is the cause of infinite evils: which contrariwise cannot be so said or alleaged, against our holy and well advised povertie, of whom learned *Seneca* speaketh honourably, saying: That the naked by this speciall meane, is out of danger of theeves, and such as are free from money, may in besieged places live at ease, not dreading the fearer of enimies. Much better then (without comparison) is franke povertie, then such slavish riches: seeing from poverty springeth infinite profits and commodities, and from worldly goods, proceedeth nothing but unhappinesse.

10

II

FOR THE HARD-FAVOURED FACE, OR FOWLE COMPLEXION.

DECLAMATION, 2
THAT IT IS BETTER TO BE FOWLE THAN FAIRE.

Who knoweth not, how much the deformitie of body and hard favoured face is to bee esteemed, principally in women (for in men it was never in so great request) hath never considered, how many amorous sparks is dayly to be seen, under an il-favoured countenance and badde composed body, choicely hid and couvered: which in a faire face finely polished, gives often occasion of ceaselesse flames and cruell passions. But the strong and invincible bulwarke, which the fowle face (not onely of olde, but likewise in these times) hath erected for it selfe, will encounter the fires of love that are so damageable. Do you beleeve (Gentlemen) if farie *Helen* the Greeke, and the gentle *Troian* Sheepheard, had beene hardfavoured or counterfeit in personage, that the Greekes would ever have taken so much paine in pursuing them. Nor had poore *Troy* endured such cruell ruine and destruction, in longe description whereof, so many skilfull wits were wearied and tyred.

And if we shall compare and unite together, the beawty of the mind with that of the body: shall we not finde a greater number of deformed people, to be more wise and igenious then the faire and well fourmed? Let *Socrates* be our witnesse, whome the historians and auncient figures represent, to be so il-favoured as might be: notwithstanting, by the Oracle of Apollo, he was acknowledged to be the wisest man of his time. *Phrigian Aesope*, the most excellent fabulist, was in forme of bodie so strange and mishapen, as the verie ougliest in his time (in comparison of him) might rightly be resembled to *Narcissus* or *Ganimede*: neverthelesse, as each one may read, he was most rich in vertues, and in spirit (beyond all other) most excellent.

Of great deformitie were the Philosophers, *Zeno* and *Aristotle*, *Empedocles* sowlie composed, and *Galba* a very ougly counterfeit: neverthelesse, they al were of marvellous and sweet disposed spirit. Could any impeach the deformity of *Philopoemen*, who after he was seene to be a good and hardie souldiour: came he not to the dignity of a most valient captain and was he not reverenced among his people, for his high & excellent vertues? Consider (Gentlemen) on such as are of faire and corpulent fashion, and ye shall commonly finde them to be sicklie, more weake, and lesse able to travaile: more soft, delicate and effeminate, then the other kind of people. Againe, ye shall sildome times see it happen, that in a beautifull body, being of great excellence, chastity agreeth in selfesame likelihood: because it is to be kept with great difficultie, being by so many sought after so earnestlie.

What shall we say of such, who (not contenting themselves with nature,) doe daily frame very great complaintes against her, making no spare of their goods of labour, to reforme (with all endevor) what seemeth best to them for fashion of their bodies: because they be not appropriate or agreeing with their curious appetites? Of such fooles I demaund, seeing nature (the most carefull and discrete mother of all things) hath given them what she thought meet and profitable in the form of their bodies: for what cause they should be displeased with her, or imagine her a bad bestower, who would never give them any part of that folly, which is so vainely set by and esteemed of by every one? Nature gives not to her friendes, the things that may quickly be wasted by sicknesse, or overthrowne by the course of age: therefore true liberalitie is knowne, by the firme and long continuance of the gift bestowen upon any one: and what see ye of lesse permanence than beawty?

Consider, how it hath headlong throwne downe yong people, into secret greefes and perillous daungers, and allured them to such hateful sins: as right happie might he count himselfe, that coulde escape them with his honor unstained. Contrariwise, note the good and profit ensuing by deformitie, when all they in generall, that of olde time have beene, & yet at this day are studious in chastitie, doe openly confesse, as nothing hath like force in them, to tame and check the pricks of the flesh, neither long watchings, grevuous disciplines, or continuall fastings; as one only looke upon an il-favoured and counterfeit person. Hence ensueth that, which is used as a common proverbe, concerning a very fowle deformed woman: that shee serveth as a good receipt and soveraigne remedy, against fleshy tentations.

O sacred and pretious deformity, deerly loved of chastitie, free from all scandalous daungers, & a firme rampart against all amorous assaults, I perceive that by thy meanes, company keeping is the easier to bee allowed, for thou takest from them all greefes & annoiances: chasing from they societie all wicked suspitions, as a very speciall remedy against desperate iealousie. O that I coulde finde wordes worthy thy praises and deserts, whence proceedeth infinit good and treasure, which with great shame hath beene (by the ignorant) despised and blamed. O what affection I have to perswade my friends, how they shoulde know (henceforth) to adorne and embelish themselves, with the beawtie that for ever endureth: and not to depart therewith from among us, either drinking, eating, waking, sleeping or breathing. I meane that beawtie, that keepes us companye even to our grave, and leaves us not till the latest gaspe: that which we may truly call our owne, no way due or attributable to our parents. Gaine-say me who shall, I will rest my selfe on this opinion, that much better it is to be adorned with such a colour, then to trust or repose only in the borrowed corporall beauty, which so easilie corrupteth, even by the least touch of any fever that may come upon us.

I remember a yong maiden of *Perigourd*, who perceiving her beauty to be a very great, suspitious, and capitall enimie to her good fame, and that in regard thereof, she was daily required and solicited by many yong younkers: her owne selfe with a rasour, or some piece of silver made sharpe for the purpose, so disfigured her faire face, that her two cheekes, which seemed before like roses of shining Carbuncles, conteyned nothing at all of their former and naturall beawty. Like act did many wife, well learned Damosels, and holy virgines of the Primitive church, of whom especiall memory is made among Christians at this day.

What say ye of our Courtezan? Whom God (by his especiall grace) having not given the gift, to bee the fairest of all other: howe daily they cease not to invent, newe and strange manners of paintinges, to counterfeit and disguise their age and first naturall shape: with false haires, Spanish white, *Pomades*, *Targon*, distilled waters, braied drugs, Oyles, Powders, and others follies too long to be recounted. Oftentimes they shave or burne their artificiall haire, and then againe, rub slick, chase and washe themselves, only to seeme faire: yet nothwithstanding, looke on them at night or in the morning, and ye shall finde them more deformed than before: but what ensueth soone after uppon this goodly industry? Sinne, Death, and the anger of God.

Now then, desire this feigned faire beawty whoe will, and such as best thinke themselves worth of it: for I hold most firmely, that it is better to hate & flie it, then to wish or affect it, seeing nothing procedeth thereof, but pride, over-weening and vaine-glorie, as also the most mishapen horned creatures of the world. Never was I of any other minde, since the time I had power of reason, to discerne and knowe truth from falshood, but that deformed people deserved more praise then the beawtifull, not is it without cause, or disagreeing with best sense, considering such as are hard favoured, are commonly chast, humble, ingenious, holy, and have ever some sweete appearance of most commendable grace.

But for them that boast of beautie, I leave to you the consideration of their behaviour, which is often times so counterfeit, as nothing can be saide to agree lesse with nature. You shall see them of lofty countenance, inconstant demeanour, wandring lookes, bold pace, and like language: nowe judge at your pleasure what ye conceive of them. Conclude then will I, that it is much better to be fowle than farie, & let no adversary party intrude himselfe to replie against my speeches, for I am both stoutlie determined, and sufficientlie furnished, to make him answer.

Had I no more but the testimony of *Theophrastus*, who hath left us in writing; that bodily beawty is nothing else but secret deceit: And he that will not heere with content himselfe, to him let me produce the advice of *Theocritus:* that beawty is an unknown detriment.

Shall we then be so unwise and sottish, that (even at the first sight) we will pursue our owne evils and misfortunes: more easilie embracing most perillous and damageable beawtie, then defomitie ten times more availing and profitable? Would God that foolish minde might not abide in any one, but rather, that we all would hate what is so unfit for us, & from which commeth no goodness of felicitie.

III

FOR THE IGNORANT.

DECLAMATION, 3
THAT IGNORANCE IS BETTER THAN KNOWLEDGE.

The more I thinke heeron, the more I resolve and rest in this opinion, that it is better to have no knowledge in letters, then to be expert of skilfull therein: considering, that such as have consumed the more part of their age in the study of sciences, have in the ende repented themselves thereof, and have oftentimes found very evill sucesse thereby.

Valerius the great, writing of *Cicero* (who by good right deserved to be called, not only the father of eloquence, but even the fountaine of all excellent lerning) saith, that in his latter years, he conceived such an hatred against letters, as if they had beene the cause of his so many greefes and travailes. The Emperour *Licinius, Valentinianus, Heraclides, Licianus* and *Philonides* of *Malta*, have openlie tearmed the skill in letters; sometime to be a publique plague, & that from great experience, esueth (oftentimes) the greatest daunger. Likewise it is certaine, that all heresies, as well ancient as moderne, came from men of knowledge: & cotrariwise, that in people esteemed idiots, or men of little knowledge, have beene visually noted express signes of vertuous workes and good examples.

I highly commend the order among the *Lucanes*, that no one professing capacity of letters, or esteemed learned, may obtaine any office, or sit as a Magistrate in their parlement: for they stande in feare, least these lettered men (by their great knowledge, which makes them presume so much on their persons) should trouble the good order and tranquillity of their common wealth. Nor may this be reckoned but to very good purpose, if we would well consider their insolencie, who under shaddow of probation in a colledge, would have every one stand bounden on beholding to them, and thinke under colour of their faire allegations, with interpretations (God wots) crooked enough sometime, to overthrow the best natural sense in the worlde, and they of dutie ought to be above all only heard, and listened to. Some of them there be, that (like *Mydas*) confound in their obstinate opinions and stiffe-necked conceits, all things whatsoever they take in hand.

I cannot imagine, to what ende are available these men so highly learned, who (in honor of their followers) are called fine, polished, curious and ingenious wits. For if they might serve to governe any publique cause; how many nations are seene, without the knowledge of lawes imperiall, or of Stoical, or Peripapetical philosophy, so to governe & entertaine themselves, that they out-goe al auncient Common weales.

To think that they may serve for the art military, I dare boldly witnesse thus much unto ye, that I have knowne more then one or two Gentlemen, and captains wel lettered, who (by the helpe of their books) have laboured and busied themselves, to point out a field, levy an armie, put men in arraie, and furnishe their squadrons; which practise never returned them any honor. For in truth in matter of warre, we daily behold to happen incident novelties, and unaccustomed strategems, which never before were registred, or put in use, by the very skilfullest writers in times past. Howe can wee then with reason affirme, the bookes of *Frontinus* or *Vegetius*, to be profitable for the art of warre? In my conceit, the good judgment of a Captaine, joyned with his long use and experience in these matters; is sufficient enough for him without troubling him to turne over bookes of the Art militarie.

That these lettered people are meet to guide a house, or governe a household (which the Philosphers called *Oeconomia*) howe can I agree thereto? When at this day is to be noted, both heere and elsewhere; how many good and honest mothers of families, who never in their lives studied in any Universitie, yet both have and doe well order their houses, & guide their household? Yea, above one or two hundred women for example, whoe (no displeasure of *Aristotle* or *Xenophon*) may learnedly reade them a Lecture, and turne them confusedly out of theyr houshold catalogue: so good and right a course doe they carry in these causes. And I doe not doubt, but it those Philosphers or Oeconomikes of times past, were at this daie present to see, how these huswives governe and content each one: themselves would avouch, that they might learne of them new precepts & instructions, that better would become their faire bookes and volumes.

May it please ye that I shew ye, how these expert fellowes in letters, even as by another *Cyres*, are transformed, and deprived of the greater part of their naturall power? Finde me out a yong man, lustie and bravely disposed of person, affable, endued and garnished with all such things, as are best beseeming his age: let him follow the studie of letters, ye shall find him in short time unlusty, sottish, unapt to al things, and as little while (for conference) can he tarry from his booke, as can the fish out of the water.

I pray ye note the lookes of poore Students, how sad they are, melancholy, grim, dreadfull, languishing, humorous and heavie, in breefe, the very neerest portrait to a deadly counterfeit, or a long dried anatomie. And as for their complexions, they are the hardest in choise that can bee amongst men: ever they are suspitious of some evill, so bad they are themselves, proud, presumptuous, despising all honest companies, mortall enimies to the so noble & inventions. Which Saint *Paule* divinely foreseeing, admonished us, not to be wise, but soberly minded: fearing, least by overplunging our selves in the depth of human doctrines, we should fall into farre greater perils & dangers: therefore he counsels us, not to seeke after high and difficult matters, but to abide in feare, without passing the bounds of obedience.

Likewise, did not he shew himselfe, to have lefte and despised all litterature and worldly knowledge, after hee had gotten the true knowledge of GOD, when he said: nothing was more to be desired, then well to know his maister crucified? That he was not come to preach, garnished with humane wisdome, or rhethoricall cunning? And that the wisdome of this world, was nothing else but follie before God? And that it did nothing else but puffe uppe the heartes of men? And that whosoever sought after things over high, should finde themselves shut quite out of glorie? And these words agree with the saying of Ecclesiasticus: that wee should seeke after nothing, which surmounteth the capacity of our spirit. To prove the same, hath not God menaced by the mouth of his Prophet, to destroy the wisedome of the wife, and to reprove the prudence of the skilfull?

What shall let me from beleeving, that the wisedome of this world, was the invention of the enimy, whom our elders called *Damon*: seeing the word *Damon*, signifieth wise and learned? This was hee that promised to poore *Adam* (so easie to be deceived,) the knowledge of good and evill, if he woulde but taste of the fruit which God had forbidden him. *Plato* rehearseth to this purpose, that an evill spirit named *Theudas*, was the first inventer of Sciences: & hence it followeth as I thinke) that we see so few learned men, but some of them are wicked, seditious, envying the glory one of another, lurking deceivers, and cruell revengers: which though it be not doone by armed in field like men, yet have they the meanes of performing the same, in Comedies, beastly Satyres, too sharpe and biting verses, cruell Iambicks, & furious Epigrames.

I woulde willinglie demaund of such, as make doubt of the disprofit and slender value of letters: if they were of such price and esteeme as they make them to be; our great Lords, who are (as every one perceiveth) very curious of the most faire and pretious things in the worlde: woulde they endure such dearth in their houses? Why doth not learning make them so rich & magnificent, as other temporal goods doe? And were it so greatly profitable for youth, as also such an honest recreation for age: I am ashamed to see, that in our great Citties and Townes, the professors therof goe from house to house, like such as begge bread with empty wallets. For in truth this is the end of letters followers and favourers, in these unahappy and accursed times: not onley to bee beggers, but (beyond al other) to be most miserable and male-content. That this is true, doe but note the very first figure, character, or letter, which wee teach our children in their infancie: it is not the Crosse? Beginning with all povertie, going on with anguishe, trouble and greefe, and ending with like dolorous death?

For example, see what was the end of *Socrates* & *Anaxgoras* as: who by sentence and decree of the Senate of their countreys, were both miserablie poisoned. *Thales* likewise, who died with thirst. *Zeno*, who was slaine by commandement of the Tyrant *Phalais*. *Anaxrchus*, who was detestably murdered by the commandement of *Nicocreon*. The great Philosopher, and most singular Mathemtician *Archmidis*, who was slaine by the souldiers of *Marcellus*. And *Pythagoras* likewise, whoe was slaine in companie of three score of his Schollers.

Thinke on the glorious recompence, made to the Philosopher *Plato*; when after his long travaile for the cause publike, he was (in the end) sold as a slave by *Dionisius* the Tyrant. *Anacharsis* died suddenlie. *Diodorus* died in despight, because he coulde not resolve a question which was proposed to him by the Philosopher *Stilpo*. *Aristotle*, when he saw himselfe out of credit with *Alexander*, he drowned himselfe in *Chalcide* in the river *Eupyrus*: and *Calisthenes* his scholar was cast forth of the windowes. *Cicero* had his hed and handes cut off, and his toong pulled out: having been before banished from *Rome*, where he sawe his house ruined, his so deerly beloved daughter ded before his face, and his wife in the armes of his utter adversary. *Seneca* died a violent and outragious death. *Averroes* the great commentator of *Aristotle*, was broken with a wheele that passed over his bodie. *Johannes Scotus*, making his Lecture in England, was stabbed to death by his schollers, with their penknives.

But leaving these auncient matters, and to speake of them of our time: let us consider the death of *Hermolaus Barbarus*, who was banished from the Signorie of *Venice*, because without the consent of them, he had accepted the Patriarches authority of *Aquilea*, he died by a cole, that tooke holde under one of his toes. *Domitius Calderinus* died also of the plague.

The learned counceller or peace-maker, was burned after he was dead, because they coulde not catch him in his life time. *Angelus Politianus* ended his daies, beating his head against the walles. *Savanarola* was burned at *Florence*, by the commandment of Pope *Alexander*. *Peter Lion* of *Spoleta*, was throwne into a well. *Johannes Tisfierus*, died in an hospitall. *Erasmus* in exile. The French Poet in like manner, by the miserable and implacable sute of the court, even in his oldest yeares. The Lord *John Fraunces Pica Mirandola*, was slaine by the people of his owne countrey. If I would stand to number all, I should undertake one of *Hercules* labours: specially, to recite the misery of them, that have beene, and even nowe are (to theyr paine) glad to go seeke their fortune, onely through the cause of learning.

Wherefore is it, that a Cooke, a Horse-keeper, a Gardener or a Peazant, shal be received more honorablie, and better provided for in the Courts of princes and great Lordes, then shall a man of great wisdome? It is because they receive more profit by such fellowes, then they do by curious students or labourers in letters: the countenance and slender service of whom, makes them in the Court so little regarded, as they are but mocked at for every worde, so that if any one of them thinke to advance himselfe in company, by pronouncing three poore words of latine: hardly can he have opened his mouth, but one is ready to cal him maister of the Towne, or School-maister of the Colledge, which are wordes of no more regard (by the report of themselves that utter them) then if one should call him poore and miserable wretch: for that is understood, without the speaking, as under the name of an unthankefull man, are comprehended all the faults that may be alleaged against him.

Did not one make a law, that whosoever shoulde speake of letters, shoulde be greevously punished and corrected? And hee that shoulde touch a booke, of what science soever, shoulde have his handes either burnt or cut off: with perticuler forbiddings to every one (under paine of hanging) no more to use paper, inke, pennes, or inke-hornes, with utter abolishing of the artes of impression, cutting, graving, or other kind of stamp, in what manner soever it should be: to the end, that learning being (by this edict) driven forth of the sight and beholding of men, by the same meanes might be prevented the unhappinesse, that from thence dailye ensueth: aswell through the greevous afflictions, that learninges followers suffer in themselves, as also in respect of the great daunger and losse in those places, where the Academies are assembled of learnings schollers.

Better it is then to be ignorant then skilfull, better to hate letters, then so deerely to cherishe and love them. Moreover, our poore ignorant people, shew not themselves astonied or confounded, of whome (God be praised) I see a sufficient competent number, and as it were infinite: but they rejoice and thanke God in their harts, for the great Fortune happening to them, by reason of their ignorance. For they remember, that when good *Socrates* was judged generally, and held by the Oracle to be wise: then him-selfe openly manifested to every one, that it was because he knewe nothing. Likewise, they forget not the goodly proverbe of Saint *Augustine*: that the simple are lifted on high, and rejoice the heavens: but the learned, with their curious lessons and sciences, shall be overthrowne. Lastly they call to mind, that which was so highly said, and reprooved to S. *Paule* by *Festus* the judge: that the multitude of Sciences, and deepe knowledge in thinges, oftentimes puts a man beside himselfe, and carrieth him quite from all good sense.

IV

FOR BLINDNESSE.
DECLAMATION, 4
THAT IT IS BETTER TO BE BLINDE, THEN TO SEE CLEERELY.

If we would in breefe, compare the commodities of sight, with the great hurts it brings to men: we should finde on the one side, all voluptuous delights and pleasures, which daily ende in bitterness, alienation of sense, provocation to envie, irritation and commotion against the heart: and on the other side we should beholde, the strength of spirit, better imagination, and contemplation of things high and heavenly, with perfection of memorie, which more excellently shewes it selfe to the blinde, then to the cleerest sighed: because that their light (which is the force of mans understanding) is neither heere or there disorderly transported.

Now, that memorie is the most noble part of the hart, it is sufficiently made plaine unto us, by the Testimony of *Cicero* in his Orator, where hee calleth it the treasure of wisedome. Also by the honour the Greeks have doone thereto, in naming it the mother of sapience. Beside this, that so many other persons, knowing themselves to be deprived of naturall memorie; in regard of the estimation they made therof: invented another, called artificiall, with very delicate and pretious oyles, sundry emplaisters, sirrops and drugs, fetcht from very farre countries.

That the blinde are of farre better apprehension and imagination, then the sharpest sighted: it is too evident unto us, if we woulde consider, that the powers of the soule are in them more equallye assembled: withall, that they have this speciall prerogative, of not beholding so many deformed and dishonest actions, which are daily to be seen in this world, whereby their spirit might be alienated or turned, from contemplation of high and heavenly matters.

First of all, when a blinde man is led by his little lad along the streets, he is free from beholding a multitude of counterfeited monsters: people but halfe made by nature, a thousand toyes on their heades, their bellies al buttons, holding uppe their noses and chins like puppets; with other such like vaine heads, so mishapen and deformed, as *Octavianus Augustus* would call, the very iestes and mockeries of Nature. He is free from seeing so many troubled with palsies, leprosies, dropsies, goutes, falling evilles, impotent with botches, biles, scabs, blaines scurffes, and such like.

What shal I say of the graces, that blindnes brings to her children? not suffering them to taste one only greefe or molestation: but gives them leisure and commodite of power (at their owne ease,) to contemplate celestiall beawties and excellences divine. Heereof was the Philosopher *Democritus* so zealous that he made himselfe blinde, regarding firmelye and stedfastlie the sun: that by the losse of his bodily eies, he might recover better use of the eies of the minde, and with more ease contemplate supernatural things, which otherwise he coulde not so well intend, when he used the obiects of this world, which alwaies constrained him to continuall laughter.

Homer, as blinde as he was, was accounted & held to be the most famous & excellent Poet in all *Greece.* Blindnesse never hindered *Dydimus Alexandrinus,* but that most elegantly he attained the Greeke & Latin languages: and which is more, (a thing perhaps incredible) he became very excellent in the mathematicall sciences. Blindnes did no waie impeache *Claudius Appius* (though he was very olde & weak), but he was daily seene in councell with the Senate of Rome: where most prudentlie hee deliberated on the affaires publique, and governed (beside) with great honour, a mightly and innumerable family. To be blinde no way offended *Lipius,* albeit hee was a most perfect Oratour. What was it the worse for *Hanibal,* that he had lost one of his eyes? did he therby loose one jot of courage, but pursued the more furiously upon the *Romaines*? perswade your selves, that if he had lost both his eyes, he woulde have been a much more valiant Captaine. See if olde *Tobias* (after he became blind) did feare of love God ever a jot the lesse, then he did before.

It was my chance one day to reason and conferre privately, with certaine of mine acquaintance that were blind, and I remember, that one among the rest, who sometime had beene a dealer in merchandise, sware and avouched faithfully unto mee: that his blindnesse did no waie grieve or offend him, but hee the more highly thanked God therefore. Because (quoth he) my sight being taken away; I have likewise lost the offence of spirit, whereinto I was drawn in divers places I frequented. And he justified, that since this good fortune befell him, he travailed about his affaires into *Spaine*: where he found himself highly contented, that he could not see the great vaunting Spaniard, nor so manye Gentlemen by the dozens, that for five shillings of yeerely rent, cause themselves to be entituled, my Lord such a one, or must be named Knights at the least.

Another tolde me, that he caused himselfe to bee led into *Germanie*, about certaine businesse hee had with the *Foulcres*: but never did he esteeme himselfe so happy, as that he could not behold the manifolde discords among the Lords of the Countrey, so many devisions, so many garrisons of Spaniards, with so many new imperiall cuts.

A third man told me, that he had beene in *France* about traffique of merchandise, where he not a little rejoysed, that he could not behold the infinite pleaders, a *Hydra* of suites and quarrels, the number-lesse throng of catchers and purloiners of benefices, a word of false accusers and masqued people, chaunging as often in opinions, as they doe in habites and attyre. Then breaking forth into a great laughter, if (quoth he) I should heereafter passe into divers places of *Italie*, where I have accustomablie haunted heeretofore: first of all, I shall no more see in *Romania* and *Lombardy*, so many partialities of *Guelfs* & *Gibelines*, so many faire buildings ruined, so many bewtifull and goodly Citties destroied by factions. I shal no more see the grosse feeding *Millanois*, the avaritious *Panoyan*, the mutinous *Playsencian*, the fanaticall *Parmesan*, the gracelesse *Cremonian*, the slothful *Mantuan*, nor the proud *Ferraran*. I shall see no more the prating *Florentine*, the dissembling *Bolognian*, the glorious *Lucane*, the usuring *Geneway*, nor the boasting *Modenan*.

And continuing his speech, he said to mee beside, that he imagined himselfe most happy, that the yeer past hee had not beene at *Rome,* no more to note the excessive pompe of infinite curtezans, who clad and decked in the habilements of Queenes, triumph on the patrimony of the poore fisher. Likewise no more to behold in *Naples*, the troopes of Moores, the bands of Ruffians, bawds and brothels: the great number of knights of the broch, [sic.] who al day doe nothing else, but walke with their noses uppe in the wind like Plovers, as well in the fieldes as the Cittye, with white wands in their hands, so expecting their Fortune, to the great detriment of their followers. Nor likewise to see in *Sicilie*, those great managers of iron-wheeled Chariots: who at the least word offered them, will counterfeit the countenance of another chollericke God *Mars*, as if they would fight with the sea & the fishes. Nor also to see so many fine dames, ready to be bought for a little, to passe the time awaye with Gentlemen.

In briefe, this good blinde man told me so much, and so sweetly lulled me asleep with his words, as he well-neere made me of the minde, to plucke foorth mine owne eies: for the greefe I have to behold in *Venice*, such a crowde of nice darlings: in *Padua*, such indiscreet lookes: in *Vincen-*

za, such beast-like demeanour: in *Treviso*, such disordered libertie: at *Verona*, such frantike fury; at *Brescia,* such miserable avarice; at *Bergamo*, such scrupulous countenances, with sundry such like qualities in other places.

Of force then must they that are cleere sighted, behold such things, as would enforce stones to starte out of the walles, by the great despight and greefe they bring to men. In witnesse of the holye man, who being newly become blinde, by chance happened to meet on the way, with *Arrius* the father of heretiques: and hearing among other talke, that *Arrius* greeved for the accident befalne the good man, the blinde father thus answered. That it was needelesse for him to greeve so much, because (quoth hee) for this blindnesse I highly thanke my God: were it not in any other respect, but only that I may not see thee, that arte suche a wicked enimie to God. Saide not good *Job*, that hee had made this covenant with his eyes, that they should content themselves with looking uppon one onely woman, and not to gaze after any other?

Hence it is, that the Prophet complained so much, that his eies robbed from beasts, saying: death entered into his heart by the windowes of the body, which are the eies, serving to overthrow mans understanding, whereto suddenly they represent and deliver (without finding any hidden ambush) all that they see and perceive abroad. And when they looke to vanity, listen what the gentle Poet saith: So soone as I had seene, I was lost.

How happened it to the holy Psalmist, when by the very seeing of *Berseba:* he was so overcome with burning and lascivious regarding her, as he wanted not much of incurring the daunger of death? The Evangelist exhorteth us, to plucke forth our eyes, if they doe scandalize or offend us: and when is it that they doe not both these to us?

If I would seeke further for the benefites of the blinde, I should finde an infinite number. First, they have no need of spectacles, wherewith to see small thinges, nor of eye glasses, otherwise called Bernacles, when they travell in windie weather. In Winter they need not feare, that the over-much whitenes of the snow, will hurt or offende their sight. They are free from subiection to eie medicines, which they have need to practise, that are subiect to the eyes inflamation, to the dilating or inlarging the apple of the eie: to helpe the disease called *Scotomie*; or when all things in view seeme to be rounde: for illusions: the eye-gellie: the web, pearle, teares fistula, rheume, bleared eies, and other such like diseases. They have no need to distill the waters of Fennell, Sage, Vervaine, or Eye-bright. They need no Aloes infused in wine, or prepared Tuthie, the whites of egges beaten in rose water, nor pilles for the sight.

Wherefore I conclude, that it is better to be blind, then to see never so well: because the blind sees nothing that afflicts or torments them; where contrariwise, the best sighted have ten thousand obiects, that molest and offendes them without pardon: which doth purchase to them so many anguishes, & brings them into such dangerous extreames, as they cannot well tell how to recover themselves againe.

How much thinke ye will it displease a poore pilgrime, when he shall see in travailing on his journey, a great many hideous horrible serpents, creeping vipers, and such like beastes? When he shall see under him quick-sandes, quag-mires, downe-fallings, and most fearefull deepe places? When he shall meete to beard him, his most mortall enemie? When he shall see himselfe mocked, scorned and railed at, with all unseemely gestures both of mouth and hands? Poor eies, of howe many evils are ye the cause, through your owne curiositie? How many follies does ye deliver to the most milde and simple spirit, only to troble the gratious rest thereof? What letters written, or what wordes engraven, are by yee represented to the poore hart, to fill him full of all bitternesse? Howe many gests and motions does yee shew to the natural sense, which soone after are the cause, that man liveth in no quiet in his conscience? How many dissimulations do ye note, aswell in the Court, as elsewhere, under a counterfeit smile, with a calfe-like made courtesie, an Italian reverence, a Judas-like kisse and embracing, and a bare voice offering service? Do ye not then account them happy, that have beleeved, and never seene any of these things? Upon these speeches and reasons, produced on my behalfe, I leave ye Getlemen to set downe such judgement, as to you shall seeme best: assuring my selfe very confidently, that after all considerations, ye will not diminish any part of my due right or equity.

V

FOR THE FOOLE.

DECLAMATION, 5
THAT IT IS BETTER TO BE A FOOLE, THAN WISE.

Albeit the like matter which I am now to prove and defende, hath beene already by two excellent men, delivered in this honourable assemblie, and by them deliberated on to their advantage: It may please ye yet not to thinke it strange, if in regarde of the occasion, which this day offers it selfe, I come as now to gleane and gather after them gone before, if so be I can finde any thinge by them left or omitted, either as unadvisedlie, or else if perhaps they had not prooves sufficient readie at hand to exchange in the cause.

For the firste advertisement, I will use the advise and opinion of the auncient Philosophers, which was, that to live securely in this world, they thought it best to use the counterfeit shadowe of a foole: and they saide, that even as he who hath some meane to counterfeit well a Prince, Lorde or Gentleman, can doe no lesse for the whyle but enter into the same travaile, solicitude, cares, paines and greefes, as the person he imitates is subject unto: so hee that in this world, will sometimes cunningly disguise himselfe with the masque of folly, as one may perceive nothing else by him, but even natural foolery: (cannot in so dooing) but participate with the happy partes and conditions of a foole, which are of such sort, as the very richest and best pleased in this worlde, are not in any thing like, or to be compared to them.

Witnesse a brave Gentleman, a younger brother, who by mishap, that his elder brother woulde not impart livings reasonably with him, became a foole: during which Fortune, he had this imagination, that all the ships which daily arrived in the Port of *Diepe*, were his owne. By meanes of which perswasion, so soone as he understoode of their coming thither, he would walke before them a mile and more on the land, using such kinde and cheerefull gestures to them, as by his words he seemed to thinke and assure himselfe, that all the marchandize on boorde in the Haven, apper-tained to himselfe. The like woulde hee doe, when any ships departed thence to Sea, eyther for *Flaunders*, *Spaine*, *Portugall*, *England*, or any other countrey: he would vaile his bonnet to them a farre of, recommending them to God, wishing them faire winde, a good voiage, and a speedy re-turne. His evill hap at length was such, that his brother (in this time of folly) returning from the warres at *Bologna*, and seeing his brother come thus before him, with such new manner of salutations: greeving (as I thinke) at this happy state of life, hee delivered him into the handes of the most skilfull Physitians he coulde finde in the countrey, by whose in-dustrie, the happy foole returned to his former disposition of good sense: which made him afterward offended with his brother, because he had de-prived him of so great recreation of sprit, which he confessed he received in his pleasing folly: whereof he yet having some small remembrance, affir-meth, that never before, or since that time, he lived more joyfully, nor bet-ter agreeing with his owne mind.

In like manner, is it not a thing highly to be commended, to see a man of meane and base condition, among the inferiour and abiect sorte of peo-ple, by vertue of this brave kind of folly, to enter into such an humour; as to weene himselfe to be a Pope, an Emperour, a King, a Duke, or some great Prince or Lord? And withal, to feele in his heart, the self-same affec-tions and contentment of mind, as accustomablie are felt by such, as truly are constituted in those high dignities?

Hereof may beare record the Lackey of a Gentleman of *Anjou*, who by the aide and comfort of his fortunate folly, imprinted in his minde the pon-tifical dignitie: for the administration wherof, at a certain hower of the day, which he had obtained by licence of his maister, he would locke himselfe apart into a chamber, with his confederates and instructed companions, who notwithstanding they mocked him, yet took great pleasure therein: and there, (after his owne mind) would he appoint a Consistorie, (lyke unto little children, that in their pastimes doe counterfeit the actions of the very greatest personages,) dispatch Bulles, give benefices, create Cardinals, send embassades, in briefe, he would doe al that he imagined beseemed a Pope: and when the houre was expired, he would returne to his wonted service.

Thinke ye that he which walked thorow *Paris*, & notwithstanding he was all dirtie bedagled, yet supposing himselfe to be a Cardinall or Legate, deserved no esteeme in his owne conceit? Hee that named himselfe to be a Prophet? He that preached & wrote himselfe the father of *Caine*? He that saide he was of the lynage of *Zabulon*? And another, who with his Scepter & Crowne of gold glistering, thought himselfe to be an Emperour? Thinke ye not (I say) that such as these are highly contented in minde, & more (perhaps) then if they were such as they ween themselves to be? What thinke ye of *Villemanoche,* whoe expected the kings daughter in marriage, and would complaine in all companies where hee came, what wrong was doone hin, in that they delaied his marriage so long? Deeme yee not such fooles have as much, or rather more pleasure in these imaginations, then such as rightlye are placed in those dignities? They have as much by these meanes, in that they partake not in the molestations, which ofte are found in the high estates of great personages, being not trobled with governing the traine belonging to theyr huge houses.

I cannot well conceive the cause, why some are so suddenly waspishe, when they are called fooles: it may be said, that they forget the number hath beene alwaies infinite, wherby some have dared to affirme, that this worlde is a very Cage or mine of such people. And if all they which holde of that race, would suffer themselves, to be written in the rowle or paper belonging to the Princes of fooles, of bee registred in the Abbey of these happy people: there should not neede so much strife and lawe, for calling one another sot or foole.

For in sooth, it is a name that may beseeme the very greatest and wisest in the worlde: yea, were it to the great king *Salomon,* who albeit he only among the Hebrewes bare the title of wise: yet beside that, hee well deserved the name of a foole, when he sacrifised to Idols, and entertained so long such a great number of Concubines. Also, of this name were capeable the seven Sages, whom ambitious and lying Greece vaunted to bring forth and nourish: their actions and behavior *Cicero* affirmeth, that whosoever will lightly runne over and cull them out, shall finde them to be more full of follie then wit.

How many have beene seene since the Creation of the worlde, that have escaped infinite daungers, only by counterfeiting folly? What might they more have doone, if they had beene fooles indeed, when the only shaddowe was to them the cause of such good? How many have we knowne and heard of, that have beene absolved of theftes, murders and other misdeeds, by supposition that they indeed were fooles? Thinke yee that heaven dooth customablye give, so faire and excellent priviledges to others, as to people divine and celestiall?

The further I wade in contemplation of follie, the more pleasing I finde it, and garnished with all faire commodities. See how a foole troubles himselfe with a kingdomes affaires, or fortifying of a Cittye. See what paine he puts himselfe to, in governing an housholde, or pertaking with one Prince or other: yet notwithstanding, we see such as are esteemed the wisest, to injury themselves heereby, and wexe very olde with such molestations of the minde. May it please ye to understand the difference, which I finde betweene the foole and wise man? Regard the passions and affections in them both. First of all the foole is not anything curious in his meate or drinke, neyther cares for fine decking and clothing himselfe: they whom we call wise, never have enough, and never are satisfied with the goods of this world: neither can all humane industry, or the very goddesse aboudance with hir great Cornet, suffice their insatiable desires.

Now judge hereby, which of these two come neerest the observation of Gods commandement: who forbiddeth us in his Gospell, not to be carefull for our food or raiment. Beside, the foole makes no esteeme of honours and worldly dignities: he condemns great preheminences, refusing the places and feates honourable in magnificent companies. Contrariwise, they that holde themselves so wise, seeke nothing at this day but worldly honour. And to attaine superiour dignities, they feare not to endure heat or cold, they forget the discommoditie of great travaile, as also losse of rest by day and night, to the hazard oftentimes of their lives so deerely beloved, and by them held in such pretious account.

The foole feeles not himselfe provoked with so many pricks of Fortune: he meddles not with fights or combats: he hath no Lawe-pleadings, nor quarrels, wherby to get or defend his goods: he hath not such paine in attending on the Court as others have, to be entertained by one or other: he yeelds not him self (for the miserable requital of two or three crowns) a buckler to ten thousand bullets of shot, musquets or harguebuzers: he breaks not his neck in riding post after offices, benefices or confiscations: he languishes not in pursuing the love or favour of Ladies: he paies no taxe or tribute: lastly, he is not subiect to any one, but liveth in perfect franchise and liberty. He is permitted and licensed, to speake what himselfe thinks good, touching the dealings of Princes & private persons, without encurring thereby any danger of imprisonment or corporall punishment. He hath no need of Rhetoricall cunning, to make him selfe attentively listened unto; but bestowes on each one the joyous pastimes of his meriments.

I stand in need of a whole source of eloquence, wherewith I might thorowlie paint foorth and discipher, the honest vertues of most pretious follie: the contrary whereof, hath beene cause of the punishing of an hundred thousand injuries, and of overthrowing the intelligence and actions of many great personages. I find, that Fortune hath evermore beene very carefull, in bestowing perticular aide upon fooles, and defended them (as her most deere children) fro infinite perils and dangers.

Likewise wee see by experience, that the greater part of fooles live longer and more happily, then the wise doe. Wherefore should we thinke this to be so: but because they give not themselves to any melancholie, never meddle with Lawe-causes, debates or quarrels, neither mollest themselves with matters publique or private? Which makes me say and affirm unto ye, that folly (even as Poesie) is somewhat celestiall, and filleth the hartes of her children, with a certaine spirite of prophesie and divine furie: by meanes, they seeme agreeable to every one, and purchase very great esteeme and favour in the eies of Princes.

You shall finde by experience, that many great & wealthy Lords, turne their faces from company and conference with wise men, yea, such as are saide to have the greatest learning: that they may intertaine pleasure with a foole, and commune familiarlie with him: yea, sometimes they will leave their best and most auncient servantes or favorites, to delight and bestow countenance on the first foole that comes before them.

Is it not marvellous, that we shall never see a man of great knowledge indeede: but hath some part of this pretious folly in him? Though ye woulde produce never so many learned men, or of what profession else so ever ye please: be they Philosophers, Orators, Painters, Statuaries, Musitians, Builders, yet they have some taste heereof, and generally all people of learning whatsoever. Where shall yee finde one singular Poet at this day, that doth not participate in this folly? Every one knoweth, that the Poet deepest skild therein, is accounted most excellent. And if the greate Philosopher *Plato* had not had, more then a reasonable portion of this divine folly; thinke yee that he had delivered so many faire & excellent matters, which we have at this day after his maner? And yet you are ashamed, to be accounted or called fools.

The inventer of the Italian Cardes, whereat they have a play or pastime called *Tarault*, did (in my conceit) very ingeniouslie, when he put the *Deniers* or monyes, and *Bastons* or clubs in combate togither, as the very encountring of force and justice. But yet he deserved more praise, for giving (in this play) the most honourable place to the foole: as we do to the Ace, which we should rather call *Nars*, that in dutch signifieth a Foole. This deviser well noted the great servitude, whereof they most commonly are subiect, that covet a place among the very wisest: for it behoves them to have so many discretions, so manye respects, so many considerations, (whewith the happie foole never troubleth himselfe;) so that they are constrained oftentimes, to submit themselves, and continue like counteneance, and daily (against theyr natures) to seeme grave and severe.

The Foole doth not repose any confidence in his owne wisedome, neither hath recourse to the subtletie and deceits of this world. He never rests himselfe on the support and favour of other, whereby anye harme may happen to him: for God hath him in his custodie and safegarde. Which is a worde, whereat (our *Catoes* at this day) will easily enter into choller. But they must lightly passe it over, and by constraint of verity confesse it true (if they will give but never so little regarde to the holy Scriptures) there they shall finde, that the wisedome of this world hath byn more sharpely taxed, and with more greevous arrests condemned, then folly, and yet our bold over-weeners, will goe contrary to this divine word: to take part with that, which God the Creator, not onelye hath reproved among men, but likewise greatly hateth.

I finde that the very greatest, and most renowned Nations in *Europe*, have (long while since) gotten some title or marke of folly. To beginne with the *Gaules*, did not Saint *Paule* call them foolish *Gallathians*? Albeit the prowesse and strength, which they have daily shewen in deedes of Armes: may sufficientlie testifie from East to West, yea, even to the *Antipodes*; at the ende and limits of which regions, hath their Ensignes beene most bravely displaied. The *Portugals* by their haughtie enterprise (who notwithstanding have been reputed foolish) passed so farre as the *Indiaes*: where with losse and damage of their men, they conquered many places in those Countryes, and got by these meanes, the commoditie to traffique with many places, before not inhabited.

This is it which makes them so proud in the trade of merchandise, and brag of the excellencie of their *Lishbone*, enritched with so faire a port of the sea, also two so wel proportioned mountaines, at the entrance, and the floud with golden sandes. As for the *Germaines*, it is well knowne that they have a large share heerein: especially they, who (in imitation of women or children,) so often change into many opinions, and maisters services. For this is may be saide, that *Caesar* in his Commentaries did them not so much honour, as to call them valiant champions, or prudent in affaires of warre.

If we will passe so farre as into *Italie*, we shall finde many goodly and noble Citties among the rest, that serve as great or very faire Cages, to fooles of all fashions, and that they are (in favour of such an esteemed matter) the most honourably situated in al the Countrey; and by the great number of fooles contained in them, they are divinely embellished and inritched, with the very cheefest excellencies, and noble privileges that can be desired. That this is true, let us consider the excellent situation of auncient *Sienna*, for the honest libertie wherof, the King (not many daies past) so earnestlie travailed. You shall there beholde, as a matter of antiquity (to preseve fooles in health) erected a pleasant & beautiful building, environed with the most sweet and gratious aire in the world, garnished with rich and honourable lodgings: villages neere hand of great receit, naturall Bathes very pure and healthfull. Moreover, as with men, so is it well furnished & adorned with Ladies gentle and courteous, young people so well disposed as may be, good musitians and Rhetoricians, as any cittie else thereabout: except the ancient Universitie adjoyning, and the newe Academie of the *Intronati,* who by the meanes of their so highlie favoured folly, do (in time of peace) thinges of incomparable pleasure and recreation.

What shall I say to ye of *Parma?* where to maintaine fooles in pastimes, is a very faire plaine of grasse, rounded & neighboured with many pleasant mountaines? How fertile is it likewise of noble and puissant families, and couragious souldiours; who by vertue of their singular follye, beeing afficted with the aide and succour of the French, are redoubted and feared of all their neighbour countries? I will hold my peace of the *Parmesane* cheese, whereof, notwithstanding that I have tasted, yet I cannot forbeare but say in my hart: that if for that meate our Father *Adam* had transgressed, in my conceit hee had beene somewhat excuseable, nor should I (after taste thereof) hath any desire to the *Nectar* and *Ambrosia* of great *Jupiter.*

O how they of *Verona, Brescia* and *Venice* were beholding to worthy folly, when they made answere to K. *Lewes* the twelfth, that they were wise inough: whereby they constrained him, to send them so many French-men as were accounted fooles, because their wisedome and magnificence, knew not how to resist th'others forse & prowesse. So were the fools of the saide king, Regentes and maisters over the wise *Venetians,* as before they had been over the *Genewaies* & *Millaineses*: & as long time before that, the fools that were led by the great French Captaine, were maisters over the mightly and wise *Romaines.*

Too long woulde the rehearsall be, of fooles and Arch fooles, that are to be found enclosed within the Cities of *Italie.* Wherefor to finishe this discourse, I will thus frame my conclusion, that fooles ought to be singularlie esteemed and commended: bicause God doth them so much favour, as he hath chosen (by them) to confound and overthrow the wisdome of this world: withall, that the most noble Cittes & puissant Nations, ought to be esteemed much more for folly, then wisdome.

VI

FOR HIM THAT HATH LOST HIS WORLDLY HONOURS AND *PREFERMENTS*.

Declamation, 6
That a man ought not to be greeved,
though he be despoiled of his goods and honours.

I am not a little abashed, for what cause the noble men of our time, make so much adoo, and moove such quarrell and contention, for the loose of their fraile and slippery estats; seeing it followeth upon necessitie, that one day they must needes be dispossessed and taken from them, if not by force, yet by the meanes of death, who, of his owne nature, imposeth an ende on all things. And I see no cause or reason, whey they (being subiect to so many humaine passions and fortunes, as even the very poorest & basest condition in the world) shoulde presume and hazard themselves, before so many persons, (of greater valour perhaps then themselves) for advancement and superiority, and yet they take scorn to be made of like mettall as they are, to whom by right of nature, they are altogither equall & semblable.

An excellent Philosopher, and of very great reputation in his time, maintained, that the rich hadde ever some occasion, to content with their riches and temporall goods, as also beautifull persons with their bodilie graces: But the greatest and most excellent contention, that men ought indeed to have among themselves, were to strive, who should surmount ech other in gentlenesse and honestie: and the very highest preheminence, that should bee sought for in this world, were to envie one another, who shoulde bee most liberall, courteous and affable.

For this cause, *Dioclesian* was praised & esteemed, among the wise men of his time, when by his modestie, he deigned to make refusall of the *Romai*n Empire, which then was farre greater and better provided, then ever it had beene before: in imitation of whom, many other great persons, have since beene moved to doe the like. Such an one was the Unckle to great king, *Charlemaine*, who became a Monke at *Mont Cassin*, where hee lived the remainder of his yeares, most holy and religiouslie: drawing (by his example) to the like, many Barons and great Lordes of the Realme of *France*.

Antiochus King of Syria, being by the *Romaines* deprived and deposed from the jurisdiction which he had by the mountaine *Taurus:* came and rendered sollemme thanks therefore to the Senate, commending them; because heereby he found himselfe well delivered and disburdened, of such a great & weightie molestation. *Heracleus* and *Galerian*, in like manner eased & discharged themselves, from the superioritie & rule they had over the people: & gave their delight altogither to the pleasure of husbandrie. And why hath not the like minde continued since then, in the harts of our Noble men to this instant? What mean our wise men, that they disswade not the fansies of great Lordes, from this endlesse heate and desire of rule; which bringeth nothing else therewith, but an over-fervent and ambitious will? That it is so, looke where such covetous and ambitious men beare sway: there is slender justice, the rich eate the poore, and the Nobles our-rage the Peasants.

The Inhabitants of the Isle *Taprobane*, hadde (in mine opinion) a very worthye and commendable custome, when they used to elect for their Prince and Governour, such an one among them; whom they had knowne and had proofe of a long time, to bee a true desirer of the profit of their weale publique: and him likewise, by right and semblable order, they would again deiect and depose, if by any meanes he swerved or changed from his right course. I have heard, that they of *Dace* and *Bohemia* went very neere this custome: but is came to passe, that since those times, they coulde not make choise of any better. I could wish, that such as deserve the governement of Signiories and common weales, shoulde be drawne and compelled thereto (as it were) perforce: and by the same meanes, the gate to be barred against covetousnesse, greedinesse, ambition, violence and deceipt.

But what makes me speake thus? Marie, because I have knowne in *Italie*, certaine Lordes & governors of the people, to lead their lives after a very strange course or manner, bearing capitall hatred to their poore subiects: Lords that have had no other care, but heere and there licentiouslie to revell, and dishonour the very honest maidens in their jurisdiction, drawing them violentlie (by meanes of certain ruffians, which they entertaine as hounds onely for this vile purpose) forth of the best houses in their townes and Cittyes.

Poore blinde men, destitute of naturall sense, is this the manner your elders taught ye, whereby to rule and guide your subiects? Was it thus, that the good Lordes of times past, the vertuous Princes, as well Ecclesiasticall as secular (whom *Homer* woulde so honourabley call, pastors of the people) were wont to doe? This so beast-like and dishonest custome, doth it any jote favour of true Christianity? They are no pastors that commit such insolencies: they are ravening wolves, and destroyers of all human societie.

Some are to be found in *Italie*, and else-where, to whom is publikely given this faire report, that they dilligently enquire after their people, not to chastise or reforme their vices and bad behavior: but contrariwise, to enquire secretlie, who amongst them hath the best pursse, and after knowledge thereof, seek some coverture to make them lose their goods: subborning false witnesses against them, who without any reason, shal enforme false plaints or quarrels against them: or else by greevous injuries and outrages, provoke them to undertakes Armes, where likewise, false villains (appointed for the nonce) taking some intended cause of offence, presently informe or complaine against them, and having seazed on their bodies, afterward (by these means) their riches comes into the Lordes hand, who (under coulour of justice,) causeth them to be condemned by Judges, in greevous paines and amercements: forgetting subtillie (yet with some colour of excuse) their goods, by way of confiscation. Crueltie well beseeming a Tragedie, and which (since the creation of the world) was never the like heard of.

A Baron of *Lombardie* one day made this brag, as for a greate proofe and example of his singular vertue & prowesse; that (not long before) he had gotten the spoile of one of his mightiest subiects, emptying his Garners, seazing on his goods perforce, proceeding even to the imprisonment of his body. The matter obiected against him, (by forged witnesses at the Lordes appointment,) was, that he had runne the Hare, and flowne the Partridge upon his land: albeit the poore honest Gentleman, was no more readie to chase a good piece of Beefe then Hares, and had never run (farre or neere) after strange beastes or birds. Yet notwithstanding this good deed, the honest minded Baron (which matter most of all displeaseth me) would make prosession of sanctitie, religion and devotion.

Lord God, that they patience is thus great, nor is it without great reason, that thou art called full of patience and longanimitie: seeing that so sweetly thou endurest the dealings, of these so cruel and insupportable monsters, brought forth & borne on the earth, only to confuse and devoure thy poore people. Assure ye, that I have seene in the kingdome of *Naples*, many monsters of this fashion and nature, having harts like Lions, and nailes like Griffons, to whome nothing seemed impossible, concerning inhumanity and impietie.

And with these few examples, I am constrained to content my selfe, without spending time to bring ye other proofes, for defence of this present occasion: because the greefe I both find and feele, in rehearsing these enormities, driveth me into overgreat affliction, making my hart so weake and feeble, as all the residue of my vitall powers want their helping use.

Now in truth let us thus reason a while. What is he who will denie, that such deedes and behaviour of life, is not sufficient to provoke the anger of God against us? And to cause, that those Lordes, through long space of time, that they have thus ruled & held their places, should in a moment be elsewhere transported? Thinke ye, if the very greatest Lordes, as wel spirituall as temporal, woulde at this daye doe their endevour, and employ themselves night and daye (as best beseemes them) to well governe and admonish their people: wee shoulde finde such a number of men, to covet and reach after kingdomes and Signjories, as now we doe? And such as are so mal-contet, to be deprived of their great charges and vextions, as now with greefe we may behold?

If is then (in conclusion) great folly in any Lord, to be displeased or offended at the losse of his honors and livings: but rather with such fortunes he ought to rejoice and be glad, as being (by so good occasion) discharged of a burden so greevous and heavy. For this is my opinion, that it were better for him to lose his worldly estate and dignitie, then himselfe to be thereby lost and destroied for ever.

VII

FOR DRINKERS.

DECLAMATION, 7
THAT DRUNKENNESSE IS BETTER THAN SOBRIETIE.

I did heeretofore (so breefely as I could) deliver unto ye, the great excellence and noble nature of wine: that I might afterward inferre, in what great honour & reputation he ought to bee, that especiallie loves it, and longest continueth in delight thereof. And albeit it seemeth to many, a verie hard and laborious enterprise, by reason of the abundance of good wordes and well convaied language: wherewith it is necessary they should bee thorowlie furnished in such a cause: yet neverthelesse, will I boldly deliver my opinion, though I am unfurnished of that divine furie, which ordinarilie worketh marvellous matters in our spirits; whereof (in this need) might I receive never so little favour, I should farre better satisfie your desires, that are bent with attention, to heare what I can say in this matter.

To proceed in our discourse, I finde that the great vertue and excellence of wine, hath beene of our elders so intirely known and approved: that the highly esteemed *Asclepiades* did it so much honour, as to couple the faculties and vertues thereof, with them of the very cheefest Gods. Which is agreeable with the consent of holy scripture, whereby was autenticallie pronounced, that wine was sent to men, as by the especiall grace and immortall gift of God, therewith oftentimes to refresh and recreate their spirites, over much weakened and travailed with long cares, which they suffer continuallie in this worlde. And heerewith altogither agreeth the opinion of good *Homer*, in many places of his divine Poesie. And whosoever shal require of me greater proofe & assurance, I pray them to consider, how that truth it selfe (which is the thing that hath, and yet at this day doth over-rule the greatest case in the world) from all antiquitie, holdeth principall consent with wine. This is it which made place for the auncient proverbe, knowne sufficiently of every one, that in *Wine is truth to be found*: wherein fooles, children and drunken men, are most accustomed to display it.

Wherefore I cannot sufficiently marvell, at the great fault of learned *Democritus*, who would sometimes maintaine, that truth lodged her selfe in the bottome of a well: this is greatly against the advise and opinion of all the Greeks, which evermore defended, that her lodging continually was in Wine. Whereto very well consenteth *Horace*, one of the most excellent Latine Poets: who so soundly confirmed this matter in his learned verses, made and composed by the helpe of this sweet liquor, wherewith his stomach so plentifully abounded, as hee coulde deliver it backe againe forth at his eies. To the same purpose, the great Philosopher *Plato* would proove and maintaine, that wine was a very firme and sure foundation of mens spirites: by the favour and vertue whereof, I may easilie coniecture, that he founde the invention of his goodly *Ideas*, of his numbers, and of his lawes so magnificent: also that with the aide of this sweet drinke, he spake so deepelie on the gratious argument of love, and likewise disposed his so well ordered Common-wealth. Withall, he defended, that the Muses flourished farre and neere, in the very smell of *Bacchus* liquor: and the Poet that drunke not profoundly therof, could frame no verse excellent, high-reaching, or of good measure.

But leaving verse and Poesie, let us come to the kind drinkers of cleere water: I would willingly demaund of them, what good they can receive in this world, by using such an unsavorie drinke? In the first place, how can a drinker of water well accomplishe householde dutie: when the naturall seede is more moist then anything else, and lesse strong for the procreation of children? Which is the cause such people are alwaies weake, feeble, sicke and colour-lesse. Likewise, ye never sawe a drinker of water, but was deprived of the true strength of all his members, and hardie courage of hart. He hath so little stomach, & so weake an appetite to digest his meates; as commonly his life is short, or else unhealthfull. For this cause it was, the Sainte *Paule*, knowing *Timothie* (albeit he was very yong, & in the strength of his age) to take delight in drinking nothing but water: admonished him, to use therewith a little wine, if it were but for the onely health of his stomach, and prevention of such diseases, whereto (by his complexion) he was overmuch subiect.

I await upon this point, the reply of some opiniative person, who will tell me, that such was not the advise of *Cistus Bullengerus*, nor yet of *Novellus Tricongius*, who dranke three measures of wine daily, called *Congii*, which contained three gallons and three pintes of our measure: for which the Emperour *Tiberius* promoted him to honour, and at the last made him Consull of *Rome*. I againe replie on the contrarie, that such was the opinion of the most wise and prudent king of all auncient memorie, who saide in his Proverbes, that wine comforteth and refresheth the hartes of men: like-wise, it is witnessed by the consent and testimonie of all Phisitians, as the most singular remedy to chase greefe from the mind of man.

But if peradventure, some misbeleeving humanist, will not give so much credit to the worde of so great a wise man, as to the precepts of auncient Phisitians: let him then consider and note well, what at this day is to be found written by *Hippocrates, Galen & Orbasus:* that wine serveth for a medicine to the cold and dulled sinewes; giveth comfort to the weary and travailed eies; bestoweth an appetite on the tast-lesse stomach; rejoyceth the sad and afflicted spirites; banisheth the imbecility of the members; gi-veth warmth to the body; provoketh urine, restraineth casting; moveth sleepe; taketh away ill digestion; consumeth moist humors; and makest a kindly consent in the bodie. *Galen* saith moreover, that wine greatly availeth against wearisome complexion of age; moveth the harts of men to force and prowesse; recreateth naturall heate; and giveth vigor to the spirits.

O how well did that good Lady *Hecuba* (of whom *Homer* speaketh so honourablie) knowe the pretious nature of wine: when (above all things) she exhorted her valiant sonne *Hector*, to cheere up and revive his mem-bers, wearied by continuall travaile he endured in Armes, with drinking of this divine liquor. The vertue whereof, learned *Pindarus* knew well en-ough, which made him a peerelesse hero call Poet: never could he have ac-complished his so highe and excellent Poeme, by the vertue and goodnes of water, but changing his stile, into the great praise & noble description of the vertue of wine: the chiefest & most notable men in the world, made likewise such price and estimation thereof, as the more part of the on his side, and marched under his Ensigne. For example, let us remember the holy man *Noah*, who first planted the vine, and the favour that hee bare to wine. Neither was it lesse loved by *Agamemnon, Marke Antonie, Lucius Cotta, Demetrius Tiberius* and their children, *Bonosus, Alcibiades, Homer, Ennius, Paccuoius, Cossus, Philip, Heraclides* and many other, who (for this cause) were never reputed the lesse wise or vertuous. And if we should need, to make a more ample discourse on this behalfe, by such nations as were addicted to this drinke: we shall finde, that the *Tartares* greatly subiected themselves thereto: and muche more the *Persians*, whose cus-tome was, to consult of their gravest and greatest matters of importance, amongst their cups and bottles of wine. And so were the *Germanes* wont to doe, according to *Tacitus* witnesseth, making the discription of their complexions. The *Macedonians* in like manner, were beyond all things else great lovers of wine: for whom, their Emperour *Alexander* instituted, the most brave fight of drinking with carowsing.

King *Mithridates* was greatly given to wine: and yet (for all that) ceased not to warre manfullle against the *Romaines*, for the space of forty yeares together. I am very sorie, that I want apte wordes, and tearmes worthye, whereby to expresse the singular vertue, which wine of itselfe bestoweth on the harts of men: I am well assured, that if I could recount them all unto yet, they would drive ye into no little marvell or admiration.

But say now in sooth, doth not wine deserve supreme praises, in making a sluggard or grosse conceited person, to become a sweet, pleasant and affable man. A Lourden or lobcock, to be a man apte and skilfull? Of a coward or faint harted craven, to make a man hardy, bold and couragious? Who (without this meane) should finde himselfe alone, and even starke naked, as it were, though he be engirt with a thousande other defences. Hath not *Greece* by the meanes of wine, wunne fame and honour thorow all *Europe*? And in like case *Bohemia* and *Germanie*? What shall I say of *Polonia*, and generally of all *Dalmatia*? What is spoken of *Italie*, I will referre my selfe to the report of *Plinie*, who writes, that drunkennesse raigned there in his time in such sort: as they would not only drinke themselves underfeet, but likewise compell heir horses and mares to drinke wine unmeasurably: so much was drunkennes (through all parts of the world) praised, celebrated, and helde in such account and esteeme, as he that would not be drunke, at the least once a moneth, was not reputed a friendly companion.

Young *Cyrus* would needes be accounted worthie to rule, because he especiallie, undertooke to drinke a greater quantitie of wine, then any other in his kingdome: yet felt he not therby any perturbation of spirit. *Plutarch,* in the life of *Licurgus*, gives this good note to the *Spartanes*, that it was a custome amongest them, to wash their new borne childrens noses and eies with wine: to make them more strong, healthfull, and the better able to endure all paines whatsoever. Infinite power of wine, in howe many kindes doest thou shew & deliver thy selfe helpeful to men? wel hast thou acquainted them with sufficient proofe of thy vertue, when the very least part of thy power, can abate and utterly destroy the strength of deadlie Hemlock.

Wherefore doe ye thinke good *Hesiodus*, recommended and joyned by his learned verses, that twentie daies before the rising of the dogge starre, and twentie daies after: only pure wine should be drunke, without tasting one drop of water? If this custome had beene entertained and observed, by the great *Lycurgus* of *Thrace*: he had not beene so dishonestlie cast headlong into the Sea, for putting water into his wine. To this effect serves us, the opinion of *Celsus*, a very excellent Physition, who among other precepts, ordained (touching the government of health) to drinke sometimes beyond measure. And to proceed a little further, let us consider, how many profitable medicines, bathes & emplaisters are made with wine: and the *Hircanes* would wash the bodies of their dead with wine, either to purifie them, or perhaps, because they imagined, that by the vertue of this good liquor, they might be recalled or broght to life againe.

Marvell not then if good drinke bee pleasing to common people, seeing we finde, that the verie wisest and best learned, have alwaies maintained the lawe, held and allowed among the Greekes in theyr meetinges and banquets, which was: that so soone as any one came among them, during their feast time, they would constrain him to drink, or get him gone: which yet at this day is observed in *Germanie*, if not of all, yet at the least of the greater number.

I will not blab, that the puissance of wine had sometime such authoritie: as to make the *Seneses* take Armes, and thereby to obtaine such victories, as are worthy to be registred in perpetuall Annales. Nor will I tell, howe in the yeere of the foundation of *Rome*, three hundred and eighteene: *Lucius Phyrrhus* was sent against the *Sarmates*, whome by the aide of wine onely, hee conquered, made subiect, and yeelded tributarie to the people of *Rome*. Wine was afterward in so great reputation with our fore-fathers: as *Mezentius*, to recover onely some quantity thereof for his disease (according as *Varro* hath left to us in writing) gave succour to the *Rutillians* against the *Latines*.

And if it were lawfull in this case, to produce holy Scripture, doe we not finde, that our Lorde, at the wedding in *Cana* of *Galile,* miraculouslie vouchsafed, to change water (being a thing lesse good and excellent) into wine most delicate and pretious? With wine were the wounds of the poore *Samaritane* washed. And beside, some say, that good olde *Abraham* made his daily offerings to God, with the best wine in his vaults.

I could willinglie proceed further in this matter, which especially pleaseth me beyond all other: were it not, I have alwaies shunned odious prolixitie: wherefore I will stay my selfe in this place; earnestlie entreating each one of ye, to embrace this so sweete desire of wine, and to forsake the simple course of sobrietie, because it maketh men so melancholy, and bestowes on them such slender strength and vigour courage.

VIII

FOR STERILITIE.

DECLAMATION, 8
THAT THE BARREN WOMAN IS MORE HAPPIE THEN THE CHILDE-BEARING.

I knowe not by what reason it should be maintained, that barrennesse is in any sort hurtfull or offensive: considering it is the meane, to make a strange affected and fantasticall woman, to become more pleasing, benigne, & ready to obey hir husband. Which contrariwise is not commonly found in a fruitfull woman: who never wanteth height of heart, and such bolde hardinesse withall, as is marvellous to note. Nor is it without reason, considering the woman beholdes so manie faire and pretty children, that depend only uppon hir commandement, and with so great reverence obey her wordes or signes: heereby shee is puffed uppe in such sort, as she thinkes she should not be a wife, or companion to her husband only, but indeed, Ladye and mistresse over her house and familie.

And if (for example) the reports of sundry places might serve, I would (above all other) willinglie perswade ye to this one. That I being one day at *Liones*, devising privately with a very faire and young woman, as is the manner in this Citty heere: we entred into talke, concerning the brave fashion of a garment, which one of his neighbours ware, and hadde caused newly to be made. When I have her councell, to have such another: she began to sigh marvelouslie. Now I knew her husband to be rich enough, able to content her in a greater desire, and not to give her one, but a doozen farre better: wherefore Lady (quoth I) why speake ye not to your husband, who can and will heerein satisfie ye: She answered, she durst not, neither would she require it, bicause she had not yet as so wel served: but if it pleased God to favour her so much, as to sende her one or twoe sweet yong babes, she shoulde have the meanes to aske of him other thinges then a new gowne. It happeneed according to her wishe, that a yeere after, she was delivered of two male children at one burthen, so soone as she saw her desire accomplished: she, who before had beene so kind and loving to her husband, began to holde all her householde in such subjection, as the poore Gentleman had no better helpe, but even to forsake his house: now beholde what fruite comes by this kind of domesticall increase.

As for the advantages that ensue by barrennesse: I finde so great a number of them, as it is impossible for me to acquaint yee with them all. First of all, if thou have a barren wife: consider, thou shalt not need to doe as many doe, nursee other folks children. It shall not displease thee, to heare the stir she makes, when they wife is sicke with childe: nor shalt thou abide the painefull trouble, during the month of her downe-lying: nor shalt thou heare the cryinges and cradle-noise, to waken thee out of they first sleepe. Thou shalt bee free from the strifes, and perpetuall molestions, of injurious and unnaturall nursses. And to conclude, thou shalt not feele that yrkesome anguish: in seeing them die by thee, or in they presence.

Witnesse heereof let serve the wise *Solon*, who being one day gone to visite his friend *Thales*, that then for more quietnes of studie, was gone not far off from the Citty of *Myletum*. And seeing no children goe up and downe before his house, he marvelled greatlie thereat, and conceived but rudely of *Thales*, that hee hadde no care of linage to ensure him. *Thales* within few daies after, would returne the like to his companion, and came to visite him even in his lodging. And while they discoursed on many thinges, there entred to them a yong Lad (who before hadde beene instructed for the purpose by *Thales*) he said, that he was come from *Athens* to see the Phylosopher, and to enquire, if he would command him any thing thither, for which cause he only came nowe to salute him. *Solon* dilligentlie enquired of him, if hee knew any matter of newes, and how all things fared at *Athens*. The yong youth answered, he knewe no other thing, but the death of an honest & wise yong man, for whom all the Cittie mourned and lamented at his departing; because he was saide to be the son of a wise Philosopher of that *Cyttie*, who as then was absent, and every one accounted well of him, but his name he had then utterlie forgotten. O poor and unhappie father (cried out *Solon*) being mooved with feare and trembling.

Then afterwarde, cariying suspition of his owne sonne in his minde, he could not forbeare from demaunding, if perhaps the name of the dead childes father, was not *Solon*? He answered, that it was *Solon*, for so he heard him called. Then the poore Philosopher began to weepe, and to beate his head against the farie walles: so that if he had not swounded in the place, he was in danger, had the doores beene open, to have runne into the fieldes, and there have raunged up and downe as madde or frantike.

Thales seeing himselfe revenged, and he had prevailed enough against him: after he had dawned him to remembrance, by the helpe of vinager and colde water, he saide. Now thou seest *Solon*, the cause which hath withheld me so carefully, from listening to the desire of children: that it can so easily offend the sense of such a man as thou art, whome I esteemed the firmest and most constant in the world. Afterward, he let him understand the fallacie, to shew hin, whence proceedeth his slender affection to have any linage.

I would faine learne of him, that is so earnestlie this way addicted: how doth a woman knowe what her children will be, when shee hath brought them foorth? For but by the issue of women, had ever the *Romaine* Empire beene tormented with such horrible monsters, as were *Caligula, Nero, Commodus,* and *Bascianus*? Had they ever lived uppon the earth, if *Marcus Antonius, Domitian* and *Septimius* had not byn married, or at least had met with barren women?

Augustus would often wish, that of his wives hee might never have children, and woulde many times call his daughter and Neece two horse-leaches, that destroied and eate uppe his daies, with great and extreame greefes. The selfe-same words might poor *Agripina* have used, who was mother to the cruel and hated *Nero*. Likewise the good father to *Phraates* K. of *Parthia*, when he beheld his sonne so cruelly slain; and at length, without any remorse of conscience, the homicidiall sworde to be sheathed, in his owne poore and over-wearied aged bodie.

Epaminondas, a king of so high spirit and most noble wisedome, lived a long time without marriyng, when being one day reproched and bearded by *Pelops*, as in the way of reprehension, for making no regard of procreation of children, for aide of the common wealth, which already declined and fell to ruine: he returned him this quicke answer. Take heed that thou hast not doone worse than I for the Common wealth, by such seed as thou shalt leave behind thee. Heereon they elected one of his sonnes: who was of such an infamous and wicked disposition, as he hoped for nothing more, then to being all thinges to confusion.

What shall I say of *Mithridates*, who by desire to succeede in the kingdome of *Pontus* (seeing the ambushes he hadde secretly prepared against his father, sorted to none effect:) made open warre against him, & assailed him very dishonorably, for to depose him? And what may be said of *Lotharius*, sonne of K. *Lewes*, who having suspition, that he was not so well beloved as his brother *Charles*: found the meanes to imprison his father? I might in this place produce the deede of C. *Thuranius Antipater*, of *Galen*, sonne to the Emperour *Valerian*: and of infinite homicides, or rather paricides. But I will not trouble yee with multitude of examples, in a matter not to bee any way gaine said.

Beleeve mee that will, but I holde it as a matter doubtlesse, that barrennesse is a most singular remedie, against the piersing thornes of householde life: which by better meanes (then this onely) cannot be escaped or prevented. And I beleeve for certainety, that this would be a sovereigne medicine, against the private mallice of children: except by good hap, the divine plant called *Hermetie* could be gotten, which whosoever useth (if *Democritus* by not a lyar) not only shall engender honest children and well disposed; but likewise very faire and gratious.

But I stand in doubt that this hearbe is lost: for which of the skilfullest, and most dilligent herballists of our time, that ever knew it? Or where is the hande that ever planted or gathered it? If nothing can be found in *Dioscorides*, in *Crescentius*, or in *Plateairus*, all good Apothecaries: I thinke assuredly, that this plant is altogither loste for our time: seeing by good proofe we new beholde, chidlren so disobedient, being lyars, Taverne hunters, Gamesters, swearers, and (for conclusion) capitall enimies to all vertue. Then doubt not, but that good *Democritus* imagined this hearbe, or dreamed on some other thing: or else that he sawe and knew it, after he had put out his owne eies, to become thereby the better Phylosopher.

I thus conclude then, that a barren woman is much better than a fruitfull: and let us not bee carefull to have such store of children, seeing they have doone harme to so manye persons. As for my selfe, I was sometime of contrary opinion: but soone after I began to repent my selfe, seeing that howe many chidren soever a man hath; if they bee strong, they are but so many servants to princes: if they be of spirite and knowe ought, then make they slender account of their parents. Some give themselves to lawe and estate of Justice, others to lay holde on benefices, & others to followe new opinions, which makes them oftentimes fall from aloft, to a hotter place then willingly they would: but if voluptuous pleasures once catch hold on them, God knowes what honor they doe then to their linage.

It was my chance sometime to be in a Countrey, thicke beset with barren mountaines, where ordinarily was to be seene, an infinite throng of Porters or drudging penny-getters, whereof daily resorted to *Venice* a very great number: so that when any child happened to be borne in that countrey, the inhabitants woulde say (as a common Poverbe) this is a young Asse for the *Venetian*.

If I should recite the latest comforts that children brings us, I must borrowe the words used in *Fraunce:* that in their youth, they besot their fathers and mothers, and when the are great, they serve for nothing but to vexe them. Consider what pleasure they bring to their parents, when newes is heard of them, that they have beene abroad all night keeping ill rule, and then come home with their heades broken, their armes shivered in peeces, their eares cut off: Or if worde bee brought their fathers, that they are in prison for some batterie, or called to the Gallies for some theft, or that they have gotten the soule disease, or (to make amends for their mis-behaviour) they have beaten the servants of the house, broken perforce their fathers counting houses, and then fledde a way with all the money. Then when they are returned againe, if the good man but shewe himselfe agreeved: answere is made, he may be ashamed in so doing.

I have at the tongues ende, an infinite number more of troubles to re-count which issue from this goodly increase: but for the present time I am content to omit them, and now to use silence, to shunne offences as well of you as my selfe, who with very ill will doe speake of such matters.

IX

FOR THE EXILED.

DECLAMATION, 9
THAT IT IS BETTER TO BE BANISHED, THAN CONTINUE IN LIBERTIE.

If such as are mightie and vertuous, take no displeasure by being banished or sent into exile: what need they feare, that have not so much to loose, their harts not reaching so high, nor their mindes addicted to so great enterprises? A Philosopher, a man of councell and prudence, exercised in affaires for the weale publique: a Captaine or ruler of a Cittye, may with some reason finde himselfe agreeved, and sorry to bee sent away thorow report, mallice or otherwise, in that he exercised his authoritie to the benefite of everie one, and notwithstanding, whatsoever paines he tooke, yet he had therein delight and pleasure.

Nevertheless, we finde left by the most expert and auncientest, that they reputed exile to be an honour and contentment of their mindes. Witnesse heereof is the honest answere of good *Diogenes*, to him that reprooved him (as with a matter ignominious) because the *Sinopians* had banished him their countrey. Quoth he, this rather ought to returne far greater shame to thee, that thou hast never byn forth of they countrey: resembling Oysters heerein, that never dare come forth of their shelles, but are continually beaten against stones and rocks. As hurtfull (in my opinion) is the want of courage heerein, and such as are ignorant of the great number of priviledges, which the banished have in their exile: whereof I will make some breefe recitall, to deliver yee from occasion of marvel, why many of our elders (with good will) made choise of exile, and did so patiently endure the same.

First of all I may say, that the banished give no cause to others, of falling into the sinne of envie, and during the time of their flight or absence, very fewe are so bolde as to aske them mony for interest: for each one knowes wel enough, that poore exiles have rather more neede of their helpe, then hinderance. Wherefore they may without blushing, of using any other conscience, borrowe the more easilie, importuning & disquieting them they have to deale withall: for under this advantage of being out of theyr countrey, and given to understand, that their goods are confiscated: they may without any other oration require the aide and succour of every one.

The banished finds himselfe not troubled with lodging strangers; nor is indebted or bound to making of banquets; to attire himselfe sumptouslie; beare Armes day and night; to goe honourably accompanied for the credit of his house; to shew himselfe brave and magnificent. But he may well vaunt, if so he thinke it good, that when he was in his countrey: he kept a table for all commers; did wonders; was rich and honourablie attired, and had the traine of a brave Cavalier after him. Beside, it will bee no dishonour to the man exiled, if hee keepe not alwaies his promise, or make deliverie of that hee standes bounde for, at the time by him prefixed. And so it happens, that many seeme satisfied, by acknowledging their good turnes, or promise of paiyng all, if ever they may returne into their long desired Countrey.

And doubt not, but many desire to pertake with this goodly priviledge, for sparing of expences, and to deliver themselves from very great troubles. For the banished are not bound, to keepe a house garnished with all provisions: they are ridde of continual keeping companie with their wives, who cease not to storme, strike and fight, first with one, then with an other, according to the quality of most housekeepers. They heare not so often their young children brawle, murmure or be peevish, demaunding firste one thing, then another: neyther see they the privie hidings of their men servants and maides, which is such an evill, as the subtillest in the house sometimes knowes not how to defend.

This the good *Anasangris* of *Sparta* well knowing, and that exile was not a matter so offensive, in regard of the priviledges before named: sent an answere in writing to one of his friends, that he tooke it in no ill part, to be sent foorth of his Countrey. But rather (quoth he) I ought to greeve the abandoning of justice, reason, and societie of all good thinges: then the countrey which thou so deerely esteemest. The parting wherewith, should be the lesse yrkesome to thee, because when thou leavest it: thou forsakest likewise infinite greefes & tribulations, which it bringeth to such as are besotted therewith.

And in sooth, lesse greevous and troublesome to us are the calamities of our countrey, when wee are farre off, then when we are neere at hand. Nor is the report, of the death or hurt of a friend, so offensive as the sight. Beeing farre from civill discordes, and sadnesse of Magistrates: we take no care for beeing called to councell; nor whether the officers of the Cittie doe their dutie, or keepe their accounts even. We shall not heare the difference of our Countrey-men among themselves, stand croutching to borrow, nor listen to the quarrels and strifes betweene neighbors. But contrariwise, we shall see ourselves free from all molestations: and oftentimes meet in the fields with better fortunes, then wee coulde have doone in the Citty.

I have knowne some, that have lived more commodiouslie and pleasantly out of their houses, then if they had continued in them: for there they could not make a little cheere, without Saint *Julians Pater Noster*, or being half crucified. Abroad is daily found some one, who hath pittie on the stranger: and or he would not imagine, what kindnesse and tendernes of hart, poore needie widdowes shewe to the banished. *Agamemnon* returning from the expedition of *Troy*, & threatned by his father *Telamon*, to be thrust from his countrey into exile: I knowe not father (quoth he) any other countrey to be affected, then that whereinto a man is best welcome. If exile had beene reputed a thing evill and hatefull, by the wisest and most prudent persons of times past (as many for want of other matter, woulde gladly alledge) should we then finde so many vertuous people, that so voluntarily and cheerefully embraced it, as didde *Metellus, Numidicus*, and many other of great renowne?

Calaster, commanded to exile by the *Athenians*, received his banishment for so great a blessing, as (at his departure) he would not have any thing knowne thereof to his very deerest freendes: and for feare by them he should be againe revoked to his coutnrey, he very strictlie forbad them by his letters, not to travaile anye iote for his returne: accounting it much better, to ende his daies in poore tranquillitie, out of his countrey: then among riches full of tribulation, and businesse of the Citty, to languish in the place of his birth.

Demetrius Phalerean, sent in exile to *Thebes*, was most highlie displeased with his fortune, and durst not shew it to *Crates* the Phylosopher; because (according to the maner of *Ciniques*) he lived very poorly and obscurely. Within a while after, the Philosopher *Crates* came to visite him, whom when hee had saluted, hee revealed to him so good a discourse, in praise and commendation of exile: as *Demetrius* (suddenly recovering his better senses) began to account it for a great glorie, that he had byn banished. So soone afterward as he came home againe, hee blamed very much the opinion, and forgetfull judgement had before, and the troublesome state of his affaires: which had so long held and detained him from joying in a life so excellent as banishment was. We shall find few men of valour or worth, thast have escaped this fortune: and if [he] wee would confesse the truth, this harme (if harme it may be called) hath more commonly and ordinarily fallen on menne of vertue, then on any other.

For proofe thereof, *Hanniball*, after hee had endured so many travailes, in service of his ingratefull common weale: was he not banished by the *Carthagenians*? Was hee not deprived of his so deere delooved Citty, by the *Athenians*? Noble *Theseus*, who hadde done so many memorable thinges, worthy of eternal honour and praise, only by meanes of his vertue: was he not chased forth of his Countrey, which hee had so amplified and enlarged? The like was doone to *Solon* by the *Athenians*: whom (in recompence of ordering their lawes and manner of life) they made to ende his latest daies in the *Isle* of *Cyprus*. The vertuous and puissant *Miltiades*, by whose meanes were vanquished about thirtie thousand *Persians*: dyed in this blessed state of exile. Like happpened as a reward to valliant *Camillus*: after he had so often given succour to his noble countrey. *Traian* the just, when hee was chosen Emperour, was in exile.

Banished was the learned *Aristotle*, and worthie *Themistocles*, constrained to gette him gone from his Countrey: the like befell to *Alcibiades*. What regard had the *Ephesians* to the vertues of *Hermodorus*, when they banished him out of their Countrey? *Rutillius* could not resist like fortune; nor poore *Cicero*, on whom the *Romaines* bestowed this favour of exile, for a recompence, because he had preserved their publique estate, beside manye other innumerable good turnes. Now what is he, that in heart woulde not with, to be in perpetuall exile, with so many good and honourable companions? Perhaps it may bee some coward and hart-lesse, strengthlesse, courage-lesse or councel-lesse creature.

I should be over-long, in shewing ye by divers waies and examples, that exiles is a thing neyther evil nor hurtfull: but at this present I am forced to forbeare, not so much for feare of offending your delicate eares: but because I remember, that the moste elloquent Maister *John Boccace*, writing to a *Florentine* friend of his, hath already discoursed very amply on this argument. Wherfore I will heere conclude this matter, after I have intreated your good willes, by that which heertofore hath beene laid: to combine the sundry profits issuing from exile and banishment, with the small greefe or harme, which a heart not over-weake and slothfull, may receive thereby.

The rather, because by reason it is more to be desired, or (at the least) liberally endured and supported: before yrkesome licence and libertie, that by testimonie of the olde *Comick* Poet, makes us ordinarily more wicked, and given to all kinde of vices: never elevating or exercising so much, the spirites of men well borne and entrusted in all vertues, as doth the pretious state of banishment.

X

FOR INFIRMITIE OF THE BODIE.

DECLAMATION, 10
THAT IT IS BETTER TO BE SICKE, THEN ALWAIES HEALTHFULL.

The advise of the most auncient wise men, hath evermore been, that
the feeble and weake complexion of our bodies; hath at al times served
as a souveraigne advertisement, to the holie life of sobrietie and parsimonie. Whefore I dare maintaine, against him that will strive to justifie the
contrary: that perpetually this vertuous dame hath beene adversarie, to
mens vaine pleasures and idle lubricities, even as the most souveraigne mistresse of all humilitie and modestie.

True it is, that (at the first sight) she seemeth scant pleasing, or rather
very offensive to some natures: but they consider not at all, the speciall
good shee dooth to men, by continuall exhorting them to all constancie,
and hope of immortalitie: bringing so many times to the memorie of the
mind, the moste pittifull and miserable frailtie of our earthly bodies. This
was it that mooved *Stilpo* the Philosopher, to make comparison of a sicke
man, to one founde in a prison sore crazed, and shivered (as it were) in
manie partes of his bodie, by meanes of the manifest ruines, from which
he speedilie hopes to passe, & enter into perpetuall liberty.

In like manner I beleeve, that sicke and infirme people, have alwaies
this good hope of quick departure from their mortall prison: when they
perceive themselves so often subiect to Catharres, weaknesse of stomach,
Collickes, Goutes, and other naturall imbecilities. For even as in a broken
or torne scabbard, many times is found a sworde or knife, of perfect mettall and good temper: so (by experience) we shall commonly see, in a sicklie
and crazed body, an excellent spirit and rich in all noblenesse, a courage
high and magnificent: ready (notwithstanding the bodies weaknesse) not
only to attempt, but to bring to passe many faire and honourable enterprises. See we not in the Gallies, that they give the Oare to the strongest
and moste mightie Galliots: when to the weakest and feeblest of members

(which oftentimes are the wisest and most skilfull) is left the charge and guide of the Rudder? Hath not the strength sooner beene overthrowne, of *Milo, Aiaz* and *Hercules*; then the abillities in *Solon, Nestor, Cato* or *Socrates*?

Even so, what other thing is the body, wherof we make so great account: but the house and poore lodging, of the most rich and noble spirite? And albeit the body be found sometimes fraile and diseased, yet dooth it no hurt to the spirit: because it is her Inne but for a little while. Poore and miserable wretches are we, who never knowing aright what wee ought especially to wish or desire: daily finde fault and are discontented; with our sicklie weake bodies, which neverthelesse are of longest life and continuance. As for proofe, the *Italians*, who for the better seething of a great turffe of hearbes, are wont to cleave & break the cover of earth wherewith they are hidden in the pot, to give them arie, better boiling and favor: yet notwithstanding, the earthen pot thus brused, will serve and endure longer time, then a sound one nothing at all broken: as if by meanes of the cleaving and rupture, it had attained a longer while of continuance. The selfe same may be saide of our bodies, the strongest and most sturdie wherof, is found to be sooner infected, then they whose skin is more thinne and soft: by reason they cannot so easilie evaporate or exhale the superfluities out of them; when ensueth, that more suddenlie and oftener strong menne die, then such whose bodies are sicklie and tender.

Plinie (in his naturall historie) makes the number infinite, of greevous and daungerous diseases, that customably take hold upon us: yet neverthelesse, we are of so simple consideration, as for a little head-ake, or one fitte of an Ague, wee enter into unspeakeable impatience. And we complaine on the fever quartaine, wherein we rather ought to rejoice, or (at the least) not greeve or offende our selves therewith so strangely: considering, that if she bee a bad mother to us one day, she is good to us for two after: and whosoever is cured thereof (say many Physitians) shall live afterward more healthfull and better disposed.

If for so little we contend with patience, we may then hazard losse of all together: if it should happen to us, as it didde to *Pherecides* the Philosopher, that from our bodies should come foorth innumerable serpents: as much as befell to good *Mecaenas*, that our eies should not shut in three yeares togither: or if we should fall into an Ethick fever, which lasteth perpetually, and never would leave us till wee came to our grave. Then would we crie out against God: howbeit, wee ought contariwise rather to rejoice, because the Apostle himselfe hath sayd: that never is the body well indeed, but when it is sicke indeed.

To prove this true, the partie afflicted with anie sicknesse, is never puffed up with pride, never buffeted with fleshlie desire, never covetous, envious, or overcome with wrath, never strangled with gluttonie, surfetting in slothfulnesse, or conquered by ambition: and would to God we were such in health, as oftentimes we promise to be when wee are sicke. The good Saint *Basill*, because he felt himselfe weake and not sounde in health, practised right well the art of medicine: wherin he profited so perfectly, as he was esteemed one of the wisest, and most expert physitians in his time.

Plato the Philosopher, because he felt himselfe strong, and over-mightie in nature, to followe his studie as he ought: chose for his place of abiding, a watrie marshie ground, a trobled & discontented ayre, where heaven shewed none other, but darke and pichie cloudes, that thereby he might become sick: and so have the meanes to refraine, the tedious and perilous assaults of the flesh, wherewith he felt himselfe sometimes pricked and moved: for his advise was, that a good mind could not flourish, if first of all the flesh were not over-maistred. And certainlie I am thus perswaded, that the weakenesse of the slender thred, whereto my poore and miserable life is fastened, makes me the more highlie to rejoice, and my heart the merrier: for the desire it hath of speedie departure, and the sooner to flie or mount alofte, where it first received her faire soule.

Now see in conclusion, of howe many felicities, the infirme and sicklie compelxion of men are the cause? First of all, it is the meane of making us live long in this world; which is the thing, that men of greatest courage wish for. For admit the case so falleth out (as there be peoples of divers complexions, some more chollericke and impatient then other) that the sicke man desireth in himselfe, to depart from this world; thorow the greefe, vexation and tediousnes he heere receiveth; yet then he happens to bee crossed with so many impeachments, as delaies and makes him tarry therein the longer. But if he would remember (setting all other troubles apart) to wishe he might live longer, for the profit and commoditie of his friends: he may then chance to escape longer, then one in perfect health never minding such matters. For the poore sicke man, considering that he is weake and diseased, will preserve himselfe very dilligentlie, from al manner of excesse: and live more soberly, then can the stiffest and strongest composed bodies.

These kind of men are such, to whom oftentimes it happeneth (thorow the over-much fiercenesse of their good disposition and strength) that boldlie or carelesly, they oppose themselves againste a thousand greefes, perils and daungers: using meates prohibited for the health of man, taking the corrupted ayre in the evening: or else (without any need) will wander into tempests, raine, snow, winde, stormes, and thus adventure themselves from morning to night. And the worse is their successe, thorowe the confidence which they repose in their bodies, which they feeling to be strong and lustie: feare not (without any discretion) to fighte heere with one, there to smite an other, spoile, outrage, and commit a thousand evils. Then, what recompence have they for al these? They fall into the rightfull hande of Justice: who without any regard of valour, strength, dexteritie, parents or riches, makes them miserablie and shamefully) to finish their daies before their expected time.

It is then great folly, to desire strength and health of body so earnestlie, seeing it is the cause of so many mishaps: were it not onely but in regarde of the warres, which we should never beholde so cruell or fierce, but by the confidence, that men suppose to be in their health and bodily strength: wherewith great and wise Lordes use to iest at each other, and make as small account thereof, as of balles running along the pent-house of a Tennis court.

XI

FOR TEARES.

DECLAMATION, 11
THAT IT IS BETTER TO WEEPE OFTEN, THEN TO LAUGH AT ANY TIME.

Not without great occasion is it, that I must assuredlie, & by good right confesse, the mourner to be in better estate then the laugher: seeing *Salomon*, in his most holy Poverbes, hath lefte us in writing, that it is better to sleepe and repose in the house of sorrowe, then in that of joy and pleasure.

By laughter, many soules have been severed from their bodies, to the infinite greefe of their good friends: but by sadnesse, not one only (which I ever heard of) at any time departed but well pleased. Laughter hath evermore beene perticularlie proper to fooles mouthes, or people without sense. And it is not read in any one place of the holye Scripture, that our blessed Saviour ever laughed at any time: but that he wept and sorrowed, is to be found in sundry passages, of the good and faithfull Evangelistes. For this cause, hath he promised eternall felicity to such as mourne, and them that laugh, he hath menaced with death.

To weepe, is a signe of penitence and compunction, whereto we are often invited and exhorted, by the voices of the holy Prophets: but laughter hath beene the cause of mocking it selfe, as the evident signe of overmuch boldnes. If we would make regard, of the commodities ensuyng by teares: howe many disdaines, and how many rages, have beene quallified, by one little teare of the eie? How manie poore lovers have they united and confirmed together, that before lived not, but in langour & distresse? How many storming hearts, fierce and cruell one against another, have they brideled, softened, & made gentle? How many great and honest recompences, have been obtained and measured, by the waight of teares? I am of this opinion, that all the force and puissance of men assembled together, cannot so soon winne or compasse what it would have: as one only teare can, yea, oftentimes it hath conqueringly obtained grace, even from obstinate and moste pittilesse persons.

For proofe heerof, *Heraclitus* was alwaies more esteemed for his weeping, then ever was *Democritus* for his laughing. See how many thinges, worthy of eternall memorie, *Crassus* by this vertue accomplished; purchasing the name of a scorner of vanities. If we should need to produce, the profit of teares & often weeping: Let us consider, that while our bodies are but young and tender, they make them to grow and encrease. Wherefore many Nursses (in regard heereof) are not very hastie to quiet their infantes, when they lie criying in the Cradle: but (by these meanes) suffer them to dilate and stretch forth their members, for so they come to the suddener growth. And if proofes should faile me against laughter, I would content my selfe with this only of good *Hypocrates*, who hath left written: that the diseases which ensure by accident of laughter, without any manifest cause; are the most difficult to be healed.

Let us then set laughing apart, seeing it bringeth such offence to man, and agreeth not with his honestie and gravitie: beside, we finde not at this daie, among so many lamentable ruines, where any place or oportunity for laughing indeed, may be graunted or suffered. And let us conclude, that laughter wrinkles and makes olde the face, counterfeits the person, makes the heart ake, woundeth the lungs & inwards of the bellie: so that after long laughing, many greefs doe follow, whereof we never make doubt, till wee feele them. So that if laughter bee not restrained, it makes the voice hoarse, and oft times shakes the bodie verie greevously.

Wherefore very excellently said the wise man, that the end of laughter, was greefe and teares: which ordinarilie endureth more space of time, & hath a longer taile behinde it, than ever had mourning. But the end of continuall teares, after this mortall life: is joy and perpetual delectation, which never hath ending, and such as are promised by him, who is onely truth it selfe.

XII

FOR DEARTH.

DECLAMATION, 12
THAT SCARSITIE IS BETTER, THAN ABOUNDANCE.

Any man of common sense and opinion, will assure yee, that for the ease and better estate of his person, as also continuance of his pleasures: aboundance of earthly goods ought well to be had in request. But for one voluptuous man ye shall finde of this opinion; I will furnish yee with an hundred of very singular spirit and perfect judgement, that liberally will maintaine: the fertillitie and aboundance of goodes in this worlde, is the mother and nursse of all evils, enimie to all modesty and honestie, and cheefe adversarie to sobrietie.

The good Lady of *Henault*, bemoned the great Dearth, which the turbulence of the warres had caused, and among other thinges, she wept for the fertilitie of the former yeares past; when as she called to minde, what store of corne and wines she had, and that before a weeke would be past, both shee and all hir house shoulde scant tell, where to gette foode or drunke once a day. But the sober and frugal *Solon-nist* faith well to the contrarie, that the lesse store of victuals are in a contrey: the lesse is the insolence of the inhabitants, who (in time of aboundance) disdain the service of their superiores: & then hath a man greater paine to get a servant (how poore soever, or bad disposed he be) then a man of wisedome, well skilde in good letters.

Moreover, what else thinke we, may be the plentie of one or two yeeres, when wee give our selves to so great feasting: but even an earnest of the dearth in them, that may or will followe soone after? The interpretation that just *Joseph* made of *Pharaohs* dream, may serve for witnesse heerof. What is it, that better gives knowledge of the price off any thing, bee it never so excellent; then the Dearth of Scarsity therof? In the East Countreys, among the Savages, no more esteeme is made of golde or pretious stones: then we in these partes, doo make of yron, lead or brasse. In *Ma-*

dera, *Cyprus* and other Islandes, where the Sugars doe grow, they give them to their Swine to eate: as we in the Countreyes neerer hande, give them great aboundance of fruites and wherefore doe they thus? Even because exceeding plently, maketh the contempt of most excellent things. For experience, when times fall out according to our owne wish: how many is there among us, that remembers God thereby, and gives him thanks with a good hart: but onely in a manner, by waye of countenance? But when times come that wee like not of: then is it that we turne unto him, and cry him mercie, then confesse we only his divine, incompaable bountie, greatnesse and excellence.

Infallibilie, the value of bread and wine, which are things needfull for nourishing the body, and to preseve the soule therein: is never knowne in the time of aboundance, when we make spoile thereof, cast it at our feete, and give it to feede filthie beastes. Nor may I forget, howe in some Countreyes stored with Vineyardes, when one plentifull yeere comes among other: they will bee so insolent, as to make waste thereof at every street corner. But when they have little store of wine and graine: then they taste, favour so well, and use them in so small quantities, as nothing at all is lost. We thinke on God, praise him and give him thankes: but then we doe it best, when we give our selves to know his geat vertues. Then our bodies are most healthfull and active, because our wine is well tempered, and we eate our wheate so pure: as they both togither may ingender the opinations of faith, and not of other matters.

And as for the vivacitie of the spirit, I say that even as in the time of fast or diet, the spirits work best and greatest causes: so in the time of scarsitie, they engenders not such huge numbers of smokes, as hinder them from dooing their divine operations. For this especiallie, among other causes, at first were the fastes and Lent time instituted: in good season and time of flowing plentie after wine, good corne, a thousand disagreements, a thousand batteries, a thousand lawe-strifes and contentions. What a poore labouring man had his halfe-peny towards a pinte of wine; then could hee make mery with his fellowes, so long as to drive away yrkesome wearinesse. Then were none so simple, but sate at the table with the house-mayster, and fed as at a franke marriage feast: and when the belly was full, then to dauncing.

Let us now make some little discourse, of Countryes fertile and abounding in all goods, comparing them with such as are barren and unfruitfull: and let us see, if their inhabitants are better natured or disposed, then they that dwell in the desarts, or regions never tilled and not fertile. First of all, in *Hircania* (if it be true, which that most faithfull Greeke hath

13

written in his historie,) one only stocke of a vine, yeeldeth about a Tunne of wine: and every foote of a figge tree, filleth wel neer forty frailes with that fruit. The wheat, although it naturallie fall to the ground from the eare on the stalke; yet without any industry or humane labour, it increaseth every yeare in mightie aboundance. The Bees doe naturallie work their honny on the trees: from whence (even as Manna from Heaven) it droppeth continually down on the earth, and there are none will take the paines to gather it. All this notwithstanding, the people of that countrey are accounted the most cruell, fierce and wickedest Nation in all the world.

In the Indian Countryes, the Earth beareth twise a yeere, and have two seasons for gathering their fruites: neverthelesse, if yee knew the people of the Countrey, ye shall finde them fantasticall, lyers and deceivers to the uttermost. In *Babilon*, every little corne of wheat, bringeth foorth two hundred other for it: beside this, the millet and other bread graine (thorow the strange and wonderfull nature of the soile) stretcheth uppe in such height, as do the trees. Yet notwithstanding all these thinges, the inhabitants of the Countrey, are more abounding in vile life and villanies, then all other nations are beside. In *Tacapa*, a great Citty of *Africa*, is to be founde such store and aboundance, of whatsoever can bee devoured, for the nourishment and life of man, & al things at so small a rate or price, as they scantlye make any reckoning thereof: in like manner is there to bee found, the verie plentifullest store that can be named, of theeves, adulterers, treasons, and infidelities.

Now let us conferre heerewith the other part, the barren regions or lesse fertile in goods; and let us see if they be not altogither industrious, freends to vertue, and greatly hardened for paines and bodily labours. In the firste, place, lette us consider what the Countrey of *Denmark* is, and what the *Franconians* and *Danes* have beene, that thence issued. Let us remember withall, the *Scythians*, that live at this day in travaile, without any certaine habitation, now in one place, then in another. What and how many brave warriours, have come from this people? Even as in our times, we have seene issued from the Isles of *Ireland, Swethen*, and Countries unfruitfull, colde, and partlie neighbors to *Scotland*. Yet in these countries, is found for nourriture of the inhabitantes, nothing more then milke and fish; but for softnesse and delicatenesee, none else like them.

But less us leave strangers, and onely make discoverie of our selves. How many men of wisedome and authoritie (thinke ye) in time of our memorie, hath issued from the untilled and mountaine countreyes of *Savoye, Daulphine, Auvergne, Gascoigne, Limosine* and *Periguelx*? Imagine ye, that the Rabulanes, Onions and Beanes of these severall soiles, could in ought diminish their goodnesse of spirit. Thinke ye for these they owe ought to our minions or the Court & elsewhere: who are nourished, and brought uppe with all wanton and lickerish thinges? How many Chancellors, Presidents, Councellors, Knights, captaines, and such like, have ye seene, and daily doe beholde, in honour of these quarters, more then any other yet their countries are of such nature; as their Coleworts, Mullets, Turneps and Chesenuts, doth there give them better nourishment, then will the moste pretious wheat or graine in the worlde. This inferreth, and prooveth well unto yee, that without this scant and frugall parsimonie, which to them is naturall; never would they have beene such, as now they are.

I agree very well with yee, that after they have once dwelt in a countrey more abounding, they become finer and foolisher, like the savage *Spaniardes*, who leaving their firste untilled region, where they wore hempen shooes, shirtes, clothes, and such like, came afterwarde to their pumpes of velvet. But all this, (proceeding from their originall nurssing) hath given them such art & industrie, as makes them nothing inferiour to other strange nations.

I say for conclusion, that the great fertillitie, of abounding in goodes of the earth, serves to no other purpose; but to stirre and move us, to attemptes of succession, Farmes, décime, rents and revenues: wherin we trust so much the most part of our time, as we become carelesse, and void of all desires of vertuous knowledge. True it is, that the over-great plentie of graine, even in such as are covetous, serves them to fatten fowles, Pigeons, Partridges and other birdes, as well as of the Garden as flight, the flesh wherof (soon after) serves to but to abridge and shorten their lives. But withall, they shoulde remember, that this huge store in lofts and garners, draweth thither a million of Rats, Mice, weevels, Fitchets and other vermin: nor is there so good a house, but heereby oftentimes it may be spoilde and consumed, beside the labour taken to separate the blasted corne, spirited and barren Oates from the other. And when all this corne is gotten together, it troubles that maister mervalously to locke it up, by reason of the aboundance: so that the torment of safe keeping, and well looking to it, makes him sometime minded, to forgoe the land for the corne, because of the displeasures, greefes and vexations he receyveth therby, in recompence of his labours.

In briefe, dearth of victuals, makes poore people carefull, and ready to their worke, contented (beside) with how little soever they get, to withstande the necessitie and daunger of time to come. It entertaineth and augmenteth good mindes, in their dutie and endevour: to the great profit of the weale publique, which otherwise would but slenderly rejoice, if by occasion of plentie, they should runne at their owne libertie. It maketh known the bountie, stregth and vertue of him, who (of nothing) raiseth mighty matters. It rebateth the pride of the highest mounted. It maketh that seeme better, which one laboureth for, or getteth by his owne paines: then if hee received it from the hand, of never so liberall affluence, or if it were given and bestowen uppon him, even for nothing. Lastlie, in times of Scarsitie, all good things augment and increase: but in the times of plentie and superfluitie, they fade, diminish and utterly die.

FINIS.

Gentlemen, heere I thought good to breake off, and conclude this first Booke, both for your ease & mine owne: least wearying you too much, you should fall in dislike of me and my labour, and so both of us misse your gentle favour, the only recompence I expect for my paines: and very unkinde are ye, if ye cannot part with so small a reward. But not despairing therof, let me intreat thus much at your hands, if ye finde any harsh English in my rude Translation, or faults unwillingly escaped in the Printing: mend the one with patience, and the other with your pennes, so both shall passe for currant, you resolved, and I sufficiently contented.

Yours to his power,
A. Mundy.

A TABLE OF ALL THE SEVERALL

PARADOXES CONTAINED IN THIS FIRST VOLUME,
GATHERED FOR READERS MORE EASIE FINDING THEM.

The ende of the Table for the
first Volume.

A TABLE OF SUCH PARADOXES,

AS ARE HANDLED IN THE SECOND VOLUME, WHICH
UPON THE GOOD ACCEPTATION OF THIS FIRST
*BOOKE, SHALL THE SOONER BE
PUBLISHED.*

For desire of Death.
That it is better to wishe speedie death, then long life.

For the Countrey man.
That the poore Husband man is more at ease, then the wealthy Cittizen.

For hard Lodging.
That the simple lodging is more to bee commended, then those in great
pallaces & houses of pleasure.

For the Wounded.
That the wounded man ought to rejoice more, than he that is whole &
sound.

For the Bastard.
That the Bastard is more to be esteemed, than the lawfully borne or
legitimate.

For Imprisonment.
That it is more healthfull and profitable to be in prison, than at libertie.

For Warre.
That warre is more to be esteemed, than peace.

For a dead Wife.
That a dead wife is most profitable vertue to hir husband, and better than a
living wife.

For Service.

That it is better for a man to serve himselfe, than to be served of any.

For Poore discent.

That the meanest place of birth, makes a man most noble.

For the Niggard.

That the niggardly sparing life, is better than the bountifull.

For Women.

That a womans excellence, is much greater than a mans.

For feare.

That it is better to live in feare, than in assurance.

For the Lawyer.

That a Lawyer is a most profitable member in a Common-weale.

FINIS

INDEX OF NAMES

TABLE OF CONTENTS

TABLE OF CONTENTS

TIBERGRAPH
CITTÀ DI CASTELLO • PG
FINITO DI STAMPARE NEL MESE DI DICEMBRE 2007

ACCADEMIA TOSCANA DI SCIENZE E LETTERE
«LA COLOMBARIA»

«STUDI»

38. CASCIO PRATILLI, G., *L'Università e il Principe - Studi di Siena e di Pisa tra Rinascimento e controriforma*. 1975, 256 pp. con 4 tavv. f.t.

39. MICHELUCCI, M., *La collezione di lucerne del Museo Egizio di Firenze*. 1975, 132 pp. con 36 tavv. f.t.

40. LESZL, W., *Il «De Ideis» di Aristotele e la teoria platonica delle idee*. 1975, 360 pp.

41. VON HESSEN, O., *Secondo contributo all'archeologia longobarda in Toscana. Reperti isolati e di provenienza incerta*. 1975, 120 pp. con 9 figg. n.t. e 34 tavv. f.t.

42. CAROBBI, G. - RODOLICO, F., *I minerali della Toscana*. 1976, XX-280 pp. con 65 ill. n.t.

43. WEISE, G., *Manierismo e letteratura*. 1976, 284 pp.

44. PATRUCCO, R., *Lo stadio di Epidauro*. 1976, 144 pp. con 40 figg. n.t. e 77 ill. f.t.

45. NEPPI MODONA, A., *Cortona etrusca e romana nella storia e nell'arte*. 1977, XX-212 pp. con 11 ill. n.t. e 28 tavv. f.t.

46. BOCCIOLINI PALAGI, L., *Il carteggio apocrifo di Seneca e San Paolo*. 1978, 224 pp.

47. PERUZZI, E., *Aspetti culturali del Lazio primitivo*. 1978, 200 pp. con 9 ill. f.t.

48. FRANCHETTI, A.L., *Il «Berger Extravagant» di Charles Sorel*. 1977, 144 pp. con 1 ill. n.t.

49. FIORE, F.P., *Città e macchine del '400 nei disegni di Francesco di Giorgio Martini*. 1978, 168 pp., 95 tavv. f.t.

50. NENCIONI, G. - SESTAN, E. - GARIN, E. - RIDOLFI, R., *Gino Capponi. Linguista, storico, pensatore*. 1977, 88 pp.

51. MORESCHINI, C., *Apuleio e il platonismo*. 1978, VI-270 pp.

52. *«Il Marzocco»* (Firenze). Indici generali. 1980, 2 tomi di complessive XIV-1010 pp.

53. PROPERZIO, S., *Il primo libro delle elegie*. 1980, 556 pp.

54. TORRINI, M., *Dopo Galileo. Una polemica scientifica (1684-1711)*. 1979, 248 pp. con 45 ill. n.t.

55. BOSCOVICH, R.G., *Lettere a Giovan Stefano Conti*. 1980, 384 pp. con 2 tavv. f.t. e numerose ill. n.t.

56. BENEDETTI, F., *La tecnica del «vertere» negli epigrammi di Ausonio*. 1980, 156 pp.

57. PARRONCHI, A., *Opere giovanili di Michelangelo. Vol. III - Miscellanea michelangiolesca*. 1981, 312 pp. con 270 ill. in 160 tavv. f.t.

58. GIOBERTI, V., *Appunti inediti su Renato Cartesio. La storia della filosofia*. 1981, 96 pp. con 3 ill. f.t.

59. DE ZORDO, O., *Una proposta anglofiorentina degli Anni Trenta. The Lungarno Series*. 1981, 268 pp.

60. PIZZORUSSO, C., *Ricerche su Cristofano Allori*. 1982, 164 pp. con 55 tavv. f.t.

61. PALMERIO DI CORBIZIO DA UGLIONE NOTAIO, *Imbreviature 1237-1238*. 1982, 356 pp. con 20 tavv. f.t.

62. BERTI, E., *Il Critone latino di Leonardo Bruni e di Rinuccio Aretino*. 1983, 238 pp. con 8 tavv. f.t.

63. RAGAZZINI, S., *Un erbario del XV secolo. Il ms. 106 della Biblioteca di Botanica dell'Università di Firenze*. 1983, 244 pp. con 44 tavv. f.t.

64. MARTINELLI, A., *La demiurgia della scrittura poetica. «Gerusalemme liberata»*. 1983, 232 pp.

65. *Accademie e istituzioni culturali a Firenze*. A cura di F. Adorno. 1983, 342 pp.

66. LUCIANI, P., *L'«estetica applicata» di Francesco De Sanctis. Quaderni napoletani e lezioni torinesi*. 1983, 196 pp.

67. MINERBI BELGRADO, A., *Paura e ignoranza. Studio sulla teoria della religione in D'Holbach*. 1983, 276 pp.

68. ORIOLI, S., *Repertorio della narrativa popolare romagnola*. 1984, 144 pp.

69. GARDAIR, J.-M., *Le «Giornale de' Letterati» de Rome (1668-1681)*. 1984, 404 pp.

70. SIMONUTTI, L., *Arminianesimo e tolleranza nel Seicento olandese. Il carteggio Ph. van Limborch - J. Le Clerc*. 1984, 176 pp. con 2 tavv. f.t.

71. SANI, B., *Rosalba Carriera. Lettere, diari, frammenti*. 1985, 2 tomi di complessive VIII-876 pp.

72. *Giuseppe De Robertis*. Giornata di studio e mostra documentaria promossa dal Gabinetto Scientifico Letterario G.P. Vieusseux. 1985, VIII-128 pp. con 5 ill. f.t.

73. PERUZZI, E., *Money in early Rome*. 1985, 296 pp. con 11 tavv. f.t.

74. *Studi su papiri greci di logica e medicina*. 1985, 216 pp. con 1 tav. ripiegata.

75. PELLEGRINI, G., *Dal Manierismo al Barocco. Studi sul teatro inglese del XVII secolo*. 1985, 168 pp. con 6 tavv. f.t.

76. *Le Pandette di Giustiniano. Storia e fortuna di un codice illustre*. 1986, 216 pp.

77. *Tecniche di conservazione degli arazzi*. 1986, 108 pp. con 56 ill. f.t. e 2 tavv. a colori.

78. FRERET, N., *Lettre de Thrasybule à Leucippe*. 1986, 446 pp.

79. CONVERSINI DA RAVENNA, G., *Rationarium vite*. 1986, 364 pp. con 2 tavv. f.t.

80. *Bernardo Tanucci e la Toscana.* Tre giornate di studio. 1986, 232 pp.

81. BULLOCK A., *Domenico Tordi e il carteggio colonnese della Biblioteca Nazionale di Firenze.* 1986, 396 pp. con 3 tavv. f.t.

82. CHIAVACCI, G., *Quid est veritas? Saggi filosofici (1947-1965).* 1986, XXX-410 pp.

83. *Protagora, Antifonte, Posidonio, Aristotele. Saggi su frammenti inediti e nuove testimonianze da papiri.* 1986, 154 pp.

84. WAZBINSKI, Z., *L'Accademia medicea del disegno a Firenze nel Cinquecento. Idea e Istituzione.* 1987, 2 tomi di 558 pp. complessive con 165 ill. f.t.

85. *Gli alleati e la ricostruzione in Toscana (1944-1945). Documenti anglo-americani.* Vol. I. A cura di R. Absalom. 1988, XII-660 pp.

86. BORTOLOTTI, A., *La religione nel pensiero di Platone dai primi dialoghi al Fedro.* 1986, 240 pp.

87. *Il contratto di mezzadria nella Toscana medievale. I. Contado di Siena, sec. XIII-1348.* 1987, 356 pp.

88. COMUCCI BISCARDI, B.M., *Donne di rango e donne di popolo nell'età dei Seventi.* 1987, 108 pp.

89. *Il contratto di mezzadria nella Toscana medievale. II. Contado di Firenze, sec. XIII.* 1988, 412 pp.

90. ROBINET, A., *G. W. Leibniz. Iter Italicum (mars 1689 - mars 1690). La dynamique de la République des Lettres.* Nombreux textes inédits. 1988, VIII-496 pp. con 4 ill. n.t. e 6 f.t.

91. *Aristoxenica, Menandrea, Fragmenta philosophica.* 1988, 136 pp. con 4 tavv. f.t.

92. MARCUCCI, M. e CREVANI, N., *Accademie e istituzioni culturali in Toscana.* A cura di F. Adorno. 1988, 544 pp.

93. UBALDINI, P., *La disfatta della flotta spagnola: 1588. Due «Commentari» autografi inediti.* 1988, 156 pp. con 3 tavv. f.t.

94. DE CONDÉ, J., *Opera.* Vol. I: *I manoscritti d'Italia.* Edizione critica a cura di S. Mazzoni Peruzzi, 1990, 2 tomi di complessive 668 pp.

95. ALBERTI, A., *Sensazione e realtà. Epicuro e Gassendi.* 1988, 180 pp.

96. TONDO, L., *Domenico Sestini e il medagliere mediceo.* 1990, 428 pp. con 20 figg. n.t. e 24 tavv. f.t.

97. RUGGIERO CORRADINI, C., *Saggio su John Ruskin: il messaggio nello stile.* 1989, 184 pp. con 5 ill. f.t. in b.n. e 2 a colori.

98. MATTIACCI, S., *I carmi e i frammenti di Tiberiano.* 1989, IV-232 pp.

99. PERUZZI, E., *I romani di Pesaro e i sabini di Roma.* 1990, VI-334 pp. con 3 figg. n.t e 17 tavv. f.t.

100. DONADONI OMODEO, M., *Giannotto Bastianelli. Lettere e documenti editi e inediti (1883-1915).* 1989, 216 pp. con 1 ill. f.t.

101. PIZZORUSSO, C., *A Boboli e altrove. Sculture e scultori fiorentini del Seicento.* 1989, 224 pp. con 15 ill. f.t.

102. ABBATTISTA, G., *Commercio, colonie e impero alla vigilia della rivoluzione americana. John Campbell storico e propagandista nell'Inghilterra del sec. XVIII.* 1989, 466 pp.

103. FABBRI BERTOLETTI, S., *Impulso, formazione e organismo. Per una storia del concetto di Bildungstrieb nella cultura tedesca.* 1989, 248 pp.

104. DARDI, A., *Gli scritti di Vincenzo Monti sulla lingua italiana.* 1990, 542 pp.

105. STURLESE, L., *Storia della filosofia tedesca nel Medioevo. Dagli inizi alla fine del XII secolo.* 1990, 244 pp.

106. MIRTO, A., *La biblioteca del Cardinal Leopoldo De' Medici.* Catalogo. 1990, 484 pp. con 4 figg. f.t.

107. *Un anonimo panegirico dell'imperatore Giuliano (Anon. Paneg. Iul. Imp.).* Introduzione, testo critico, commento a cura di A. Guida 1990, 176 pp. con 13 tavv. f.t.

108. *Varia papyrologica.* 1991, 136 pp. con 5 tavv. f.t.

109. MINUTELLI, M., *«La miraculosa aqua».* Lettura delle Porretane Novelle. 1990, 264 pp.

110. *Logica, mente e persona. Studi sulla filosofia antica.* A cura di A. Alberti. 1990, 260 pp.

111. SQUILLONI, A., *Il concetto di 'Regno' nel pensiero dello ps. Ecfanto. Le fonti e i trattati Περὶ Βασιλείας.* 1991, VI-222 pp.

112. LINGUITI, A., *L'ultimo platonismo greco. Principi e conoscenza.* 1990, 132 pp.

113. FERRARI, M., *I dati dell'esperienza. Il neokantismo di Felice Tocco nella filosofia italiana tra Ottocento e Novecento.* 1990, 466 pp.

114. BORTOLOTTI, A., *La religione nel pensiero di Platone dalla Repubblica agli ultimi scritti.* 1991, 300 pp.

115. DEL LUNGO CAMICIOTTI, G., *La nozione di lingua standard nella cultura inglese del Settecento.* 1990, 166 pp.

116. MENSI, E., *La Fortezza di Firenze e il suo territorio in epoca romana.* 1991, 216 pp. con 12 tavv. f.t.

117. BULLOCK, A., *Il Fondo Tordi della Biblioteca Nazionale di Firenze. Catalogo delle appendici.* 1991, 180 pp.

118. MUGNAI CARRARA, D., *La biblioteca di Nicolò Leoniceno. Tra Aristotele e Galeno: cultura e libri di un medico umanista.* 1991, 248 pp.

119. OLIVIERI, A., *Felice Tocco. Le carte e i manoscritti della Biblioteca della Facoltà di Lettere e Filosofia dell'Università di Firenze.* 1991, 496 pp.

120. ABSALOM, R., *A Strange Alliance. Aspects of escape and survival in Italy 1943-45.* 1991, 346 pp.

121. DONADONI OMODEO, M., *Giannotto Bastianelli. Lettere, documenti editi ed inediti (1915-1927).* 1992, 204 pp. con 3 tavv. f.t.

122. MAIOLINO BISACCIONI, *Il Demetrio moscovita. Istoria tragica.* A cura di E. Taddeo. LXXII-256 pp. con 4 tavv. f.t.

123. JANÁČEK, K., *Indice delle* Vite dei filosofi *di Diogene Laerzio.* 1992, 380 pp.

124. *Il contratto di mezzadria nella Toscana medievale. III. Contado di Siena, 1349-1518. Appendice: la normativa 1256-1510.* A cura di G. Piccinni. 1992, 484 pp.

125. PARRONCHI, A., *Opere giovanili di Michelangelo. Vol. IV, Palinodia michelangiolesca.* 1992, 84 pp. con 1 ill. a colori e 79 ill. f.t.

126. ANGIULLI, A., *Gli hegeliani e i positivisti in Italia ed altri scritti inediti.* A cura di A. Savorelli. 1992, 314 pp.

127. *Le Raccolte della «Colombaria». I. Incunaboli. Con un saggio sulla libreria Pandolfini.* 1993, 320 pp. con 4 tavv. f.t.

128. BELLANCA, N., *La teoria della finanza pubblica in Italia, 1883-1946. Saggio storico sulla scuola italiana di economia pubblica.* 1993, 350 pp.

129. *Studi su codici e papiri filosofici. Platone, Aristotele, Ierocle.* 1992, 254 pp. con XIV tavv. f.t.

130. *Il manoscritto fiorentino di J.J. Winckelmann. Das Florentiner Winckelmann-Manuskript.* Herausgegeben und kommentiert von M. Kunze. 1994, XIV-266 pp. con 2 ill. f.t.

131. CIPRIANI, G., *Gli obelischi egizi. Politica e cultura nella Roma barocca.* 1993, 206 pp. con 44 figg. f.t.

132. VERGA, M., *La Sicilia dei grani. Gestione di feudi e cultura economica fra Sei e Settecento.* 1993, 258 pp. con 1 tav. f.t.

133. BENCINI, A. - MALESANI, P., *Fiume Arno. Aque, sedimenti e biosfera.* 1993, VIII-116 pp. con 26 tabelle e 56 grafici nel testo.

134. FANTAPPIÈ, C., *Il monachesimo moderno tra ragion di chiesa e ragion di stato. Il caso toscano (XVI-XIX sec.).* 1993, 444 pp.

135. SALIBRA, L., *Il toscanismo nel* Maestro Don Gesualdo. 1994, 240 pp.

136. BARTOLI, L., *Il disegno della cupola del Brunelleschi.* 1984, II-204 pp. con 82 figg. n.t., 5 tavv. f.t. a colori e 18 ill. f.t. in b. e n.

137. WAZBINSKI, Z., *Il Cardinale Francesco Maria del Monte (1549-1626).* 1994, 2 tomi di complessive VI-698 pp. con 59 tavv. f.t.

138. *Un patrizio toscano alla corte di Napoleone. Diari di Paolo Lodovico Garzoni.* A cura e con introduzione di C. Pellegrini e F. Giovannini. 1994, 284 pp. con 6 ill. f.t.

139. GIOVANNI DI GARLANDIA, *Epithalamium Beate Virginis Marie.* Testo critico, traduzione e commento a cura di A. Saiani. 1995, 684 pp.

140. *Realtà e ragione. Studi di filosofia antica.* A cura di A. Alberti. 1994, 222 pp.

141. *Lettere inedite a Cosimo Ridolfi nell'Archivio di Meleto. I (1817-1835).* A cura di R.P. Coppini e A. Volpi. 1994, 212 pp.

142. ANTONIO BENIVIENI, *De abditis nonnullis ac mirandis morborum et sanationum causis.* A cura di G. Weber. 1994, 292 pp.

143. *Storia dell'Istituto d'Arte di Firenze (1869-1989).* A cura di V. Cappelli e S. Soldani. 1994, LXII-306 pp. con 78 figg. f.t. di cui 2 a colori.

144. GIOVANNI DA FALGANO, *Ippolito, Ecuba, Christus Patiens. Volgarizzamenti inediti dal greco.* Saggio introduttivo ed edizione critica a cura di L. Caciolli. 1995, 286 pp.

145. NANNINI, S., *Nuclei tematici dell'Iliade «Il duello in sogno».* 1995, 190 pp.

146. BARONE, C., *La parlata croata di Acquaviva Collecroce. Studi fonetico e fonologico.* 1995, 206 pp.

147. *Studi linguistici per i 50 anni del Circolo Linguistico Fiorentino e i secondi mille dibattiti (1970-1995).* 1995, XVI-310 pp. con figg. n.t. e 4 tavv. f.t.

148. SODINI, C., *I Medici e le Indie orientali. Il diario di viaggio di Placido Ramponi emissario in India per conto di Cosimo III.* 1996, 120 pp. con 24 ill. f.t.

149. STURLESE, L., *Storia della filosofia tedesca nel Medioevo. Il secolo XIII.* 1996, 304 pp.

150. *Dall'Accademia neoplatonica fiorentina alla riforma. Celebrazioni del V centenario della morte di Lorenzo il Magnifico.* Convegno di studio. 1996, 146 pp. con 2 tavv. f.t.

151. FERRARI, M., *Ernst Cassirer. Dalla scuola di Marburgo alla filosofia della cultura.* 1996, 344 pp.

152. GEMELLI, B., *Aspetti dell'atomismo classico nella filosofia di Francis Bacon e nel Seicento.* 1996, 434 pp.

153. PARRONCHI, A., *Opere giovanili di Michelangelo. Vol. V: Revisioni e aggiornamenti.* 1996, 68 pp. con 46 tavv. f.t.

154. WEBER, G., *Areteo di Cappadocia. Interpretazioni e aspetti della formazione anatomo-patologica del Morgagni.* 1996, 154 pp.

155. BALDI, S., *I piaceri della fantasia. Versioni con testi originali.* Con un saggio di O. Macrì. A cura di A. Celli. 1996, 186 pp.

156. LA PENNA, P., *La fortezza e la città. Bonaiuto Lorini, Giulio Savorgnan e Marcantonio Martinengo a Palma (1592-1600).* 1997, 206 pp. con 4 ill. f.t.

157. *Carteggio Giordani-Vieusseux (1825-1847)*. A cura di L. Melosi. 1997, 274 pp. con 4 figg. f.t.

158. LAPINI, W., *Il POxy. 664 di Eraclide Pontico e la cronologia dei Cipselidi*. 1996, 220 pp.

159. CORRADINI BOZZI, M.S., *Ricettari medico-farmaceutici medievali nella Francia meridionale*. Vol. 1. 1997, 506 pp.

160. PASTA, R., *Editoria e cultura nel Settecento*. 1997, XIV-298 pp. con 6 tavv. f.t. Ristampa 2007.

161. WEBER, G., *Aspetti poco noti della storia dell'anatomia patologica tra '600 e '700. William Harvey - Marcello Malpighi - Antonio Cocchi - Giovanni Maria Lancisi. Verso Morgagni*. 1997, 172 pp.

162. LUCREZIA MARINELLA, *Arcadia felice*. Introduzione e note a cura di F. Lavocat. 1998, LXX-220 pp. con 11 ill. f.t.

163. *Papiri filosofici. Miscellanea di Studi. I*. 1997, 154 pp. con 10 ill. f.t.

164. COSTA, G., *Le origini della lingua poetica indeuropea. Voce, coscienza e transizione neolitica*. 1998, 506 pp.

165. PERUZZI, E., *Civiltà greca nel Lazio preromano*. 1998, 196 pp. con 15 tavv. f.t. e 9 figg.

166. GIOVANNI DA FALGANO, *Opre et giornate, Scudo di Hercole, Theogonia. Volgarizzamenti inediti dal greco*. Saggio introduttivo ed edizione critica a cura di L. Caciolli. 1998, 196 pp.

167. MANFREDINI, I., *Saint-Simon. Les manuscrits de «L'industrie»*. 1999, 152 pp.

168. *La famiglia Chaplin. Storia di un'epoca. I, 1884-1918. Il carteggio*. A cura di A. Bullock. 1998, XXXVI-534 pp.

169. VOLPI, A., *La "filosofia della chimica". Un mito scientista nella Toscana di inizio Ottocento*. 1998, 202 pp.

170. *La cultura ebraica all'epoca di Lorenzo il Magnifico. Celebrazioni del V centenario della morte di Lorenzo il Magnifico*. A cura di D. Liscia Bemporad e I. Zatelli. 1998, XIV-168 pp. con 5 ill. f.t.

171. WEBER, G., *L'anatomia patologica di Lorenzo Bellini, anatomico (1643-1704)*. In appendice: *il Methodus historiarum anatomico-medicarum* (1678) di J.K. Peyer. 1998, 170 pp. con 3 figg. n.t. e 2 tavv. f.t.

172. MIATO, M., *L'Accademia degli Incogniti di Giovan Francesco Loredan. Venezia (1630-1661)*, 1998, 298 pp. con 5 ill. n.t.

173. *Pulpiti medievali toscani. Storia e restauri di micro-architetture*. Atti della Giornata di studio a cura di D. Lamberini. 1999, 214 pp. con 81 figg. n.t.

174. TOCCHINI, G., *I fratelli d'Orfeo. Gluck e il teatro musicale massonico tra Vienna e Parigi*. 1998, XVI-368 pp. con 21 ill. f.t.

175. *Lettere inedite a Cosimo Ridolfi nell'archivio di Meleto. II (1836-1840)*. A cura di R.P. Coppini e A. Volpi. 1999, 248 pp.

176. SORBI, L., *Aristotele. La logica comparativa*. 1999, 204 pp.

177. *Papiri filosofici. Miscellanea di Studi. II*. 1998, 184 pp.

178. *Giacomo Devoto nel centenario della nascita*. Atti del Convegno «Giacomo Devoto e le istituzioni» (Firenze 24-25 ottobre 1997). Ricerche e documenti. Scritti minori. A cura di C.A. Mastrelli e A. Parenti. 1999, 408 pp.

179. MIRTO, A., *Lucas Holstenius e la corte medicea. Carteggio (1629-1660)*. 1999, 328 pp. con 2 tavv. f.t.

180. PARIGINO, G.V., *Il tesoro del Principe. Funzione pubblica e privata del patrimonio della famiglia Medici nel Cinquecento*. 1999, 242 pp. con 4 tavv. f.t. a colori.

181. FARA, G.M., *Albrecht Dürer teorico dell'architettura. Una storia italiana*. 1999, 226 pp. con 21 ill. n.t. e 46 f.t.

182. MORELLI TIMPANARO, M.A., *Autori, stampatori, librai. Per una storia dell'editoria in Firenze nel secolo XVIII*. 1999, VI-724 pp. con 14 tavv. f.t.

183. *Aspetti della terapia del Corpus Hippocraticum*. Atti del IXe Colloque International Hippocratique (Pisa 25-29 settembre 1996). A cura di I. Garofalo, A. Lami, D. Manetti, A. Roselli. 1999, VI-718 pp.

184. COSTA, G., *Sulla preistoria della tradizione poetica italica*. 2000, 180 pp.

185. WEBER, G., *Autopsie, edite e inedite, di Giovanni Targioni Tozzetti ed esplorazione di un codice «medico-anatomico» del XVI secolo*. 1999, 244 pp. con 6 tavv. di cui 4 a colori.

186. KÜHN, W., *La fin du Phèdre de Platon. Critique de la rhétorique et de l'écriture*. 2000, 138 pp.

187. ROTZOLL, M., *Pierleone da Spoleto. Vita e opere di un medico del Rinascimento*. 2000, 130 pp.

188. *«Opuscoli e schede mineralogiche», manoscritti e lettere di Ottaviano Targioni Tozzetti. Conoscenze naturalistiche a Firenze tra Sette e Ottocento*. A cura di C. Cipriani, C. Nepi, L. Poggi. 2000, LIV-130 pp.

189. BERISSO, M., *La raccolta dei poeti perugini del Vat. Barberiniano Lat. 4036. Storia della tradizione e cultura poetica di una scuola trecentesca*. 2000, XXIV-352 pp.

190. † JANÁČEK, K., *Sexti Empirici Indices. Editio tertia completior*. 2000, X-265 pp.

191. *Agricoltura e sviluppo sostenibile nel Chianti Classico*. Atti del Convegno - Volpaia, 29 maggio 1999. A cura di R. Cianferoni e A. Innocenti. 2000, 142 pp.

192. *La famiglia Chaplin. Storia di un'epoca. II, (1919-1930). Il carteggio*. A cura di A. Bullock. 2000, 2 tomi di complessive XLIV-732 pp.

193. *Gli alleati e la ricostruzione in Toscana (1944-1945). Documenti anglo-americani.* Vol. II. A cura di R. Absalom. 2001, 2 tomi di complessive XVI-766 pp.

194. *Perugia liberata. Documenti anglo-americani sull'occupazione alleata di Perugia (1944-1945).* A cura di R. Absalom. 2001, VIII-666 pp.

195. TIMPANARO, S., *Virgilianisti antichi e tradizione indiretta.* 2001, XVIII-184 pp. con 1 tav. f.t. a colori.

196. MORELLI TIMPANARO, M.A., *Il Cavalier Giovanni Giraldi (Firenze 1712-1753) e la sua famiglia.* 2001, 100 pp. con 4 ill. f.t.

197. REBUFFAT, E., Ποιητὴς Ἐπέων, *Tecniche di composizione poetica negli* Halieutica *di Oppiano.* 2001, 274 pp.

198. *L'Accademia Toscana di scienze e lettere "La Colombaria" (1735-2000).* A cura di L. Sorbi. 2001, 258 pp.

199. CONTINI, A., *La reggenza lorenese tra Firenze e Vienna. Logiche dinastiche, uomini e governo (1737-1766).* 2002, XXVIII-432 pp.

200. MOSCA, A., *Via Cassia. Un sistema stradale romano tra Roma e Firenze.* 2002, XVI-264 pp. con 5 figg. e 34 tavv. n.t. e 41 ill. f.t.

201. SORBI, L., *Aristotele. La logica comparativa - II. La distribuzione del bene negli enti.* 2002, 224 pp.

202. PAGNINI, M., *Letteratura e ermeneutica.* 2002, VI-358 pp.

203. RUOCCO, I., *Il Platone latino. Il* Parmenide: *Giorgio di Trebisonda e il cardinal Cusano.* 2002, 108 pp.

204. CASPRINI, M., Le Antellesi. *Il Decamerone di Bindo Simone Peruzzi. Un documento inedito del Settecento trascritto e commentato.* 2002, 112 pp. con 12 ill. f.t.

205. DE PALMA, C., *Il paese dei Tirreni. Serona toveronarom.* 2003, X-196 pp. con 32 figg. e 9 tavv. n.t. e 1 tav. f.t.

206. *L'imprenditoria cinese nel distretto indutriale di Prato.* Scritti di M. Colombi, S. Guercini, A. Marsden. A cura di M. Colombi. 2002, IV-108 pp.

207. MISSAGGIA, M.G., *Stefano Jacini e la classe politica liberale.* 2003, 456 pp.

208. TOSTO, E., *Edmondo De Amicis e la lingua italiana.* 2003, 188 pp.

209. DE PETRIS, A., *Prometeo, un mito.* 2003, 148 pp.

210. NARDUCCI, E., *La gallina Cicerone. Carlo Emilio Gadda e gli scrittori antichi.* 2003, XII-152 pp.

211. LAPINI, W., *Studi di filologia filosofica greca.* 2003, 280 pp.

212. *Religione, cultura e politica nell'Europa dell'età moderna. Studi offerti a Mario Rosa dagli amici.* A cura di C. Ossola, M. Verga, M.A. Visceglia. 2003, VI-708 pp.

213. *La cartografia europea tra primo Rinascimento e fine dell'Illuminismo.* Atti del Convegno Internazionale *The Making of European Cartography* (Firenze, BNCF-EUI, 13-15 dicembre 2001). A cura di D.R. Curto, A. Cattaneo, A.F. Almeida. 2003, XXIV-428 pp. con 35 tavv. f.t. a colori.

214. PARRONCHI, A., *Opere giovanili di Michelangelo.* Vol. VI. *Con o senza Michelangelo.* 2003, 132 pp. con 132 tavv. f.t.

215. ERMINI, M., *La cultura toscana nel primo Settecento e l'origine della Società Colombaria fiorentina.* 2003, 98 pp. con 15 tavv. f.t.

216. MUZIO, G., *La Capponiera. Ms. Ricc. 2139.* A cura di B.P. Strozzi. In preparazione.

217. HEYWOOD, E., *Il Moro.* A cura di P. Grimaldi Pizzorno. 2003, XXX-74 pp.

218. *Aspetti di letteratura gnomica nel mondo antico.* I. 2003, XVI-304 pp.

219. SQUILLONI, A., *Libertà esteriore libertà interiore. Due aspetti del pensiero greco.* 2003, X-174 pp.

220. *Vivere a Pitti. Una reggia dai Medici ai Savoia.* A cura di S. Bertelli e R. Pasta. 2003, XXIV-578 pp. con 50 tavv. f.t. di cui 31 a colori.

221. *Luigi Sturzo e la democrazia nella prospettiva del terzo millennio.* Atti del Seminario Internazionale, Erice, 7-11 ottobre 2000. A cura di E. Guccione. 2004, 2 tomi di complessive XXIV-960 pp.

222. SCALA, A., *Girolamo Rorario. Un umanista diplomatico del Cinquecento e i suoi «Dialoghi».* 2004, 310 pp. con 12 tavv. f.t. di cui 3 a colori.

223. PANICHI, N., *I vincoli del disinganno. Per una nuova interpretazione di Montaigne.* 2004, XXXIV-468 pp.

224. MINUTO, E., *Il partito dei parlamentari. Sidney Sonnino e le istituzioni rappresentative (1900-1906).* 2004, 210 pp.

225. *Aspetti di letteratura gnomica nel mondo antico.* II, a cura di M.S. Funghi. 2004, 470 pp. con 6 tavv. n.t.

226. MONTUSCHI, C., *Il tempo in Ovidio. Funzioni, meccanismi, strutture.* 2005, 464 pp.

227. DE PETRIS, A., *Del vero e del falso nel Sofista di Platone. Con un saggio sul Cratilo.* 2005, 190 pp.

228. *Philosophy and doxography in the imperial age.* Edited by A. Brancacci. 2005, VIII-188 pp.

229. FERENTE, S., *La sfortuna di Jacopo Piccinino. Storia dei bracceschi in Italia (1423-1465).* 2005, XX-236 pp.

230. SIMONETTI, C.M., *La vita delle «vite» vasariane. Profilo storico di due edizioni.* 2005, 178 pp. con 10 figg. n.t. c 12 tavv. f.t.

231. MELANI, I., *Il tribunale della storia. Leggere la* «Methodus» *di Jean Bodin*. 2006, XVI-356 pp.

232. MARTINELLI TEMPESTA, S., *Studi sulla tradizione testuale del* De Tranquillitate animi *di Plutarco*. 2006, XVIII-276 pp. con 14 tavv. f.t.

233. WEBER, G., *Sensata Veritas. L'affiorare dell'anatomia patologica, ancora innominata, in scritti di anatomisti del '500*. 2006, 164 pp.

234. TAFANI, D., *Virtù e felicità in Kant*. 2006, XIV-142 pp.

235. LENZI, M., *Moderatismo e amministrazione nel Granducato di Toscana. La carriera di Luigi Serristori*. 2007, XVI-246 pp.

236. DE PETRIS, A., *Riletture dell'Apocalisse. Riconsiderazioni sull'idea del Regno*. 2007, XII-186 pp.

237. RANOCCHIA, G., *Aristone*, Sul modo di liberare dalla superbia, *nel decimo libro* De Vitiis *di Filodemo*. 2007, XVIII-438 pp.

238. *La famiglia Chaplin. Storia di un'epoca. III, (1931-1935). Il carteggio*. A cura di A. Bullock. 2007, XXXIV-306 pp.

239. CIPRIANI, C. - SCARPELLINI, A., *Un contributo alla mineralogia settecentesca. La collezione di Giovanni Targioni Tozzetti*. 2007, VIII-200 pp. con 4 figg. n.t.

240. BEVILACQUA, G., *Una questione hölderliniana. Follia e poesia nel tardo Hölderlin*. 2007, 172 pp.

241. GRIMALDI PIZZORNO, P., *The ways of Paradox from Lando to Donne*. 2007, 212 pp.

242. LANDI, M., *Per un'organologia poetica. Gli strumenti musicali nella poesia francese romantica e simbolista*. Tomo I: *Aerofoni e cordofoni*. In preparazione.

243. BRANCACCI A., *Studi di storiografia filosofica antica*. In preparazione.